TH
TRAFALGAR CHRONICLE

Dedicated to Naval History in the Nelson Era

New Series 2

~~~~~~~~

Journal

of

THE 1805 CLUB

Edited by

PETER HORE

In association with The 1805 Club

Seaforth
PUBLISHING

Text copyright © individual contributors 2017

First published in Great Britain in 2017 by
Seaforth Publishing,
An imprint of Pen & Sword Books Ltd,
47 Church Street,
Barnsley S70 2AS

www.seaforthpublishing.com

British Library Cataloguing in Publication Data
A catalogue record for this book is available from the British Library

ISBN 978 1 4738 9976 6 (PAPERBACK)
ISBN 978 1 4738 9978 0 (EPUB)
ISBN 978 1 4738 9977 3 (KINDLE)

Designed and typeset in 10/12 Times New Roman by M.A.T.S, Leigh-on-Sea, Essex
Printed and bound in China by 1010 International Ltd.

CONTENTS

Colour Plate section between pages 96 and 97

The 1805 Club

President's Foreword

The Royal Marines, who trace their foundations to 1664, and the United States Marine Corps, who had their origins in 1775, both rose to preeminence in the Great War of 1792–1815. Marines, or sea soldiers, became a key component in the naval armoury in the eighteenth century, present at every important action of the fleet, afloat and ashore.

Though sometimes at odds during that war, the two corps have in the intervening two hundred years developed at operational and tactical level into fundamental exemplars of the special relationship. Side by side, both corps developed in the twentieth century into naval infantry in the First World War and specialists in amphibious warfare in the Second World War. They continued these roles throughout the Cold War, and it seems likely that they have an enduring part to play in future operations.

In the age of sail, marines formed a significant part of the complements of most British and American warships, they took part in all fleet and ship-on-ship actions, therefore it is appropriate that an edition of the *Trafalgar Chronicle*, the leading resource on the history of the of period, should be themed on and dedicated to the Royal Marines and to the United States Marine Corps.

Once again, the editor has assembled a cast of international writers, including some of the leading scholars of the genre and amateurs from the ranks of The 1805 Club, and I thank them, and others who kindly offered papers, most warmly for their contribution to this second in the new series of the *Trafalgar Chronicle*.

ADMIRAL SIR JONATHON BAND GCB DL
Former First Sea Lord
President of the 1805 Club

GREAT ENCOURAGEMENT.

AMERICAN WAR.

What a Brilliant Prospect does this Event hold out to every Lad of Spirit, who is inclined to try his Fortune in that highly renowned Corps,

The Royal Marines,

When every Thing that swims the Seas must be a

PRIZE!

Thousands are at this moment endeavouring to get on Board Privateers, where they serve without Pay or Reward of any kind whatsoever; so certain does their Chance appear of enriching themselves by PRIZE MONEY! What an enviable Station then must the ROYAL MARINE hold,--who with far superior Advantages to thefe, has the additional benefit of liberal Pay, and plenty of the best provisions, with a good and well appointed Ship under him, the pride and Glory of Old England; furely every Man of Spirit muft blufh to remain at Home in Inactivity and Indolence, when his Country and the beft of Kings needs his Assistance.

Where then can he have fuch a fair opportunity of Reaping Glory and Riches, as in the Royal Marines, a Corps daily acquiring new Honours, and there, when once embarked in the BRITISH FLEET, he finds himself in the midft of Honour and Glory, furrounded by a fet of fine Fellows, Strangers to Fear, and who ftrike Terror through the Hearts of their Enemies wherever they go!

He has likewise the infpiring Idea to know, that while he fcours the Ocean to protect the Liberty of OLD ENGLAND, that the Hearts and good Wifhes of the whole BRITISH NATION, attend him; pray for his Succefs, and participate in his Glory!! Lofe no Time then, my Fine Fellows, in embracing the glorious Opportunity that awaits you; YOU WILL RECEIVE

Sixteen Guineas Bounty,

And on your Arrival at *Head Quarters*, be comfortably and genteely CLOTHED.--And fpirited Young BOYS of a promifing Appearance, who are Five Feet high, WILL RECEIVE TWELVE POUNDS ONE SHILLING AND SIXPENCE BOUNTY and equal Advantages of *PROVISIONS* and *CLOATHING* with the Men. And thofe who wish only to enlist for a limited Service, fhall receive a Bounty of ELEVEN GUINEAS, and Boys EIGHT. In Fact, the Advantages which the *ROYAL MARINE* poffeffes, are too numerous to mention here, but among the many, it may not be amifs to state,--That if he has a WIFE, or aged PARENT, he can make them an Allotment of half his PAY; which will be regularly paid without any Trouble to them, or to whomsoever he may direct: that being well Clothed and Fed on Board Ship, the Remainder of his PAY and PRIZE MONEY will be clear in Reserve for the Relief of his Family or his own private Purposes. The Single Young Man on his return to Port, finds himfelf enabled to cut a Dafh on Shore with his GIRL and his GLASS, that might be envied by a Nobleman.--Take Courage then, seize the Fortune that awaits you, repair to the ROYAL MARINE RENDEZVOUS, where in a FLOWING BOWL of PUNCH, in Three Times Three, you shall drink

Long live the King, and Success to his Royal Marines

The Daily Allowance of a Marine when embarked, is—One Pound of BEEF or PORK.—One Pound of BREAD —Flour, Raisins, Butter, Cheese, Oatmeal, Molasses, Tea, Sugar, &c. &c. And a Pint of the beft WINE or Half a Pint of the best RUM or BRANDY: together with a Pint of LEMONADE. They have likewise in warm Countries, a plentiful Allowance of the choiceft FRUIT. And what can be more handsome than the Royal Marine's Proportion of PRIZE MONEY, when a Sergeant shares equal with the First Class of Petty Officers, such as Midshipmen, Assistant Surgeons, &c. which is Five Shares each; a Corporal with the Second Class, which is Three Shares each; and the Private, with the Able Seamen, One Share and a Half each.

☛ For further Particulars, and a more full Account of the many advantages of this invaluable Corps, apply to Sergeant Fulcher, at the Eight Bells, where the Bringer of a Recruit will receive THREE GUINEAS.

S. AND I. RIDGE, PRINTERS, MARKED PLACE, NEWARK.

Nearly contemporary recruiting posters of the nineteenth century for the Royal Marines and the United States Marine Corps. Both posters emphasise the opportunity for winning prize money, while the British poster, printed during the War of 1812 or as the British then called it 'The American War', advertises the bounty paid to recruits. Note that American eighteen-year-old recruits were 4½in taller than their British boy rivals.
(Royal Marines Museum and courtesy of USMC)

PRIZE MONEY! PRIZE MONEY!

RESPOND TO YOUR COUNTRY'S CALL!

Wanted for the U. S. Marine Corps
ABLE-BODIED, SOBER, INTELLIGENT MEN,

Between the ages of 18 and 40 years, not less than five feet four and a half inches high, and of good character.
Soldiers serving in this Corps perform duty at Navy Yards, and on board Vessels of War on Foreign Stations.
Term of service, four years. Minors will be enlisted with the consent of their Parents or Guardians.

	PAY PER MONTH.		PAY PER YEAR.		PAY FOR 4 YEARS.
ORDERLY SERGEANT,	- $20	-	$240	-	$960
SERGEANTS,	- 17	-	204	-	816
CORPORALS,	- 13	-	156	-	624
MUSICIANS,	- 12	-	144	-	576
PRIVATES,	- 13	-	156	-	624

In addition to the above pay, each Soldier receives $1.50 per month whilst serving on board Ships, and an ample supply of Clothing, from which he can save from $60 to $75 during his enlistment, besides medical attendance during sickness, and $100 Bounty when discharged; also, the chances of Prize Money!
A Soldier who may re-enlist at the expiration of his term of service, will receive $2 per month in addition to his former pay.

A Premium of $2 will be paid immediately to any person bringing an accepted recruit.
Apply at the OFFICE, No. 18 BOWERY.
D. M. COHEN, Capt. Command'g.

BAKER & GODWIN, Printers, Printing-House Square, opposite City Hall, N. Y.

Editor's Foreword

This *Trafalgar Chronicle*, whose focus is very much on those two historic and heroic corps, the Royal Marines and the United States Marine Corps, will I trust, meet the reader's expectation of new research and new images about the men and women, and the navies – and marines – of the age of sail. Following the international motif of the *Trafalgar Chronicle*, I am pleased to report that half of the writers are from overseas, mostly from North America. Naturally, much of the action which is narrated takes place at sea or abroad, and, in this edition, this means in North America, during what in Britain was called the American Wars.

Contributors include members of The 1805 Club, distinguished historians from across the world, and enthusiasts writing and being published for the first time. I especially welcome as readers members of the Royal Marines Historical Society who may be seeing the *Trafalgar Chronicle* for the first time, and the large number of new readers in North America to whom the *Trafalgar Chronicle* is available through the United States Naval Institute Press.

Tony Bruce opens the core of this edition with a detailed description of the Battle of Bunker Hill, a victory for British marines, but a battle so well-fought that many Americans count it as a battle honour. Charles Neimeyer and 'JB' Armstrong outline some of the earliest actions of the USMC and the USN, and Britt Zerbe tells us of the marines' role at the Battle of Trafalgar. Two of this year's contributors, Allan Adair and Thomas Fremantle, have ancestors who fought at Trafalgar, and a third contribution is a rare survival of a memoir by a Royal Marine, Stephen Humphries, who also fought at Trafalgar. Humphries' memoir contrasts with John Rawlinson's life, told through pictures, of an almost contemporaneous marine officer.

The Royal Marines were so successful that they were formed into battalions who fought in the Peninsular War and the War of 1812, as Bob Sutcliffe and Alex Craig show the reader. Many readers will know of references in literature to the Sea Fencibles and others will have read about 'blue colonels', naval officers who held commissions in the Marines: here

David Clammer explains through the biography of a Dorset captain who the Sea Fencibles were, and John Bolt unearths a 200-year-old scandal which involved the most senior naval officers of the age.

Sim Comfort describes a unique sword which is probably the earliest exemplar of a Royal Marines sword and the extraordinary achievements of its owner.

Royal Marine uniforms worn in Canada during the War of 1812.
(Collection of Alexander Craig)

Louis Ferreiro's article about the navies of France and Spain in the years before Trafalgar reminds us of the context in which much of this action took place, and another article by Jann Witt reminds us that while the great powers fought, others tried to make a living at sea – by fair means or foul.

Major-General Julian Thompson has kindly written the introduction and I wish to thank him, and to express my gratitude and great thanks to a wide variety of others, Brian Carter, Sim Comfort, Anthony Cross, Agustín Guimerá, Joan Thomas and Peter Turner among them, who have helped me to identify writers and source pictures, and to several referees who shall remain anonymous. Special thanks go to Geoff Hunt for allowing the publication of his painting *Lobsters*. All have given freely and readily of their advice and services. I also wish to thank the contributors who responded to my calls and questions and suffered patiently my 'red spider'.

This year I received a large number of excellent articles which I have not been able to fit in, and which I hope to hold over for another year. I thank these contributors too. Also, a great debt of gratitude goes to a first-class editorial team at Seaforth.

The editor's appointment is for three to five years, and this is my third edition. Given that the lead-time for each edition is about eighteen months, I am looking for a successor. A job description is available and a small honorarium is payable. You need to be an experienced editor, knowledge-able about the period, and to have a wide network of colleagues and contemporaries in the field. The appointment is made by the council of The 1805 Club, but in the first instance and for more information, please contact me at tc.editor@1805club.org.

As for the *Trafalgar Chronicle* in 2018, I have already announced plans to theme the next edition on women and the sea in the age of sail. Women have, for various reasons, left a light footprint in the sands of history – nevertheless, I have long thought that historians (mainly men) have unfairly overlooked women and their important role in the tide of events. My views were reinforced when I read Dr Margarette Lincoln's words in a recent book that 'Women's contribution to British naval supremacy in the long eighteenth century tends to be neglected or sensationalised', and in the next edition I intend to redress the balance. I have promises of some excellent contributions and I am looking for more. First-time papers by undergraduates and by students of the period are particularly welcome, and proposals should be made to the editor at tc.editor@1805club.org. The deadline for copy for the next *Trafalgar Chronicle*, number 3 in the new series, is 1 May 2018.

PETER HORE
Rabanal del camino
1 June 2017

The Marines: The Early Days

Julian Thompson

Kipling was wrong. The marines are not 'soldier and sailor too'. They are soldiers who go to sea; not sailors who go ashore. Originally, marines in the British service were raised as army regiments, beginning on 28 October 1664. At a meeting of the Privy Council, King Charles II directed:

> That twelve hundred land soldiers be forthwith raised to be distributed into his Majesty's Fleets prepared for sea service. Which said twelve hundred men are to be put into one Regiment, under One Colonel, One Lieutenant Colonel and One Sergeant Major, and to be divided into six companies, each company to consist of two hundred soldiers; and to have One Captain, one Lieutenant, one Ensign, one Drummer, four Sergeants and four Corporals ... The care of all of which is recommended to the Duke of Albemarle his Grace Lord General of his Majesty's Forces.

The regiment was raised as the Duke of York and Albany's Maritime Regiment of Foot. Their first colonel was the Lord High Admiral, James, Duke of York, hence they became known as the Admiral's Regiment, but were part of the army under George Monck, Duke of Albemarle, head of King Charles II's army. Later, as will be related, the Marines were to become part of the naval service, but remained soldiers who go to sea, as they are today. The Admiral's Regiment saw service afloat and ashore in the Second and Third Dutch Wars. The regiment was first alluded to as 'Marines' at the start of the Third Dutch War, after the Battle of Sole Bay in 1672, when Captain Taylor wrote to his master, the Secretary of State, Lord Arlington, 'Those Marines of whom I so oft have wrote you, behaved themselves stoutly'.

From 1664 until 1755, marine regiments were raised when Britain went to war, and disbanded on conclusion of hostilities. The numerous engagements involving marines over a period of eighty-one years showed the need for a permanent force of soldiers for sea service: for landing parties, amphibious operations, and a trained, disciplined body of men on board ship. When embarked in a warship, marines brought down musket fire on the deck of enemy ships, and took part in boarding parties and cutting-out expeditions (seizing enemy ships while at anchor or in harbour). However, being part of the army but employed by the navy exposed problems, mainly administrative. When ashore, marines were quartered in dockyard towns, billeted, as was the army custom, all over town, in small detachments in public houses. This made it difficult to muster marines quickly and embark them quickly.[1] Another problem was pay. Marines sometimes found themselves owed months, and even years of back pay because, as Britt Zerbe tells us:

> Marines were paid as land forces from the paymaster assigned by each colonel of his respective regiment. This meant that the paymaster had to keep a vast array of accounts because of the very nature of a regiment's entanglement among the fleet, scattered among many ships in several locations. The paymaster was required to return these accounts to the Treasury and the Marine Paymaster-General in London.[2]

Notwithstanding these complications, the marine regiments raised by the army took part in the wars of the late-seventeenth and first half of the eighteenth centuries: at Beachy Head, Barfleur, La Hogue, and off Lagos. In 1697, peace brought disbandment, and most marines were turned out into the streets, along with 68,000 fellow soldiers. In 1701, the War of Spanish Succession brought reprieve for some marines awaiting disbandment. Among the fifteen new army regiments authorised by Parliament, six marine regiments were included: Fox's, Villiers's, Shannon's, Mordaunt's, Saunderson's, and Holt's, following the army system of the time, taking their titles from the names of their colonels who commanded them, rather than princes or royal appointees. A seventh marine regiment, Seymour's, survived the 1697 cuts.

An attempt to seize Cadiz in 1702 by 10,000 marines and foot, landed from an Anglo-Dutch fleet under Sir George Rooke, failed thanks to poor planning and execution. Rooke was able to redeem himself in 1704 by leading the expedition to capture Gibraltar, landing 1,900 English and 400 Dutch marines. The combined landing force seized the isthmus connecting the Rock with the mainland, cutting off the fortress from Spain. Following bombardment from the Anglo-Dutch fleet anchored off the waterfront, landing parties raced ashore in boats, and having seized all exits from the town, the Spanish governor surrendered. The fighting was not over, for three months later the men who had seized Gibraltar found themselves under siege in their turn by a 14,500-strong combined French and Spanish force. The Marines, reduced to 1,000 men fit for duty, were reinforced by

2,000 men of the Guards, Foot, and Dragoons. After seven months and much fighting, which failed to overcome the garrison, the Franco-Spanish force abandoned the siege. A report of the defence of Gibraltar stated: 'the garrison did more than could be humanly expected, and the English Marines gained an immortal honour'. At one stage, Captain Fisher of the Marines with seventeen men successfully defended the Round Tower against the continued assaults of 500 French Grenadiers. There was no respite for the garrison after the siege had been lifted. Fresh troops from newly raised regiments replaced the veteran defenders, who in their turn went on to capture Barcelona.

Early in the War of Spanish Succession, the Lord High Admiral assumed control of all marine regiments, with the same chaotic administrative outcome related earlier. Officers had to find funds from their own pockets to pay their men. Captains of ships tried to use marines as seamen, and restrict command of marine detachments embarked in their ship to one junior officer. The end of the War of Spanish Succession in 1714 saw the disbandment of some marine regiments, while four became line infantry in the army and remained there as numbered regiments of foot.[3]

In 1739, a conflict which began over Spanish abuse of British seamen in the Americas, known as the War of Jenkins's Ear, expanded into the War of the Austrian Succession, which lasted until 1748, involving Austria, France, and Prussia as belligerents, along with Britain and Spain.[4] At the outbreak of war, six marine regiments were raised by transferring men from the Guards and the Line, with another four raised in the American colonies. In 1747, following the precedent of the previous war, the marine regiments (provided by the army), were under the direct command of the Admiralty, resulting in the administrative problems discussed above. Admiral Anson, preparing his squadron for action in the Pacific, encountered difficulty in finding marines for his ships. He was sent 500 Chelsea pensioners. Those who could walk deserted at Portsmouth. The bedridden remaining 259 all died on the voyage. To replace the deserters, Anson was given 240 marines from the new regiments. In the course of circumnavigating the world, only four of Anson's men were killed in action, but 1,300 of his ships' companies, including marines, died of disease – mostly scurvy. The difficulties Anson had experienced finding marines for his voyage made an impression on him that was to bear fruit later. The War of Jenkins's Ear was the start of the most intense period of naval warfare in British history; the Royal Navy would be at war for fifty of the next seventy-five years. The Marines, at sea and ashore, played a leading role in the events that saw Britain rise to what we would now call a superpower.

In 1741, all six marine regiments took part in the expedition against Cartagena, in what is now Colombia. Colonel James Wolfe, commanding 1st Marines, intended that his thirteen year-old son, James, should join the expedition. But young James fell sick and was left in England. Had he gone to Cartagena, he might not have survived to win at Quebec in 1759. The force arrived in Jamaica with 1,500 sick, 600 having died on the voyage. After a promising start, the attack on Cartagena failed, mainly because of disease. Eventually, only one man in ten survived this enterprise.

In 1747, on the prompting of Admiral Anson, mindful of his unhappy experience in obtaining marines for his squadron, it was decided that marine regiments and any additional ones should be under full Admiralty command. In 1748, peace was signed, and all marine regiments were disbanded. On 23 January 1755, the fleet was mobilised in anticipation of war with France. On 3 April 1755, a new Corps of Marines was sanctioned by the King's Council at the Court of St James.[5] Parliament approved the establishment of 5,000 marines divided into fifty independent companies, to be based in the three naval port divisions of Chatham, Portsmouth and Plymouth. The divisions were administered by the Marine Department and Marine Pay Department, both situated in the Admiralty Building in Whitehall. The 'new' corps was to be 'formed into something truly new and distinct from their previous formations'.[6] In the years that followed, barracks were built, or existing ones taken over, to provide a home for each 'division' of marines: Chatham, Portsmouth and Plymouth, and later for a while at Woolwich. This would allow the swift embarkation of marines into ships of the fleet at these ports. The divisional barracks provided a base where marine recruits were trained, and a headquarters to administer the officers and men of the division. The division was not a tactical formation, like an army division, but an administrative organisation. This divisional organisation was much more flexible than the army regiment when it came to providing marine detachments for ships. A first rate, 100-gun battleship had a marine detachment of a captain and two lieutenants and over 150 NCOs and privates; a sloop's detachment of fifteen privates might be commanded by a sergeant. The detachments in two-decker 74-gun ships of the line, frigates, sloops and brigs, were all of different size.

Until 1755, marine officers purchased their commissions like every guards, line infantry, and cavalry officer in the army. Throughout the eighteenth century, and until 1871, when purchase of commissions was abolished, promotion was a matter of having the necessary funds to buy the next step up the ladder, as well as finding someone who wanted to sell out.[7] Commissions in the Artillery and Engineers were obtained by nomination, and entrance to the Royal Military Academy, Woolwich, where artillery and engineer cadets were trained, was by competitive examination. A commission was a valuable investment. During George II's reign, an ensign's commission in a line regiment would sell for £400 to £500 and a captain's for around £1,100 (equivalent to over £20,000 and £40,000 today), and in the Guards or cavalry considerably more. An ensign's commission in the Marines was worth only about £250. By the middle of the eighteenth century, the Marines had become a poor man's regiment and hence low in the social pecking order. This low status continued after 1755, for in the navy neither obtaining a commission nor promotion was by purchase. Many officers joined the Marines because they could not afford to buy a commission in the army, or obtain a nomination to the Artillery or Engineers. Becoming part of the navy resulted in even worse promotion prospects for the officers. The paralytic promotion of marine officers after 1755, and the sinecure of appointing naval captains and admirals to 'blue colonels' and generals of marines respectively, at the expense of promoting marine officers, are covered in John Bolt's chapter.

The marines on board ship were not required to go aloft, and usually performed tasks such as heaving round the capstan, pulling on halyards and other running rigging, and keeping part of the ship clean: jobs that required little training or seamanship. Their tasks in battle are fully covered by Britt Zerbe in his chapter 'That Matchless Victory'.[8] They also fought ashore, landed from single ships, or squadrons, often supported by seaman landing parties. Sometimes a squadron would form its marine detachments into a battalion under a major or lieutenant-colonel sent out for the purpose. Despite the low social standing of the marine officers, there was nothing wrong with their or their men's fighting spirit, as subsequent events would show.

The first major action by the new Corps of Marines was in 1761, when a force commanded by Commodore Keppel and Major-General Hodgson attacked Belleisle, off the French coast. Hodgson had nine army regiments. Keppel landed two marine battalions, one from England and one constituted from detachments in ships. When asked which troops had been the most active, the French replied, 'les petits grenadiers', who wore the grenadier caps, but were not as tall as grenadiers. The laurel wreath in the corps badge is believed to commemorate the Marines' action at Belleisle.

Marines served at sea and ashore during the American War of Independence. Two marine battalions took part in the Battle of Bunker Hill which, as Anthony Bruce reminds us, is a memorable date for the corps. It was a tactical victory for the British, as he says, but rightly, because of the steadfastness of the American defenders, celebrated in the USA.

The war against France, lasting from 1793 to 1815, with a short respite from March 1802 to May 1803, saw the Marines, later Royal Marines, serving both at sea and ashore in a myriad of actions round the globe. This war provides one of the, if not the most, outstanding examples of the exercise of sea power. It was perhaps the golden age of fighting under sail. The key part played by the Marines was recognised above all by Admiral of the Fleet, Earl St Vincent. When, on 29 April 1802, King George III directed that the Marines should be styled Royal Marines, St Vincent said:

> In obtaining for them the distinction of 'Royal', I but inefficiently did my duty. I never knew an appeal to them for honour, courage, or loyalty, that they did not more than realize my highest expectations. If ever the hour of real danger comes to England, they will be found the country's sheet anchor.

On 18 August 1804, a new task was given to the Royal Marines: Royal Marine Artillery companies, one to each division, were formed to man the 13in mortars on bomb vessels. These replaced Royal Artillery mortar detachments, which had been the source of disputes over who had the right to discipline them.

Ninety-two officers and 2,600 men of the Royal Marines were in Nelson's fleet at Trafalgar when he defeated the larger combined French and Spanish fleets on 21 October 1805. There are three chapters covering what Britt Zerbe calls 'That Matchless Victory'.

Three Royal Marine battalions fought ashore in the war with America from 1812 to 1814. One Royal Marine battalion formed part of a force under General Ross, which defeated the Americans at the Battle of Bladensburg. The force entered Washington and set fire to government buildings, including the White House. Taking advantage of British superiority at sea, marines were landed to raid key places on the Atlantic coast of the USA. Chesapeake Bay, which gave access to several rivers leading inland, was kept in turmoil by raids destroying American military stores. The coast from New York to Boston was subjected to similar incursions. Marines also fought at sea in single-ship engagements between British and American frigates.[9]

The experiences of two marine officers exemplify the variety of service of the corps in the latter half of the eighteenth and early-nineteenth centuries. Lieutenant Charles Menzies, having joined the Royal Marines in late 1805, spent twenty-two months commanding the detachment in the frigate *Minerva* from 1806 to 1808. He was awarded the Lloyd's Patriotic Fund sword for 'his intrepidity and zeal when commanding the Marines of the ship, at the storming of Fort Finesterre, and in capturing five Spanish luggers'. A raiding party had been sent to cut out the Spanish ships, which were lying under the cover of the guns of the fort, and, led by Menzies, took the fort by surprise at the point of pike and bayonet. A month later he led an attack on a Spanish privateer, *Buena Dieha*. The approach to *Buena Dieha* involved a forty-five-mile row in *Minerva's* barge. Menzies was wounded in the right arm, and it was amputated. This did not deter him from leading another cutting-out expedition in October, capturing a Spanish ship in Arosa Bay, and subsequently landing to take the enemy commodore prisoner.

Edward Nicholls was commissioned in 1795, and in 1803 volunteered to command a cutting-out expedition. With only thirteen men he took the French cutter *Albion*, his second foray that year. In 1804, he took part in the unsuccessful attack on Curaçao. In 1807, he led a landing party from *Standard* during Vice-Admiral Sir John Duckworth's passage of the Dardanelles, burning a Turkish frigate, and storming a redoubt to spike the guns. These actions, and others by landing parties, allowed Duckworth to transit the narrows. His successor 108 years later was not so fortunate.[10] In 1809, Nicholls commanded the landing force that captured the Danish island of Anholt. In the war of 1812 in America, he and seventy marines formed a force of Creek and Choctaw Indians in eastern Louisiana, to draw off American forces from the defence of New Orleans. Nicholls was in action 107 times, wounded six times, court-martialled twice, but survived to be knighted and, by 1854, promoted to full general. Little wonder that he was nicknamed 'Fighting Nicholls'.

Although the exploits of Menzies and Nicholls are among the most colourful among the Royal Marines of the period, plenty of other officers and men had similar adventures. The French Revolutionary and Napoleonic Wars saw the high point of daring operations mounted with such frequency from ships of the Royal Navy. The Royal Marines played an honourable and sometimes leading part in these raids.

The first 151 years of the corps' existence are important, for they set the pattern for the subsequent 202 years right up to the present. Richard Brooks's assessment cannot be bettered: 'Its [The Royal Marines'] reputation, like that of the French Foreign Legion, has been won through years of arduous, often ill-rewarded service in out of the way corners of the world. Their traditions are the more potent for having been hard-won in the face of many difficulties'.[11]

Battle of Bunker Hill, see colour plate 4

The Marines in Boston, 1774–75

Anthony Bruce

One of the main responsibilities of the British Marines (they were yet to become the Royal Marines) in the period following their re-formation in 1755 was the policing of the North American colonies. The Marines' regular duties included the defence of the colonies, the protection of sea trade and anti-smuggling operations, but the number deployed was small until North America drifted towards war.

In 1771, there had been only 186 marine officers and men serving in the North American squadron, 172 of them in the Boston area.[1] In October

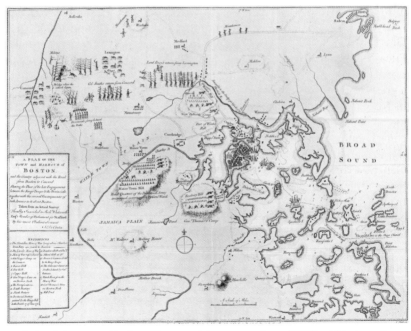

A plan of the town and harbor of Boston and the country adjacent (1775), which shows the locations of the battles of Lexington and Concord, Chelsea Creek and Bunker Hill in which the Marines participated. (Library of Congress)

1774, as rebellion increased, General Thomas Gage, commander-in-chief of British forces in North America, wrote to William Legge, Earl of Dartmouth, Secretary of State for the Colonies, requesting reinforcements. In response, the Cabinet decided to 'send two or three ships of war, with as large a detachment from the Marines as can be conveniently accommodated'.[2] The Admiralty assembled 600 men under the command of Major John Pitcairn, who had served as a marine since 1746, for service ashore in Massachusetts. They were organised as an army regiment, with grenadier and light infantry flank companies. The ships taking the battalion to Boston were allocated their normal complement of shipboard marines to ensure they had operational flexibility while stationed there.

The first batch of marines arrived in *Asia* (64) on 5 December 1774, but at first Vice-Admiral Samuel Graves, commander-in-chief of the North American station, refused to land them as they were needed for seaborne operations and the prevention of smuggling. Marines were also required to carry out their established role in preventing desertion and protecting official property. It was only after General Gage forced the issue that most of the marines were released for battalion formation training in conjunction with the army and for operations to disarm the Americans.[3] However, Graves still retained some of the marines and, in February 1775, Major Pitcairn felt compelled to write to John Montagu, Earl of Sandwich, First Lord of the Admiralty, explaining that 'this distresses me greatly, as I have a great desire to convince everybody of the utility of keeping a large body of Marines, who are capable of acting by sea and land as the public service may require'.[4] Pitcairn wrote a further letter to Sandwich a few weeks later complaining that Admiral Graves still had fifty of his best men and was trying to persuade him to return several more to his ships. However, General Gage had rejected this request as 'he was every day threatened with being attacked by many thousands [and] could not part with any of his troops'.[5] Pitcairn also gave Sandwich his advice on how the American crisis could be resolved: 'I am satisfied that one active campaign, a smart action, and burning one or two towns will set everything to rights'.[6]

The Marines had an early opportunity to demonstrate their value in land operations during the battles of Lexington and Concord which marked the start of the American War of Independence, 1775–1783.[7] The aim of the expedition to Concord, a town about twenty miles northwest of Boston, was to locate and destroy the large quantity of rebel arms and ammunition which was stored there. The force, which was led by Colonel Francis Smith, with Major Pitcairn as second in command, consisted of some seven hundred grenadiers and light infantry who were drawn from the garrison

Vice-Admiral Samuel Graves (1713–1787), Commander-in-Chief, North American Station,
who was reluctant to release marine reinforcements from his warships for service
in Boston in 1774–75. (Christie's)

regiments and from the 1st Battalion of Marines. At 10.30pm on 18 April,
the force left Boston by boat and moved up the Charles River to the landing
point a mile away. After they had been organised and supplied, they
marched overnight through Cambridge to Menotomy (the former name of
Arlington) in Massachusetts.

At this point, six light infantry companies under Pitcairn's command were ordered to take two bridges to the north of Concord. But an advance guard led by a marine lieutenant learnt that some two hundred militia, under Captain John Parker, had assembled on Lexington Green, barring the way to Concord. News of the expedition had already reached Lexington and more militia were on their way there. As the British approached, the Americans 'began to file off towards some stone walls on their right flank … the Major instantly called to the soldiers not to fire but to surround and disarm them. Some of them who had jumped over a wall, then fired four or five Shot at the troops'.[8] The light infantry returned fire without orders. In the exchange, a soldier was wounded and Pitcairn's horse was hit by two balls; eight Americans were killed as they ran for cover in the first bloodshed of the war. Major Pitcairn signalled a ceasefire by striking 'his … sword downwards with all earnestness',[9] but order was only fully restored when Colonel Smith and the grenadiers arrived.

The British then marched on to Concord, which was six miles away, and as they approached, the militia withdrew across the North Bridge about a mile from the centre. They took possession of the bridge while a search for weapons was underway. Major Pitcairn, who was attacked by a resident, discovered three cannon barrels, one of the few finds that day, but most of the rebel stores had already been dispersed. A few hundred yards separated the 100 British regulars on the bridge and their American opponents. By 9am there were up to five hundred militiamen holding a hill overlooking the river and the British commander called for reinforcements. Reacting to rumours that Concord was about to be burnt, the Americans advanced towards the bridge as a first step in rescuing the town. The British withdrew across the bridge and fired the first shots, but they were in an exposed position and there were losses on both sides. The Americans stopped firing when British reinforcements arrived and there was no sign that Concord was on fire.

With little to show for their efforts, the British were ordered to begin the march back to Boston at noon. Flank guards – groups of up to a hundred light infantrymen – protected the main column by keeping the surrounding area free from snipers. At a hill outside Lexington, they were attacked by a militia company and, according to a British participant, 'we were totally surrounded with such an incessant fire as it's impossible to conceive'.[10] British casualties mounted and Major Pitcairn was thrown from his horse and injured. The British retreated in disarray, but at Lexington they met a relief force which had been dispatched to cover their withdrawal. Under the command of Lord Percy, it consisted of the battalion companies of three infantry regiments and the Marines, a total of some eight hundred men, and saved the expeditionary force from 'inevitable destruction'.[11]

The Americans planned to surround the departing column in 'a moving circle of incessant fire', but concentrated on attacking it from the back, its most vulnerable point. According to Lord Percy, the militia had 'men amongst them who know what they are about ... nor are their men devoid of the spirit of enthusiasm'.[12] Losses on both sides mounted and Percy decided to head for Charlestown rather than returning directly to Boston, thus avoiding a certain ambush on his original route. However, skirmishes continued, with the marines defending the column against a final attack as they entered Charlestown at 7.30pm. A detachment of marines, under the command of Captain-Lieutenant James Johnston, from HMS *Somerset* (70), had been landed at Charlestown in the afternoon to cover the retreat. The warship – and the assembled marines – 'so intimidated its Inhabitants that they (tho' reluctantly) suffered the Kings Troops to come in and pass over to Boston'.[13]

The Concord expedition had drawn militia forces into the Boston area and they remained to blockade the city. However, supplies could still be brought in by sea and livestock could be acquired from the Boston harbour islands. The Americans were unable to stop shipments by sea but, in an action that led to the Battle of Chelsea Creek, they ordered all livestock to be moved from Noddle's Island and Hog Island, near Chelsea on the northeast side of Boston harbour, so that it was out of British reach.[14] Vice-Admiral Graves, who had received information about a possible attack, ordered guard boats (which included marines) to patrol off the islands but they were difficult to defend.[15] There were also forty marines stationed on Noddle's Island with orders to protect the livestock.

On 27 May, at about 11am, rebel Colonel John Stark landed on Hog Island with 300 armed men and he ordered them to round up the livestock. He crossed Crooked Creek to Noddle's Island accompanied by thirty men, who were ordered to kill the livestock and set fire to haystacks. Columns of smoke from burning hay alerted the British and the nearby warships were ordered to send their marines ashore and expel the Americans. Some 170 marines were landed in total. The schooner *Diana* (6) was ordered to support the operation and prevent the Americans' escape.

When the Americans returned to Crooked Creek they fought a pitched battle with the marines and withdrew to Hog Island at 5pm. As *Diana* advanced upstream she deployed her cannon against the enemy, but was 'greatly annoyed' by heavy small arms and artillery fire from General Isaac Putnam's forces in the first action in which the Americans used field pieces.

When *Diana* experienced unfavourable winds, barges manned by marines were sent to rescue her but the schooner drifted and ran aground in Chelsea Creek. The marines refused an American offer to surrender, but were forced to abandon the rescue when the tide went out. *Diana* was captured and set on fire shortly after midnight on 28 May; it was the first British ship to be lost to the Americans during the war. Soon after the action ended, 200 soldiers landed on Noddle's Island, but as a source of food supply it no longer had any value.

As the military situation deteriorated, 2,000 reinforcements, including a second marine battalion of 600 men, under the command of Major John Tupper, arrived during May. They were accompanied by three major generals – William Howe, Henry Clinton and John Burgoyne – who had been sent to assist General Gage in managing a larger garrison. They advised him on a plan to seize the unoccupied hills surrounding Boston before advancing and breaking the siege.[16] The southern flank – Dorchester Neck – would be taken first and then Charlestown heights to the north would be occupied. The Charlestown peninsula, which was dominated by Bunker Hill to the west and Breed's Hill to the east, was connected to the mainland by a narrow strip of land (the Charlestown Neck). At the southern end of the peninsula, which was about a mile long, the small town of Charlestown faced Boston across the Charles River.

These plans soon became known to the Americans, who decided to occupy the Charlestown peninsula as a counter-stroke, despite the presence of a powerful army and fleet. During the night of 16 June, 1,200 men, under the command of Colonel William Prescott, crossed the Neck and constructed a redoubt on Breed's Hill. Although it was not as high as Bunker Hill, Breed's Hill was closer to Boston and well positioned to fire on British positions and ships in the harbour. The redoubt was square – each side was 136ft – with ditches and earthen walls about 6ft high. The centre of the redoubt at the front, which was in an arrow shape, looked towards Charlestown, while the eastern side commanded the most likely route of an attacking force. A wooden platform enabled the defending troops to fire over the walls. Defences were added to the unprotected left flank to the east as far as the Mystic River, and included a breastwork, rail fence and stone wall on the beach, but the Americans were unable to construct a defensive line to the west of the redoubt.

In the early hours of 17 June, the British became aware of the noisy construction on Breed's Hill as they were only separated from the peninsula by 300yds of water. At 4am, *Lively* (20) opened fire on Breed's Hill and soon other British guns joined in. General Gage and his three senior officers decided that a direct assault on the redoubt should be undertaken without delay and dismissed the idea of attacking the unprotected Neck, which would have cut off the Americans' line of retreat. They assessed the redoubt as being vulnerable to an attack on the American left, but underestimated the rebels' fighting capabilities and other difficulties. Under the British plan, 2,400 troops and marines would be landed, with the navy providing covering fire. Warships would also bombard the Neck to disrupt the supply of American reinforcements.

It took several hours to organise the British force, which was under the command of General Howe, and twenty-eight loaded barges did not depart from Boston until 1.30pm. Landing unopposed in two waves at Morton's point to the east of Breed's Hill, it consisted of ten companies of grenadiers and ten companies of light infantry together with the 5th and 38th regiments; 1,500 men in total. The 1st Marines and the 47th Regiment, which were to form part of Brigadier Robert Pigot's left wing, had been on standby, but were embarked as soon as the barges returned: General Howe had assessed the strength of the American defensive works to the east of the redoubt (including the rail fence) and had requested reinforcements. Operations were delayed until the marines arrived, giving General Howe 2,200 men in total.

Under the British plan, Howe was to lead the main assault on the American left, while Pigot on the British left would feint an assault on the redoubt. Howe and Pigot each had a line of ten companies, with a second line close behind. The marines – together with Pigot's light infantry – assembled to the south of Charlestown and then advanced directly towards the redoubt on the extreme British left. Even before the attack began, the marines suffered casualties from snipers firing at long range from Charlestown, and in response the navy fired 'red-hot balls' on the town and it was quickly set on fire. General Burgoyne reported that 'our battery [on Copp's Hill, Boston] ... kept an incessant fire on the heights; it was seconded by a number of frigates, floating batteries and one ship of the line. And now ensued one of the greatest scenes of war that can be conceived'.[17]

The dense cloud of smoke produced by the burning of Charlestown was not the only problem the heavily-laden troops faced as they advanced up the hill towards the rebel defences at about 3pm. Hot weather, waist-high grass and fences made progress difficult, despite supporting artillery fire. As the British approached the enemy lines, the cannonade ceased, to avoid causing them injury. Howe's light infantry mounted the main attack along the Mystic River beach, with the aim of taking the stone wall and then attacking the rail fence, breastwork and redoubt from the rear. At the same time the grenadiers led a frontal attack on the rail fence. As they advanced towards the stone wall, the light infantry were cut down by a 'continued sheet of fire' and, sustaining heavy losses, they retreated in disorder. Further to the west, Howe's attack against the fence fared no better. The Americans had been ordered to hold their fire 'until they could see the whites of their enemies' eyes' and did not launch an attack until the enemy was within 50ft. The British suffered heavy casualties and were forced to withdraw back to the shore, while the Americans, who had the advantage of having some cover and could use the fence to fire their muskets, maintained their position. On the British left, Pigot's forces, including the marines, faced rebel skirmishers and 'were unable to mount a real attack on the redoubt, and when they saw what happened to Howe he called them back'.[18]

Howe quickly reformed his troops and decided on a revised plan for a second assault. His grenadiers and light infantry would attack the rail fence rather than making a second advance along the beach. Pigot would make a direct attack on the redoubt rather than a feint, but without any support from a flanking movement on his right. The assault on the rail fence resulted in heavy British casualties (including every member of Howe's staff) from an 'incessant stream of fire … from the rebel lines'. The Americans' destructive power 'was too much to endure', and suddenly the decimated ranks turned and ran. Pigot's advance also collapsed and his forces were ordered to retreat. Despite the failure of the second assault, it 'afforded an opportunity of signalizing the discipline and intrepidity of the Battalion of Marines, which dealt destruction and carnage around them'.[19]

Undeterred by heavy casualties, Howe prepared for a third attack which would require more men and a different plan. General Clinton, who arrived on the peninsula to rally the British left, sent 400 men of the 2nd Marines across from Boston. Howe decided that his main force would concentrate on the redoubt and breastwork rather than the rail fence and it would advance in a column before launching the final bayonet charge. The troops were permitted to remove their coats and heavy packs. The attack on the American left would be no more than a feint.

The third assault began when the artillery moved forward and raked the enemy lines. The Americans were forced to withdraw from the breastwork and the grenadiers started to work their way around the fort from the east. Grenadiers led by General Pigot were moving towards the other side of the redoubt. In a flanking movement, the marines advanced towards the western side of the redoubt: 'a battalion reduced to a handful led the way, followed by the Marines, with the 47th in the rear'.[20] The Americans, whose ammunition was running low, did not open fire until the British were about

15yds away when the leading battalion wavered. The marines, according to Adjutant John Waller, were 'checked by the severe fire of the enemy, but did not retreat an inch'.[21] At this point, a captain of marines commented to Major Pitcairn 'that of all the actions he had been in, this was the hottest; first, from the burning of the houses in Charles-Town; next, the heat of the day; and thirdly, from the heat of the enemy's fire'. In reply, Pitcairn said that 'soldiers should enure themselves to all manner of hardships, not to regard either heat or cold'.[22] Soon afterwards Pitcairn, who had been trying to rally the troops, was mortally wounded and died two or three hours later.[23]

In the confusion, Adjutant Waller did all he could 'to form the two [marine] companies ... which I at last effected, losing many of them while it was performing'.[24] They were ordered to stop firing and prepare for a bayonet charge with Waller fearing that 'had we stopped there much longer, the enemy would have picked us all off'. Heavy American fire continued as the marines rushed forward. Together with part of the 47th Regiment, the two marine companies were the first British troops to cross the ditch and scale the walls of the redoubt, with the grenadiers advancing from the right.

The shooting of Major Pitcairn (who had shed the first blood at Lexington) by the colored soldier Salem. Marine Lieutenant John Pitcairn, who also served at Bunker Hill, was standing by his father when he was shot by Peter Salem, a former slave. Pitcairn carried him from the battlefield before returning to the fight. (New York Public Library)

As 'the redoubt filled up with a chaotic mixture of British and American soldiers', the rebels, who had now run out of powder, were unable to escape 'the carnage that followed the storming of this work'. The marines 'tumbled over the dead to get at the living, who were crowding out of the gorge of the redoubt' and 'drove their bayonets into all that opposed them'.[25] Although they did not have bayonets, the Americans engaged in hand-to-hand fighting, but it soon became clear that they were overwhelmed and the redoubt 'nearly became a death trap for them'.[26] They were ordered to retreat and even though the Americans had failed to create a second line of defence on Bunker Hill, 'it was no flight; it was even covered with bravery and military skill'.[27] By 5pm the British were in control of the peninsula.

The Battle of Bunker Hill was a tactical victory for the British and remains one of the Royal Marines' ten most memorable dates. According to an official report submitted to the Admiralty by Major Tupper:

the Officers and Men of the Marine Corps shewed ... the greatest Intrepidity and Valour, for notwithstanding the incessant fire of the Rebels, they Surmounted every difficulty that is usual in this inclos'd Country, and were some of the first that got into the Redoubt tho they were oppos'd by a great body of Men and a heavy fire from the place, the taking of which decided the Affair in our favour.[28]

However, there is no doubt their achievement was the 'dearest bought and barrenest victory ... of the war ... The conquerors remained more closely besieged than before [and] their losses forbade the execution of any movement to raise the blockade'.[29] There was a total of 1,054 British casualties, including six marine officers and twenty-four other ranks killed and eighty-seven wounded. The loss of Major Pitcairn, an effective and courageous marine, was 'greatly regreted [sic] by the whole Corps who held him in very great Estimation'.[30]

The Royal Marines' motto '*Per Mare Per Terram*' accurately describes their flexible dual role by land and at sea which was much in evidence during the opening stages of the American War of Independence. They were deployed rapidly in Boston to bolster the garrison at a time when it was coming under increasing rebel pressure. American experience confirmed the importance of battalion formation training if the Marines were to operate effectively in land-based operations. The joint exercises carried out with the army early in 1775 helped to ensure that the two services worked seamlessly together, although they were to achieve mixed results. Effective leadership, as well as strong discipline and morale, help to explain the Marines' major role in facilitating the British withdrawal from Lexington, as well as their decisive contribution to the final assault on Breed's Hill. In 1775, priority was given to the Marines' service with the army, but at the same time they made a wide-ranging contribution at sea, which included the successful amphibious operation to maintain control of the islands in Boston harbour, and the interception of rebel shipping. When the Marines left Boston in 1776, they continued to serve in North America but reverted to their 'more traditional wartime operational sphere of combined operations and raiding, and removed from land-based battalion duty'.[31] However, the Marines' more flexible role in 1775 resulted in greater public recognition of their wider importance, leading eventually to their promotion as the Royal Marines in 1802.

Leathernecks: The US Marine Corps in the Age of the Barbary Pirates

Charles Neimeyer

United States Marine Corps legend holds that its contemporary nickname, 'Leatherneck', dates back to the time in the early 1800s when the Marine Corps and US Navy were engaged in conflict with the Barbary pirates. The nickname actually came much later. Nevertheless, today's US marines are taught that their early ancestors were issued a thick 3½in leather stock collar to protect them from the slash of an enemy cutlass during boarding operations – hence the name 'Leatherneck'. While it is true that for a number of years early US marines were indeed issued such a collar, this device would have done little to stop a cutlass slash. More likely the leather stock was provided to give the average marine an erect military posture by physically forcing him to hold his chin up. In remembrance of their ancestors' neckwear, present day US Marine Corps dress uniforms incorporate a high stock collar, except they are made of cloth instead of leather. The collars, however, are still as just uncomfortable as they ever were.

The traditional birthdate of the American Marines is 10 November 1775. However, few are aware that the last Revolutionary War era marine (along with what was left of the Continental Navy) was discharged in 1783. Both organisations were eventually resurrected in the 1790s. George Washington, then in his final term as the first president of the United States, strongly urged Congress to re-establish a modestly funded United States Navy to better protect American interests on the high seas. A major reason for Washington's urgency was that a truce between Portugal and Algiers, brokered by the British, had been recently concluded. The truce enabled the Dey of Algiers to now send his ships into the Atlantic in search of new prey. Lacking a national navy, unprotected American commercial shipping headed for Mediterranean ports was an easy and obvious target. It was not long before American vessels were being seized by Algerian corsairs, and their captured crews interned for ransom or sold into slavery. In order to further influence the Algerians, in June 1792 George Washington appointed the well-known American naval hero John Paul Jones to become the US consul in Algiers. Unfortunately for Washington and the United States, Jones died en route from Paris before he could assume his office.

Without John Paul Jones or the US Navy to worry about, in 1793 the Dey of Algiers decided to raise the stakes. According to David Humphreys, one of the US ministers in Portugal, the Dey sent a fleet of at least 'four frigates, three xebecs, and a brig of 20 guns past the straights [Gibraltar] into the Atlantic ... probably to cruise against the American flag'.[1] The Americans, on the other hand, had not a single purpose-built frigate ready for overseas combat duty. The European powers had long been plagued by similar piratical activity, but were able to mitigate these depredations through a combination of tribute payments and stationing powerful men-of-war off the ports of Algiers and Tripoli.

Many Yankee merchant houses suspected the Europeans, and especially their British commercial rivals, of secretly encouraging the predatory stance of the Algerians, in order to keep American competition out of the Mediterranean. In a panic, the US consul in Lisbon, Edward Church, wrote to Secretary of State Thomas Jefferson that 'the Portugueze [*sic*] Ships of War, which were stationed on that Coast, [were] obliged to quit it, to follow the orders of *their Masters* the English'. Church worried that the 'tribute paid by other Nations far exceeds the Sum prescribed by the U.S.' He urged that the government quickly establish a fighting navy so that:

> we can appear in the Ports of various Powers, or on the Coast, of Barbary, with Ships of such force as to convince those necessary to keep faith with Us, then, and not before, We may probably secure a large share of the Mediterranean trade, which would ... speedily compensate the US for the Cost of a maritime force amply sufficient to keep all those Pirates in Awe, and also make it their interest to keep faith.[2]

Indeed, unchecked Algerians corsairs on the high seas terrified US merchant captains, and caused maritime insurance rates to skyrocket, thus making American trade in the Mediterranean a nearly impossible task. In the months of October and November 1793 alone, the Algerians had captured '10 American Vessels, the Masters & Crews to the number of 110 Men is brought into Algiers and is made Slaves of this Regency, these and all other American Captives is in a distressed and naked situation'.[3]

The American schooner *Jay* was one of the ships captured by the Algerians. Her captain, Samuel Calder, described for his employers what had taken place on 30 October 1793 off Cape St Vincent:

I am very sorry to inform you of my present Situation which is most deplorable. I was taken by an Algerine Cruizer [along with 10 other American merchant ships] – we was stript of all our Cloaths & some Came on shore even without a shirt, we was put to hard Labour, with only the allowance of three small loaves of black bread per day & water & as it will take some time to get any supply from America, & its not possible to Live long, in this situation, I am under the Necessity of beging you to supply me with about 100 dollars, throu the hand of the Spanish Consul, for which I will send you bills ... [4]

Due to pitiful letters from people like Samuel Calder and other imprisoned Americans, Congress eventually agreed with Church's security assessment and authorised the construction of six new frigates in 1794. In order to get congressional approval, the vessels were to be built in a variety of shipyards up and down the American eastern seaboard. The Frigate Act of 1794 established the organisational structure for each frigate. Naturally, the crew list included a marine detachment of at least one officer and 'between forty-four and fifty-four enlisted men'.[5] However, ship construction was so slow that it was not until French privateers began preying on American commercial shipping in the Caribbean in 1797 that Congress moved to get the new ships completed, fully manned, and into the water. In fact their haste was now so great and much to the embarrassment of gathered dignitaries and onlookers, the new 44-gun frigate *United States* ran hard aground as she was being launched into the Delaware River, severely damaging her hull and rudder. In the meantime, American diplomats made entreaties to the Dey about what sort of tribute might please him and, until the new frigates were operational, this was the best the United States could do.

By 1798, relations between the Directory of France and the United States had also greatly deteriorated. On 11 July, Congress passed an additional Act for Establishing a Marine Corps to complement the sailors already recruited for the nation's new frigates. On this same date, the Secretary of the Navy, Maryland-born Benjamin Stoddert, authorised a number of US Navy captains who had vessels ready to go to sea to take armed French naval vessels wherever they might be found. However, Stoddert reminded the aggressive Captain Stephen Decatur Sr, commanding officer of the 20-gun converted merchant ship *Delaware*, that while he was encouraged to attack armed French ships, he was not authorised to interfere with 'Vessels, Citizens & Subjects of Nations, with whom We are at Peace, [they] are entitled to the same Civility, Respect & Friendship from Us, which We wish to receive from Them ... You are not even authorized by the Law of Nations nor by our own Laws, to recapture an American Vessel taken by the armed Vessels of any Nation but France'.[6] Just a few days before receiving this letter, without official sanction, Decatur's *Delaware* had taken the French privateer *Croyable* off the coast of Egg Harbor, New Jersey. Stoddert decided it was wise to write similar letters to nearly every US Navy captain with an active commission to make doubly sure that no American warship be accused of violating neutral nation rights, a point of international law the US government was quite serious about in the early nineteenth century. Thus began what became known in the United States as the Quasi-War with France – an undeclared naval war that would test the mettle of the newly re-established United States Navy and Marine Corps.

The first new frigate fully ready for sea turned out to be the Baltimore-built 38-gun USS *Constellation*, commanded by Captain Thomas Truxtun (or Truxton). Truxtun was one of the few American captains who knew what to do with his US marine detachment. He simply copied the British model for his own shipboard marines. Expected to demonstrate the highest level of discipline and loyalty, Truxtun's US marines were required to drill and practice musketry, keep their clothing clean, and their arms ready at all times. Marine sentries would provide shipboard security, man the fighting tops, assemble on the quarterdeck during a general action, form as part of a boarding party or to repel enemy boarders, and from time to time form as part of expeditionary forces during operations ashore. In general, marines were not supposed to perform the duties of the ship's sailors unless emergency circumstances called for it. Nevertheless, many early US naval captains used their marine detachments as they personally saw fit, such as having their leathernecks run errands for the ship's officers ashore, man the ship's boats, or act solely as seagoing ceremonial troops. In many cases, the marines themselves were at a loss as to what their actual role was aboard a US Navy frigate. However, it was the test of combat during the Quasi-War with France that settled this question and most (but not all) US Navy captains eventually copied Truxtun's British-based model for their own marine detachments.

The most sensational moment of the short-lived Quasi-War took place near the island of Guadaloupe – said to be the primary location for the Directory's Caribbean-based privateers. Cruising off the Lesser Antilles, on 9 February 1799, Thomas Truxtun's *Constellation* approached a similarly sized vessel first thought to be British. Instead, the ship turned out to be the French frigate, *Insurgente*. Once recognised, Truxtun immediately beat to quarters. Truxtun's marines were commanded by First-Lieutenant Bartholomew Clinch, USMC. Some of Clinch's leathernecks scrambled up

Commodore Thomas Truxtun USN (1755–1822), painted in 1817
by Bass Otis. (Navy History and Heritage Command)

the rigging to man their battle stations in the fighting tops. Others formed on the quarterdeck with their muskets and bayonets at the ready. Thanks to holding the weather gauge, Truxtun was able to quickly close with *Insurgente* and was soon within pistol-shot range. The French captain shouted at Truxtun for a parley but due to prior depredations against American shipping, including the recent capture of an American naval schooner *Retaliation* (the former *Croyable*), Truxtun was not inclined to grant one. Instead, he fired *Constellation*'s 24pdr main guns as they bore on *Insurgente* 'in the English fashion', and aimed for the Frenchman's hull. *Insurgente* returned fire and partially damaged one of *Constellation*'s masts. In reality, *Insurgente* was at a tremendous disadvantage throughout her running fight with *Constellation* since this vessel traded weight of ordnance for speed and was armed with only 12pdrs – half the size of *Constellation*'s main battery. A ship of *Constellation*'s size usually mounted 18pr guns at best, but the Department of the Navy had insisted on a much heavier 24pdr main battery which caused *Constellation* to heel extremely while under sail – so much so that her lee gun ports had to remain closed nearly all the time, unless Truxtun

USS *Constellation*, depicting the action of 9 February 1799, when, under the command of Thomas Truxtun, she fought the French frigate *Insurgente*, painted in 1981 by Rear-Admiral John William Schmidt. (Navy History and Heritage Command)

was willing to surrender the weather gauge to an opponent – something that *Constellation* was required to do in this particular fight.[7] In fact, over-gunning ships became a consistent American problem throughout the early years of the US Navy and often made their vessels exceptionally top heavy. However, in a close-up gun fight, the American frigates, with their heavier ordnance and hulls made out of stout southern live oak, were usually more than a match for any ship of similar size and complement.

Meanwhile, both ships continued to fire into each other. When in range, Truxtun's marines poured musket fire onto *Insurgente*'s weather deck as *Constellation*'s main battery exacted a horrific toll on the French frigate's gun crews. For a short period of time, both vessels drew apart to assess their own damage. The French 12pdrs had scarcely damaged *Constellation*'s stout hull, whereas Truxtun's heavier ordnance had made a shambles of *Insurgente*'s decks and rigging. With over three dozen casualties and temporarily immobile, *Insurgente*'s officers watched as Truxtun manoeuvred *Constellation* across her stern in order to rake the now-helpless French vessel. At this point, *Insurgente*'s captain, Michel-Pierre Barreaut, struck his colours and was soon boarded by members of *Constellation*'s crew. The

French captain, however, demanded the return of the frigate, since technically America and France were not officially at war. Truxtun rejected any notion of returning his valuable prize and, after making repairs, set sail for Norfolk, Virginia. The news set off an explosion of celebration throughout the United States and Truxtun became an instant national hero.

Throughout the remaining months of 1799, many of the new American frigates (sometimes called 'super 44s' due to their larger than normal size and armament for a frigate) searched the Caribbean for French privateers or men-of-war. During this time, *Constellation* fought another bloody single-ship engagement against the French frigate *Vengeance*. This time, however, Truxtun was less successful. During the interim between the *Insurgente* and *Vengeance* fights, *Constellation*'s main gun battery had been retrofitted with more weight-appropriate 18pdr guns. Running down *Vengeance*, the aggressive Truxtun engaged the French frigate in a four-and-a-half-hour running gunfight at night. Unlike *Insurgente*, this particular French vessel was nearly the same size and armament as *Constellation*. After exchanging dozens of broadsides, the vessels edged closer to each other. At this point, *Vengeance*'s captain, F M Pitot, prepared to board *Constellation*. Truxtun's marines, firing their muskets and lobbing grenades from the fighting tops, along with grapeshot from *Constellation*'s powerful deck carronades, drove the French boarders back with great loss of life. Both vessels drifted away from each other. Toward the end of the violent combat, Truxtun believed *Vengeance* had struck her colours, but in the darkness it was too hard to tell. It did not matter because before he could send a boarding party over, *Constellation*'s mainmast collapsed. All the mainmast topmen save one were drowned. Seeing the Americans were now busy clearing away the debris and temporarily immobile, the heavily damaged *Vengeance* was able to limp away in the darkness. The ship eventually found a safe temporary harbour at Curaçao, only to be captured a year later by HMS *Seine*. The engagement between *Vengeance* and *Constellation* had cost both sides horribly. Truxtun had at least fifteen men dead and around two dozen wounded. The French had lost at least sixty men themselves.[8]

If the short Quasi-War with France did anything for the new United States Navy and Marine Corps, it was to establish the military reputations of a number of up-and-coming combat leaders in both services. Moreover, toward the end of the conflict, Navy Secretary Benjamin Stoddert believed he finally had enough naval strength to send ships out of the Caribbean and toward the Algerian corsair-infested Mediterranean and North African coast. There were a few other lessons learned, such as the folly of one-year enlistments for sailors and marines, and the continual fractious behaviour of America's newly minted naval heroes. However, thanks to the effective administration of Secretary of the Navy Benjamin Stoddert, the early US Navy and Marine Corps became a respectable naval force, but on the whole still far below the level of the European powers.

The US Navy and Marine Corps did not have time to rest on their Quasi-War laurels. The Americans had appointed James Cathcart as US consul to Tripoli, while the post at Tunis went to a former military officer with no diplomatic experience, William B Eaton. During the early spring of 1801, newly elected President Thomas Jefferson received news from the reigning Bashaw of Tripoli, Yusuf Karamanli, that he intended to attack American shipping in the Mediterranean unless the United States provided him with an immediate payment of $250,000, to be followed by an annual tribute of $20,000 a year thereafter. In order to underscore his point, the Bashaw ordered his men to invade the grounds of the American consulate in Tripoli and chop their flagpole down – a clear symbol in the North African world that a state of war now existed between the two nations.[9] The Bashaw gave the United States six months to respond, or face the consequences of non-payment.

Yusuf Karamanli was certainly one of the region's more unstable Barbary leaders. He had come to power in Tripoli by murdering his oldest brother Hassan at an alleged reconciliation meeting prearranged by their own mother. When a copy of the Koran was called for, Yusuf received instead two loaded pistols from one of his bodyguards, whereupon he discharged them into the chest of Hassan and killed him. In 1793, following the brief capture of Tripoli by a Turkish pirate, Yusuf and his next eldest brother Hamet combined forces and ousted the Turks from the city. Both brothers thereby entered into a power-sharing arrangement. However, Yusuf then tricked Hamet into leaving the city of Tripoli, and once he had departed declared himself the sole Bashaw and permanently exiled his older brother, who then fled to the protection of the Bey of Tunis. It was here that Hamet met the US consul, William B Eaton, for the very first time.[10]

To make matters even more complicated, the United States had concluded an earlier (1796) non-aggression treaty with Yusuf Karamanli for the one-time sum of $56,000. In 1801, it seemed that treaty was at an end and despite previous tribute agreements, all the North African Barbary powers might possibly join in declaring open season on American commerce in the Mediterranean. The reason for the renewed American concern was that the Dey of Algiers was supposed to make sure this event did not happen. He had been paid much more by the United States than the other Barbary powers. This included a substantial payment in gold, naval stores, and even the delivery of a new purpose-built light frigate called *Crescent*. It was thought by American diplomats that the more powerful Algerians, not wishing to risk their lucrative arrangement, might keep the lesser Barbary powers in line. By 1801, however, the Bashaw of Tripoli and the Bey of Tunis clearly wished to make a new deal for themselves along the lines of what the Algerians were receiving, and the Dey did nothing to stop them.[11]

Jefferson resented these new demands, since he thought there would be no end to them. He now believed it might be more cost-effective to send a squadron of warships to the Mediterranean to protect American interests, and it was not long before a small American naval squadron had established a loose blockade over the harbour of Tripoli. However, due to a lack of attentiveness on the part of early commanders such as Richard Dale and Richard Morris, who largely kept their vessels in the vicinity of Malta, or even as far away as Gibraltar, Tripolitan corsairs continued their aggression against American shipping in the region. Both sides attacked each other's commerce and American prisoners of war began to accumulate in Tripoli. Most of the time the prisoners were harshly treated. While exchanges of prisoners were sometimes made, the Bashaw believed that holding large numbers of captured sailors would pay off for him, and that the Yankees would pay dearly to get their countrymen back.

Events continued to conspire against the United States in the Mediterranean when in 1804 the American frigate *Philadelphia*, commanded by the unlucky Captain William Bainbridge, ran hard aground at the entrance of Tripoli harbour. *Philadelphia* had been part of the small American Mediterranean squadron under Commodore Edward Preble in USS *Constitution*. Desperate to get away, Bainbridge had *Philadelphia*'s crew toss casks of water, cordage, and even the ship's heavy guns overboard in a desperate effort to lighten his vessel. Seeing Bainbridge's predicament, the Bashaw sent out nine gunboats that swarmed around *Philadelphia* like angry bees and fired into the stricken vessel with little to fear from any American counter-fire. After four hours of close-quarters fighting and with his ship still firmly lodged on the rocks, Bainbridge surrendered to the Bashaw of Tripoli. It was not long before he and his men were prisoners of war. Bainbridge and his officers were treated fairly well in captivity, the enlisted men far less so, many of whom were forced to endure hard labour unless they converted to Islam, which at least two of *Philadelphia*'s crew, John Wilson and Thomas Prince, apparently chose to do.[12]

37

While the Bashaw waited for the Americans to pay a ransom for the officers and crew of *Philadelphia*, Preble had other ideas in mind. Instead of paying ransom, he planned a daring commando operation to burn *Philadelphia* as she rested at anchor inside Tripoli harbour. The dashing Lieutenant Stephen Decatur, whose father had performed so well during the Quasi-War with France, volunteered for the assignment. Employing a captured vessel the Americans had renamed *Intrepid*, Decatur and his raiding party slipped into the harbour under the cover of darkness. It was not long before he and his men had retaken *Philadelphia* and killed or driven off the Bashaw's guards. While Preble had initially thought that Decatur might be able to cut out the American ship and get her underway, he decided to order her destruction, due to the difficulty of getting the ship away from the Bashaw's fortified shore batteries at night. Decatur had combustibles pre-positioned aboard *Intrepid*, and it was not long before flames had engulfed the *Philadelphia* from stem to stern. The Bashaw watched in frustration as *Philadelphia*'s burning masts and sails lit up the night sky over Tripoli harbour, the ship's loaded cannon booming one final salute when the flames finally reached them. Preble, however, was thrilled with the results of the operation. In order to keep better watch on Tripoli, Preble stationed what was left of his American squadron at nearby Syracuse. He then had his ships continue the loose blockade of Tripoli while he pondered another way to put pressure on Yusuf Karamanli.

No longer worried about *Philadelphia*, Preble rented some 'gunboats and mortar vessels' from the Kingdom of Naples and he was anxious to use them against Tripoli. In August 1804, Preble's squadron of fifteen ships shelled Tripoli, while his gunboats went into the harbour to engage the enemy corsairs then at anchor. The now famous Stephen Decatur led one of the American gunboat divisions, while his colleague Lieutenant Richard Somers commanded the other. The fighting in the harbour was extremely violent and hand to hand. Stephen Decatur's younger brother James boarded a Tripolitan gunboat that had struck her flag. However, as James Decatur stepped aboard the boat to take possession, the Tripolitan captain shot him in the head with a pistol just as he cleared the gunwale. Enraged, Stephen Decatur led a storming party of eleven sailors and marines to attack the boat he believed was responsible for the death of his brother. This decision nearly cost Decatur his own life. As he and his men boarded the gunboat, they found themselves outnumbered by thirty-six Tripolitans who seemed willing to fight to the death. The Tripolitan captain, a large man, stabbed at Decatur with a boarding pike and inflicted several wounds, but none were fatal. Decatur flung the weapon away and he and the captain wrestled on the deck. Another Tripolitan tried to hack at Decatur with a scimitar sword, but the blow was parried by the skull of a nearby American sailor who, incredibly, survived the fight. Grappling with the captain, Decatur saw him pull a large curved knife from his sash. Before the captain could plunge the weapon into his chest, Decatur pulled out a pocket pistol and shot the Tripolitan through his body, instantly killing him.[13] Decatur later wryly remarked to a friend that hand-to-hand combat was not for the faint of heart.

Truth be told, Decatur's sailors and marines performed magnificently throughout the hours-long close-quarters fight. While this was going on, Preble manoeuvred the super-44 USS *Constitution* to shell the city and keep other gunboats from attacking the Americans then struggling against the corsairs in the harbour. The Americans eventually captured three Tripolitan gunboats without much damage in return. The only American killed was James Decatur, although at least two dozen others had been seriously wounded. The Tripolitans lost at least forty-five men killed in action. However, just four days later, an American gunboat commanded by Lieutenant James Caldwell blew up when a lucky shot from an enemy cannon penetrated her powder magazine, killing ten men, including Caldwell himself. Just days afterward, Preble was surprised to learn that he was to be replaced by a more senior commodore, Samuel Barron, who was bringing five frigates from the United States to add to the fight with the Tripolitans. Nevertheless, until superseded, Preble continued his attacks against Tripoli with the utmost vigour.

Commodore Samuel Barron arrived off Malta on 7 September 1804 in USS *President*. Aboard he had a special passenger, the former US consul to Tunis, William B Eaton. After surviving some financial trouble of his own making, Eaton was given the title of US Navy Agent for the Barbary Regencies. Eaton had also conceived a vague plan with limited approval from the US Secretary of State, James Madison, to place pressure on the Bashaw at Tripoli by playing up the rift between him and his exiled elder brother, Hamet Karamanli. Eaton's ideas were opposed by many of the more conservative US Navy commanders already on station in the Mediterranean as risky and unsupportable. Undeterred, in letters back to the Secretary of State, Eaton wrote a 'harsh indictment of the management of naval affairs' there. He was also highly critical of the lax blockade of Tripoli. Needless to say, many of these same navy officers found Eaton and his opinions highly contemptible. Nevertheless, Eaton pressed ahead to resolve the situation in Tripoli, and did so without much support from Barron's Mediterranean squadron. On his own volition, in November 1804,

Eaton travelled to Egypt to find Hamet. Both men then began to make plans to unseat Yusuf Karamanli as the Bashaw of Tripoli and Hamet's animosity against his younger brother would become Eaton's means to an end. From this point forward, Eaton was very careful to refer to Hamet as 'the rightful Pasha of Tripoli'.[14]

It is clear in the correspondence between Eaton and Samuel Barron, that the commodore was uneasy about this increasingly ad hoc enterprise ashore, over which he had little or no control. In his role as Naval Agent for the Barbary Regencies, Eaton believed he had been empowered to appoint persons to positions and then consult the federal government about it afterward. One such appointment was given to Dr Francisco Mendrici, a gentleman whom Eaton befriended when he was the US consul at Tunis. Eaton conferred upon the Doctor the title of 'Agent of the United States in Grand Cairo'. He also stated that while 'he was not authorized to engage that any salary will be annexed to this appointment but am nevertheless free to assure you that in case, of any events which shall render our establishment permanent here, you may rely on my influence with my Government to obtain for you the Consulate of the United States in Egypt'.[15]

On his own, Eaton drew $13,000 from the Briggs Brothers merchant firm in Alexandria and then had their company 'inform' Samuel Barron how much the government of the United States owed them. Eaton seemed unconcerned about the rising cost of his expedition. This was probably due to an earlier arrangement he had made with Hamet Karamanli, where the once and future Bashaw of Tripoli magnanimously pledged the 'Tribute of Sweden, Denmark, and the Batavian Republic', to underwrite the cost of the expedition. This included setting Captain William Bainbridge and the incarcerated crew of the frigate *Philadelphia* free without ransom. Of course, this meant that the expedition needed successfully to oust Yusef Karamanli. Eaton also penned a note to the Secretary of the Navy that he had requested of the commodore 'a hundred stand of arms, with cartridges, and two field pieces with trains and ammunition; and also a detachment of one hundred marines, if necessary, to lead a coup de main'.[16] The US Department of State did provide Eaton with a minimal amount of monetary support, which Eaton believed was far below what was necessary. However, due to all his other responsibilities in the region, it is doubtful that Samuel Barron much appreciated Eaton drawing upon his own scarce resources. He had no idea where he was going to get Eaton's requested field artillery. Furthermore, a levy of 100 marines would require Barron to strip his squadron of a significant portion of his own shipboard leathernecks.

Barron cautioned Eaton against any experiments in regime change. He wrote:

> you must be sensible, Sir, that in giving [governmental] sanction to a cooperation with the exiled Bashaw, [the] Government did not contemplate the measure as leading necessarily and absolutely to a reinstatement of that Prince ... they appear to have viewed the cooperation in question as a means, ... without meaning to fetter themselves by any specific or definite attainment *as an end*. ... I fear by the convention you were about to enter into with Hamet and by the complexion of other measures that a wider range may have been taken than is consistent with the powers vested in me for that particular object'.[17]

Eaton and the 'rightful Pasha' Hamet Karamanli nevertheless pressed on with their expedition across the scorching Libyan desert. They set up their jumping-off point at a place sixty miles west of Alexandria, Egypt, known as the Arab's Tower. Eaton made contact with the American brig *Argus* lying just offshore. *Argus* was commanded by Lieutenant Isaac Hull, who had been ordered by Samuel Barron to support Eaton's expedition.

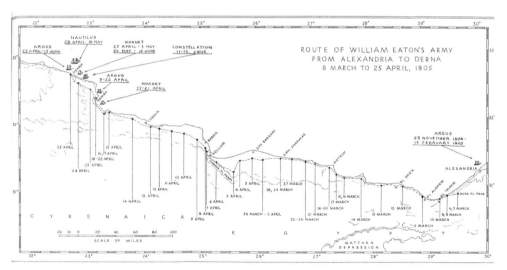

Map showing the advance of William Eaton (1764–1811), former United States Army officer and the US consul to Tunis (1797–1803), during the First Barbary War – a route similar to that taken by the British Army in 1942/3. (Author collection)

Lieutenant Presley Neville O'Bannon, United States Marine Corps (1776–1850),
the hero of Derna, famous for his exploits in the First Barbary War. (USMC)

The small brig was the best Barron could do. The rest of his squadron continued with their blockade duties. Moreover, Eaton did not get the 100 marines he had asked for, but was provided the services of an enterprising Marine Corps officer named First-Lieutenant Presley O'Bannon, a sergeant, and six US Marine privates. A youthful US Navy midshipman named Paoli Peck went along as well. Eaton and O'Bannon secretly recruited as many soldiers of fortune around the Alexandria area as they could find. They eventually got about seventy Christian mercenaries to sign on. By the time the expedition began to move, not counting Eaton's

Christian soldiers, Hamet had recruited a total force of approximately four hundred men, all of whom were of the mercenary variety.

Meanwhile, Eaton and Hamet planned to take the coast road with their polyglot column from the Arab's Tower all the way to the Bashaw's fortress at Derna. It was nearly a five-hundred-mile journey. In order to get there, *Argus* was supposed to rendezvous with Eaton's column to resupply them with food and water at a coastal location known as Bomba – about sixty miles from his target destination of Derna. As it turned out, Eaton vastly underestimated the amount of water and food he actually needed for the expedition. Moreover, as they went along, his restive Bedouin allies clamoured for their pay, of which Eaton had little to give.

After an initial delivery of around $11,000, Isaac Hull warned Eaton that he did not have any more money aboard *Argus* to continue to pay Hamet's growing body of Bedouin mercenaries. On the first day of their journey, Eaton and Hamet's forces did not get more than fifteen miles before the Bedouin camel drivers demanded their pay upfront. Only when Eaton threatened to take his own troops back to Alexandria did the drivers agree to continue the campaign. This near-mutiny was the first of several that would take place during the long journey to Derna.[18] Eaton's problem was that he was leading a predominately mercenary army on a highly difficult five-hundred-mile march without funds to pay the soldiers until after the reigning Bashaw had been deposed. Fortunately for Eaton, he could count on his small US Marine contingent and the indefatigable Lieutenant Presley O'Bannon USMC.

Midshipman Paoli Peck later described the journey to Derna. In a letter published on 9 October 1805 in the *National Intelligencer*, Peck wrote that he would have given 'thousands' for a 'gill of water'. Their rations were limited to a handful of rice and two biscuits per day 'and every day [we were] perplexed and harassed by the Arabs for money, who finding us in their power, endeavoured to extort everything from us'. At one point, Peck stated that provisions became so low that 'we killed a camel for subsistence'. Nearly out of food, water and money, the unhappy Arab mercenaries, often aided and abetted by the mercurial Hamet Karamanli, threatened to mutiny on several occasions and were only thwarted due to the timely intervention of O'Bannon's disciplined marine guard. With the entire expedition on the verge of starvation, early in the morning of 17 April 1805, the Americans were thrilled to spot a sail on the horizon. It turned out to be that of USS *Argus* – full of fresh provisions and water for the expedition. At that point, Midshipman Peck was convinced he had participated in one of the 'most extraordinary expeditions ever sat on foot'.[19]

However, before the resupply took place, the lowest moment of the expedition had occurred just nine days earlier. It was here, just outside the Bomba rendezvous point, that Hamet and his mercenaries refused to go any further. Eaton suspected that Hamet did not believe the promised American relief from the sea was going to arrive at all and in reality was planning to seize what was left of the provisions and depart for the mountains. In order to present a show of force, Eaton ordered O'Bannon's marines to run through the manual of arms in the immediate presence of the restive Arab troops. This proved to be a mistake. The Bedouins saw this martial display as a provocative act and aimed their weapons directly at the marines and Eaton himself. It was a critical moment. Eaton wrote that he then coolly 'advanced towards the Bashaw and cautioned him against giving countenance to a desperate act'. The Bashaw was so angry that he attacked one of his own retainers with the flat of his sword because the man had the temerity to ask him if 'he was in his senses'. Fortunately, other Arab officers intervened and Eaton was able to get the agitated Bashaw away from the crowd. Only then did the Bashaw's anger begin to subside. Hamet told Eaton that if he would 'give the orders to issue rice it would calm everything down'. Eaton did as requested and wrote that:

> confessions of obligation and professions of attachment were repeated as usual on the part of the Bashaw and his officers – and the camp again resumed its tranquillity. The firm and decided conduct of Mr. O'Bannon, as on all occasions, did much to deter the violence of the savages by whom we were surrounded, as well as to support our own dignity of character. After the affair was over the Bashaw embraced him with an enthusiasm of respect, calling him *The Brave American* [italics in the original].[20]

On 27 April 1805, Eaton's army had finally reached the vicinity of Derna. Although nowhere near Tripoli, it was thought that if this valuable city was taken, the government of Yusuf Karamanli might possibly fall and the people then flock to this brother Hamet. Eaton boarded *Argus* out in the bay in order to confer with Isaac Hull. *Argus* was soon joined by two other similarly armed but slightly smaller American vessels, *Hornet* and *Nautilus*. The reigning governor, Mustapha Bey, was sent a message by Eaton that 'with me is advancing the legitimate sovereign of your country' and he was offered the opportunity to peaceably surrender the town. Mustapha, however, was not a man to be trifled with and according to Eaton, the 'flag of Truce was sent back to [him] with this laconic answer, "my head or yours!"' With this, Eaton began his assault. Isaac Hull then moved his three ships within range and placed the enemy shore batteries under a devastating fire. Eaton stated that Lieutenant O'Bannon commanded his marines along with 'a company of 22 Cannoniers [*sic*] and another of 26 Greeks including their proper Officers ... together with a few Arabs on foot'. Eaton personally led a second group, while Hamet Karamanli's mercenaries attacked the town from a third side. While Hull's well-directed naval gunfire eventually succeeded in silencing the enemy batteries, many of Mustapha's men continued to lay down a heavy volume of musket fire against their attackers. Eaton did manage to laboriously land a single artillery piece, but 'in their excitement' his gunners had shot their rammer staff down range.[21]

With pressure building, Eaton felt the crucial moment in the battle had arrived. He ordered his men to charge. 'At this moment I received a Ball through my left wrist, which deprived me of the use of my hand and of course my Rifle.' Eaton then described what happened next:

Mr. O'Bannon, accompanied by Mr. Mann of Annapolis urged forward his Marines, Greeks, and such of the cannoniers ... [who] passed through a shower of Musketry from the Walls of houses, took possession of the Battery, planted the American Flag upon its ramparts, and turn'd its guns upon the Enemy ... Of the few Christians who fought on shore I lost fourteen Killed and Wounded, three of Whom are Marines, one dead and another dying, the rest chiefly Greeks, who, in this little affair well supported their ancient character.[22]

Eaton believed the timely capture of Derna was fortunate, in that a relief column from Tripoli was only two days away. He also thought that the rest of the country would soon turn on Yusuf Karamanli. In Eaton's fevered mind, the conquest of Tripoli was within sight. However, once again, events beyond Eaton's immediate control worked against him. First, the Tripolitans did not flock to Hamet's banner. Instead they joined the forces of Yusuf Karamanli and counter-attacked Hamet's mercenaries on 13 May 1805. Eaton was only able to stop the assault by firing his artillery into the attacking columns. In reality, Eaton and Hamet were themselves now under siege. Fortunately for them, Tobias Lear had been previously dispatched by the US State Department to conclude a peace with Bashaw at Tripoli. The fall of Derna may have put Yusuf Karamanli in a better frame of mind to negotiate, but he was still going to retain his position as the Bashaw of Tripoli. In exchange for peace, the Americans would pay $60,000 for the ransom of Captain Bainbridge and the crew of *Philadelphia*, and Yusuf

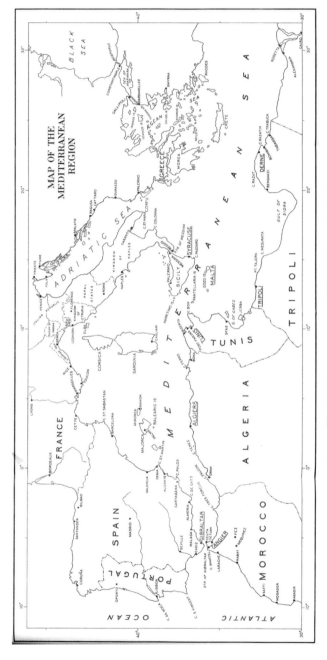

A map of the Mediterranean in about 1805. (Author collection)

Karamanli promised to make no more claims for tribute. By mid-June 1805, full diplomatic relations were finally restored between the two nations.

The United States Navy and Marine Corps would return to deal with the recalcitrant Dey of Algiers just one more time after 1805. During the War of 1812, the Dey took advantage of American naval weakness in the Mediterranean and declared war against the United States in 1814. Once the Treaty of Ghent was signed that ended that particular conflict, President James Madison was able to send the American navy once again back to the Mediterranean. This time, Stephen Decatur was now a commodore on board the new 44-gun frigate USS *Guerriere*. On 17 June 1815, Decatur's *Guerriere* caught up with 46-gun Algerian frigate *Mashuda*. The powerful American vessel blasted the hull of *Mashuda* and when a cannonball cut its commander in half, the Algerians surrendered, with over thirty men killed in action. Decatur lost only a single man killed. He then sailed into Algiers and coolly informed the Dey that in the future the United States would pay no more tribute. In fact, Decatur demanded that the Algerians compensate America $10,000 and immediately release all US prisoners of war without payment of ransom. He then proceeded on to Tunis and Tripoli and did the same thing to them. Even the wily Yusuf Karamanli, still on the throne at Tripoli, paid the United States an indemnity of $25,000. Because he held no Americans, Karamanli agreed to release ten European prisoners instead.[23]

Fighting the Barbary powers had been expensive for the United States – far more so than if it had simply paid tribute and ransom. It is estimated that the cost to America for maintaining a Mediterranean squadron to fight the Barbary powers came close to $3 million overall – a massive sum for the young nation to bear at that time. During the course of fighting, the Americans lost thirty-five sailors and marines killed in action, and sixty-four were wounded.[24] Nevertheless, although a relatively young maritime power, the willingness of the United States to resist the blackmail of the Barbary powers proved that the new US Navy, along with a few good marines, was ready and able to defend American interests abroad. Never again did the Barbary pirates attempt to attack American commerce in the region, and it was not long before other nations such as Great Britain and the Netherlands in 1816 also ended their own tributary relationship with the Dey of Algiers forever. In 1830, France made Algeria part of its colonial empire and it would remain so until they liberated themselves from the French in the early 1960s.

Fighting tops, see colour plate 5
Assault on Derna, Tripoli, see colour plate 6

'Against the Common Enemies': American Allies and Partners in the First Barbary War

Benjamin Armstrong

The maritime conflict between the still-young USA and Tripoli at the start of the nineteenth century is a favourite of American historians. At the end of 2015 yet another book has reached our shelves purporting to tell the story of how, alone and unafraid in their daring, the heroes of the early US Navy faced down the Islamic terrorists of the north coast of Africa.[1] Other historians have labelled the conflict as 'the birth' of the American navy, despite the fact that it was the second conflict in which the service fought (having followed the 1789–1801 Quasi-War with France). With its exciting stories of swashbuckling raids and its place in US Marine Corps lore, the hyperbole surrounding the conflict can be dramatic, including poorly constructed parallels to the twenty-first-century challenge of Islamic terrorism. One of the dominant narratives of both the popular and scholarly study of the conflict has been that American forces faced the corsairs alone. Ostensibly, the old world powers of Europe refused to do anything about the depredations against peaceful shipping in the Mediterranean and eastern Atlantic. However, a look at the archival record and the efforts of naval diplomacy conducted by Commodore Edward Preble shows that the Americans were not quite alone. Support from allies and partners in the Mediterranean, including British interests and the Kingdom of the Two Sicilies, played an important part in the year of the heaviest fighting, 1804.

A most daring act

On 17 February 1804, the American flagship *Constitution* (44) lay anchored in the harbour at Syracuse at the eastern end of Sicily. When lookouts spotted a pair of sail on the horizon, Commodore Edward Preble ordered the signal 227: 'Have you completed the business you were sent on'. The commodore was on edge. The two ships he had sent to Tripoli harbour in a daring raid to burn the captured frigate *Philadelphia* (36) were two weeks overdue and he knew that strong gales had swept the seas north of Tripoli. To his relief, the ships returned the signal with 232: 'I have completed the

Commodore Edward Preble. Engraving by T Kelley. (Franklin D Roosevelt Collection, Naval History and Heritage Command)

business'. The captured coastal raider, and former Napoleonic bomb ketch, *Intrepid* (4) had slipped into Tripoli in the night and burned the frigate which Captain William Bainbridge had run aground and surrendered three months prior. Sailing in company with the brig *Syren* (16), the American raiders returned to Syracuse victorious. The mission, led by Lieutenant Stephen Decatur, went down in naval legend and was reputed to have been called 'the most daring act of the age' by Lord Nelson himself.[2]

The excitement over the successful raid into Tripoli harbour was palpable. Midshipman Ralph Izzard, who participated in the attack, wrote to his mother that 'we are astonishing the folks in these parts ... the Commodore has new schemes in his head ... I expect to go to Naples shortly and then we will have hot work off Tripoli'. The young officer, soon promoted to lieutenant, was right. The mission into Tripoli served as an operational

Contemporary sketch of the US ketch *Intrepid* by Midshipman William Lewis with a description of the vessel. (Naval History and Heritage Command)

turning point for the American squadron, which had suffered from questionable leadership and poor results under previous commodores, Richard Dale and Richard Morris. Preble was ready to go on the offensive, but to do so he needed the right kinds of ships. He had heavy frigates, as well as medium-sized sloops and brigs, which had made the Atlantic crossing. But in order to conduct an assault on Tripoli itself he needed smaller combatants to move into the shallows and take the fight into the harbour and within range of Pasha Yusuf Karamanli's forts.[3]

Preble made efforts along several lines to obtain the gunboats he needed for attacks on the harbour and the corsairs. He worked closely with James Leander Cathcart, the American consul in Leghorn, on the possibility of building gunboats for the squadron there. The two men exchanged design notes and Cathcart began looking for potential builders. Of course, the biggest challenge was the money necessary for new construction. Preble had a line of credit with bankers in London, but that only went so far. The commodore pursued a second route by applying directly to the Kingdom of the Two Sicilies to lease or borrow some of their small combatants, since there were 'a great number of very fine boats at Palermo and Messina'.[4]

Preble had already established a good working relationship with the Sicilians when he moved the American base of operations to Syracuse in

Stephen Decatur boarding a Tripoli gunboat during the attack on Tripoli, 3 August 1804. Oil by Dennis Malone Carter. (Naval History and Heritage Command)

November 1803, and the kingdom was also at war with Tripoli, even if they had not really been pursuing the conflict militarily. The previous American commodores had used Gibraltar and Malta as their main bases, but these harbours had downsides. First, Lord Nelson's forces in the Mediterranean regularly cleared those ports of all their stores and water, with the much larger British force's massive appetite for supplies and victualling. Secondly, having American and British ships in close proximity had resulted in plenty of friction, with each side signing on and protecting deserters from the other, and duelling between officers. Dale had first established a relationship with Syracuse and primarily used it for watering. Preble's move of the American rendezvous to Syracuse achieved two things: it gave the Americans their own base of operations and, by adding some distance between the two, it made co-operation with the British easier.[5]

In Syracuse, Preble worked out arrangements to send American prizes for adjudication at the Sicilian Admiralty Court. Governor Marcello de Gregorio offered up the use of his magazines and the empty space in his storehouses for the Americans to stow their provisions and ammunition, and welcomed the establishment of a rendezvous for his new allies in the

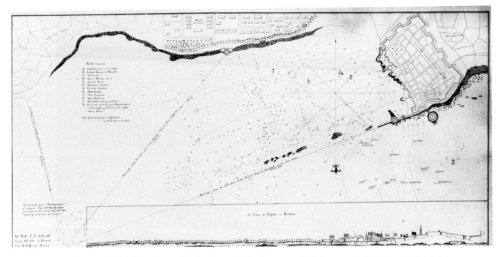

Chart of Tripoli harbour, September 1804, drawn by Midshipman F C Dekrafft. (Naval History and Heritage Command)

harbour. Receiving such positive terms, admittedly with benefits for the local economy, Preble moved his stores and provisions ashore and began watering his ships. With a solid relationship set in Syracuse, based on common interest and a growing alliance against the Pasha in Tripoli, Preble began corresponding with the court of King Ferdinand in Naples. It was there that he found a helpful ally in Sir John Acton, a Briton serving as Ferdinand's prime minister.[6]

Sir John Francis Edward Acton had risen through the ranks in the Neapolitan court after first joining the naval service of Tuscany under the auspices of his uncle. He commanded a frigate in the joint Spanish and Tuscan expedition against Algiers in 1775 with some success, rose to command Ferdinand's maritime forces, and finally became prime minister. During 1803 and 1804, he was a regular correspondent with both Preble and Nelson as the two naval commanders manoeuvred in the Mediterranean. In his pursuit of gunboats, Preble first contacted Abraham Gibbs, the American consul in Palermo, to try and obtain some of the vessels stationed there. But when Gibbs enquired about it with the viceroy, Alessandro Filangieri, the Sicilian prince told him that only Acton in Naples could authorise the leasing or borrowing of the ships. Gibbs believed that the alliance was an obvious one, and that Acton would agree, so long as Preble promised only to use the vessels in the conflict with the common enemy in Tripoli. John Broadbent, the consul in Messina, received the same response from the governor there when he asked about that city's gunboats. He also spoke to the Sicilian Minister of Marine, who promised all the assistance he could provide, but also pointed toward Acton for final permission. Preble turned to James Cathcart in Leghorn to appeal to Acton, and the consul made a formal request for access to four gunboats and four mortar boats on 5 March 1804. The next day Broadbent forwarded news of Decatur's successful raid to burn *Philadelphia* to Acton as well, telling Preble that 'atchievments [*sic*] of this nature cannot be too well known; it will have a good effect on the Court of Naples'.[7]

After several weeks of correspondence, Preble decided it was time to see Acton himself. However, he had already planned to depart with *Constitution* for a patrol off Tripoli. He wrote to his agents in Leghorn and to Broadbent and told them that he planned to sail for Naples at the end of March, after his patrol, and he would personally apply to the court for their assistance at that time. As Preble sailed off Tripoli, Acton decided to help the Americans and took the issue to the King. The two men readily agreed to the lending of boats, but there was some discussion of the limited naval guns available for the ships, which gave pause over a total agreement. Acton wrote to Cathcart that if Preble came to Naples himself to complete the negotiation, he believed the King would agree to loan the vessels and the guns.[8]

Delayed by an unsuccessful attempt at negotiation with the Pasha over the release of the *Philadelphia* captives, Preble was a month late and did not arrive at Naples until evening approached on 8 May. The next morning Cathcart came aboard to meet the commodore and the two men went ashore to see Acton. Preble recorded in his journal that he was 'favorably received' by the prime minister and Cathcart had already received word that the boats and guns would be forthcoming. The day following their meeting, Preble sent Acton a written request for eight gunboats and two mortar boats, their guns, powder, shot, shells, and muskets and sabres for the crews. He asked for them as a loan, promising to return them in the same condition in which they were received and to pay for any that were damaged or sunk. In the request he gave a brief operational description, saying that he intended to use them for an attack on the harbour at Tripoli, and also to make assaults on the other major seaport towns of Benghazi and Derna, finally saying that 'the season is now arriving when Gun Boats can be employed to most advantage'.[9]

The King agreed to Preble's request, but limited the gunboats to six instead of eight. Acton wrote that the King was pleased to be in alliance with the government of the United States and 'seconding its operations against the common enemies'. The prime minister promised to write out orders to the Minister of Marine to turn over the requested vessels, guns, and stores. He provided Preble with a copy of those orders that afternoon. As a demonstration of goodwill, Acton also successfully made efforts to cut the quarantine time for American ships pulling into Naples, a noted complaint of American merchants in the Mediterranean.[10]

Sailing for the Gulf of Sidra

Having maintained a blockade for years, patrolled the Mediterranean and made captures of blockade-runners and corsairs, the American squadron began offensive operations in earnest. On 25 July 1804, Commodore Preble approached the city of Tripoli with an assault force made up of his flagship frigate *Constitution*, the brigs *Argus* (16), *Syren* and *Scourge* (16), the schooners *Enterprise* (12), *Vixen* (12) and *Nautilus* (12), two bomb ketches, and six gunboats with over a thousand officers and men. The Sicilians in Palermo and Messina had even sent sailors to man the boats the King had loaned the Americans, which were augmented and officered by the Americans. Preble's intelligence told him that the fortress walls, batteries mounting 115 guns, with nineteen gunboats, two galleys, two schooners and a brig, protected Tripoli. The Americans did not envision the attack on the harbour as an effort to take the city, but instead to destroy the Pasha's means of defence by entirely eliminating his naval forces and coastal defences. Once completed, the blockade could be tightened, and regular and easy bombardments of the city would be possible, thus giving American naval forces the chance to force a resolution. The shallows of the harbour and the arrangement of the channel made it impossible for *Constitution* to get in close, which left the main fighting to the shallow-draught vessels, with the frigate's heavy battery providing support if Tripolitan gunboats came in range.[11]

As July came to a close, and Preble waited for the right conditions to attack, a gale blew off the North African coast and sent the American squadron back into the blue water to weather the storm. The squadron returned to its close position on 3 August and at noon Preble signalled his commanders to come within hailing distance. A group of Tripolitan gunboats had ventured out of the channel and into the open water beyond the rocks that protected the port. Preble intended to make them pay for their boldness. After days of planning and conferences with his junior officers, he knew his intent was clear and he ordered them to beat to quarters and prepare to attack. At 2.30pm, *Constitution* hoisted the signal to commence the assault and the small ships sailed in for Tripoli. The bomb ketches commenced action fifteen minutes later, after moving eastward into position, hurling shells into the city itself. The two divisions of gunboats, under the command of Lieutenants Stephen Decatur and Richard Somers, advanced on the Tripolitan gunboats, and a heavy and general battle ensued.[12]

At 4pm, as the sun sank toward the horizon, Preble signalled the retreat from *Constitution*. He wrote in his report to the Secretary of the Navy that 'our grape shot made havoc among their men, not only on board their shipping, but on shore', and concluded 'the enemy must have suffered very much in killed and wounded'. The attackers sank three Tripolitan gunboats outright, and raked several more with grapeshot and musket fire which cleared their decks of any living resistance, and took three as prizes. The Americans did not lose a single ship or boat, had thirteen wounded, and one sailor killed in action. The death was Lieutenant James Decatur, the younger brother of the now celebrated captain and a well-regarded officer in his own right, which moved the entire American force toward a desire for vengeance.[13]

On 7 August, Preble received a letter from the French consul in Tripoli suggesting that the Pasha was ready to negotiate. However, when the Americans sent a boat into the harbour under a white flag, no reciprocating flag was raised above the palace and the boat withdrew. Preble, incensed, elected to mount another assault. With his gunboats reinforced by the three prizes taken and manned with sailors borrowed from the ships of the squadron, the two divisions under Decatur and Somers launched a second assault under sail and sweeps. With the gunboat losses the Tripolitans suffered in the first attack, the enemy boats remained deep in their harbour and Decatur and Somers took their boats up point-blank to Tripoli's western shore batteries. While the first attack had had few repercussions for the shore defences, the second assault appeared to have a greater effect on the batteries by dismounting guns and killing gun crews. However, this increased effect ashore also came with a greater loss. Firing hot shot, one of the Tripolitan gun crews hit *Gunboat 9* (1), one of the prize boats under the command of Lieutenant James Caldwell. The super-heated ball ripped through the boat's magazine in the stern and it exploded, taking with it ten Americans on the aft end of the boat, including the commander. Sailors rescued eleven members of the crew after the bow section of the ship sank, but not until after they continued to return fire from their bow gun, under the command of Midshipman Robert Spence, even as the shattered hull foundered. The attackers retreated on the commodore's signal, a little after 5pm as the wind began to shift.[14]

During the second attack on Tripoli, the corvette *John Adams* (24) appeared on the horizon and joined the American squadron. Fresh from the

United States, Master-Commandant Isaac Chauncey brought dispatches from Washington, which included the formal commission for Stephen Decatur's promotion to captain. However, the dispatches also brought bad news for Preble. The administration was organising a new squadron under Captain Samuel Barron, with reinforcements of more heavy frigates, to sail not long after *John Adams*. Barron was senior to Preble and would take command in Mediterranean.[15]

On 9 August, the squadron lay offshore, resupplying the gunboats and bomb ketches with ammunition and stores in order to prepare for another attack. On the following day, Preble sent a boat into the harbour under a flag of truce with letters for Bainbridge and the American prisoners of war. The boat returned with a letter from the Pasha offering to negotiate a peace. Tripoli would accept a ransom of $500 a head for the prisoners, end the war, and give up the demand for increased tribute. It was a significant concession, but Preble thought it was a sign that he was approaching total victory. In total, the Pasha's offer would have cost nearly $200,000. Preble made a counter-offer of $100,000 total ransom for the prisoners, and a $10,000 consular gift, and no tribute. The Pasha rejected the counter-offer and the squadron continued preparing for a final attack that Preble planned to execute when Barron arrived with the reinforcements.[16]

Water, water, everywhere ...

Already at sea for a month, with multiple attacks on the harbour and almost the entire American squadron present and more attacks to come, Preble faced a logistical challenge. His squadron was so small that detaching ships to return to Syracuse for supplies and ammunition would degrade his force. Instead, he decided to take advantage of the positive relationship he had developed with Sir Alexander John Ball, the British governor of Malta. The previous January, after he announced the close blockade of Tripoli's harbour, Preble had responded to a request for help from Ball. While the governor promised that the British would respect the blockade, and do what was in their power to discourage trade with Tripoli, he had a thousand bullocks that had been purchased by the British prior to the blockade which were still in Tripoli. These cattle represented a significant element of the food supply for Malta's military garrison and victualling for the Royal Navy. Preble, as a token of goodwill, gave passports to the ships which Ball sent to pick up the cargo so that they could pass through the blockade. Several months later, as his logistical challenges off Tripoli mounted, Preble turned to Ball and the British forces at Malta to repay the favour.[17]

Malta was the closest port for the American squadron, and the transit time of only a few days was about half what it would take to Syracuse and back. Preble instructed his naval agent in Malta, William Higgins, to co-ordinate with the British authorities to lease several local vessels to use as supply ships.[18] The biggest challenge was watering the entire squadron at sea. The American vessels did not have enough water casks to store their own water and to run a supply chain between the squadron and Malta at the same time. Preble turned to the British authorities to borrow some of the water casks which the Royal Navy had on the island. Ball and Captain Charles Schomberg, captain of the Malta guard ship *Madras* (54), agreed to supply the casks and to do what they could to help Higgins find the supplies he needed. The chartered vessel *Conception* sailed on 12 August with 105 iron-bound casks from the Royal Navy, full of fresh water, as well as a full hold of other victuals, including thirty sheep and ten dozen fowl. The store ship *San Giuseppe*, which Higgins kept rotating out to the squadron with holds full of water casks, food, and ammunition, quickly joined her.[19]

With some of Preble's ships having been on station off Tripoli for nearly five months, the squadron still needed more supplies. Malta remained the only place they could go quickly and on 16 August, Preble could not help but detach one of his ships. He sent *Enterprise* to Malta with orders to quickly hire more transports, stock them, and escort them back to the squadron. Three days after *Enterprise* left, the commodore ordered his captains to reduce the rations and water allowances for their men as the remaining stocks in their holds dwindled.[20] But that same afternoon, a glimmer of hope arrived as *Intrepid* sailed into view with a full hold. Over the next few days, the leased supply ships began arriving and offloading their holds before cycling back to Malta, and the squadron remained on station.[21]

Despite Isaac Chauncey's report that the new American squadron was leaving within days of his own departure from the United States, days stretched into weeks. In his diary, Preble recorded day after day his readiness to attack, and concerns that a shift in the weather which normally came with the end of summer would push his assault force further offshore and make a new operation impossible. After waiting for weeks, the commodore decided he could not wait for the arrival of reinforcements and prepared for a night attack. On 24 August, the conditions were right and the Americans launched the night gunboat assault, but it failed again to force the Pasha to terms. On the evening of 27 August, *Constitution* and almost the entire squadron bombarded the city. While they appeared to wreak havoc on the shore defences and the population, it still had no effect on the Pasha.[22]

On 11 August, *Intrepid*, the captured ketch which had carried the raid to burn and sink *Philadelphia*, had sailed from Syracuse with a cargo of stores to help resupply the squadron off Tripoli. The month prior, *Intrepid* had been converted to a hospital ship to support Preble's attacks on Tripoli over the summer. In between the combat operations she carried supplies to augment the leased store ships. After the ketch arrived with the squadron, Preble placed her under the command of Midshipman Joseph Israel as the ship moved around the squadron distributing supplies. But there was more in store for the captured ketch. Following the failure of the bombardments to force a resolution, the crew brought *Intrepid* alongside *Syren* and began outfitting for a new mission as an 'infernal': an explosive-laden fire-ship directed into the harbour to destroy the remainder of the Pasha's naval defences.[23]

On the evening of 4 September, after repeated false starts because of rising seas or contrary winds, some of the squadron's ships conducted a brief bombardment of the shore and *Intrepid* sailed for Tripoli, escorted inshore by the schooners *Argus*, *Vixen* and *Nautilus*. The winds were favourable and Master Commandant Richard Somers and the crew headed into the channel. As the escorting schooners watched through their night glasses, the white canvas of the ketch's sails, full with an easy breeze out of the east, ghosted into the darkened port. Suddenly, well before the expected time for the detonation, the air and water around Tripoli filled with the light and crashing madness of a massive explosion. Witnesses reported seeing the masts of the infernal ketch rocket into the sky as the harbour was lit up bright as day. Preble wrote 'the shrieks of the inhabitants informed us that the town was thrown into the greatest terror'. Shells and shrapnel flung from the explosion began raining down in all directions. But *Intrepid* had exploded in the outer section of the harbour, and while the attack appeared to strike fear into the city and silenced the guns of the enemy for the rest of the night, the material damage was negligible.[24]

In the morning of 5 September, the seas began to rise. Preble's crews continued re-arming the gunboats for another attack, but the winds shifted out of the north, northeast and began pushing a heavy swell toward shore. The volatile weather that Preble had been worrying about for the past few weeks was setting in. He ordered the men to reverse their work, taking the heavy shot and shell out of the gunboats and bomb ketches and stowing it back aboard the larger *Constitution* and *John Adams*, which would ride the heavy seas more safely. Over the next two days, as the crews worked to make their ships safe, the weather continued to deteriorate. Preble took stock of the ammunition and stores that he had left. There was hardly even enough to maintain three ships for the blockade, never mind the entire force he had on the Tripolitan coast. Barron still had not arrived with reinforcements or more resupply, and Preble decided that his window to force the Pasha's hand had closed. On 7 September, he ordered *John Adams*, *Syren*, *Nautilus* and *Enterprise* to take the gunboats and bomb ketches in tow and head for Syracuse. He took the remaining ammunition and stores from the departing ships and remained on station with *Constitution*, *Argus* and *Vixen* to hold the blockade.[25]

Partners, allies and the 1804 campaign

In the afternoon of 10 September, lookouts on the blockaders spotted sails and the frigates *President* (44) and *Constellation* (38) finally arrived from America. The blockaders rendezvoused with the new ships and the captains joined Barron aboard *President* for a conference that afternoon. Barron was 'mortified extremely by the contrary winds which has lengthen'd our passage in an uncommon degree', and stopped at Malta for water and stores before meeting Preble off Tripoli. Preble began briefing his replacement on what the squadron had accomplished over the summer. Secretary Smith's orders expected Preble to remain in the squadron, giving up his position as commodore, but staying on as captain of *Constitution*. Preble, however, had other ideas. Captain John Rodgers had sailed with Barron, and he was also senior to Preble. The outgoing commodore was tired after such intense combat operations over the summer and he was not about to accept a position as third in command of the squadron. Answering to Barron was one thing, but Preble and Rodgers had a long-standing animosity and Preble had sworn never to serve under him.[26]

Barron agreed when Preble told the new commodore that he intended to go home. He also listened to Preble's advice, letting the departing commodore order the newly promoted Captain Stephen Decatur to command of *Constitution* as one of his final acts in command of the squadron. After hearing about the success of the summer gunboat attacks and harbour bombardment, Barron asked Preble for one thing before he sailed for home: return to King Ferdinand's court and attempt to get more gunboats for the next year's operations. The agreement with the King had been that the Americans would return boats used in 1804 at the end of that season, and they clearly needed more small ships. Preble agreed to work his naval diplomacy one last time, but was unsuccessful. Ferdinand was under pressure from somewhere else to withhold support from the Americans. Preble suspected the French. Before sailing for America he sent one last letter to Barron suggesting buying more gunboats in Malta, where he could build on the relationship with Governor Sir Alexander Ball and the Royal Navy captains.[27]

The American squadron never obtained more gunboats from allies in the Mediterranean. William Eaton, the former consul in Tunis, had returned to the Barbary Coast with Barron's reinforcements and orders to explore the possibility of an overland campaign in support of the Pasha's older brother and his rightful claim to the throne. The success of that campaign, and the taking of the city of Derna in April 1805, put enough pressure on Yusuf Karamanli that he acceded to peace terms in June. Eaton was beside himself, forced to abandon the brother Hamet Karamanli, but the war was over.[28]

The history of the United States' First Barbary War is commonly accompanied by exaggeration and hyperbole by popular historians, but sometimes by academics as well. The regular portrayal of the American effort as being a solitary one, forsaken by Europeans who were happy to keep paying tribute to the corsairs, is not entirely accurate. Success depended upon partnership and alliances built through solid naval diplomacy. Central to the American fighting in the summer of 1804 was the contribution in men and equipment of the Kingdom of the Two Sicilies, and, despite the antagonism that characterised Anglo-American relationships in that era, the support of the British to overcome Preble's logistical challenges. These were ad hoc coalitions of the willing, or partners with 'kinship' of interests as Alfred Thayer Mahan would describe them, central to the exercise of sea power, which allowed a small navy (the US Navy in this case) to play a central and effective role in naval operations.[29]

Marines at the Great Gate, Tripoli, see colour plate 8

Captain Ingram, the Sea Fencibles, the Signal Stations and the Defence of Dorset

David Clammer

When the war with Revolutionary France broke out in February 1793, Captain Nicholas Ingram was without employment. At his home in Burton Bradstock, near Bridport, he was on the beach and anxious to be doing something in the country's defence. Made a lieutenant in 1778, he had served aboard *Royal Oak*, Rear-Admiral Hyde Parker's flagship, and had been promoted commander in 1780, and commanded the *Star* brig until the peace of 1782. During the Nootka Crisis of 1790, he commanded the sloop *Shark* and was made post-captain in the general round of promotions in November of that year.[1] So he was not without experience. For two years the Admiralty had nothing to offer him, and such was his frustration that on 8 March 1795 he wrote to Their Lordships stating that as he had had no naval employment since the outbreak of the war, 'and wishing to serve my King and Country in some mode or another', he had enlisted in the ranks of the Dorset Volunteer Rangers, the local cavalry regiment which had been raised the previous year by Lord Dorchester.[2]

Ingram was commissioned on 9 May and the regimental muster roll shows him as a lieutenant in the 6th Troop under the command of Richard Travers of nearby Uploders.[3] This was a considerable commitment for a half-pay naval officer. The Rangers made a point of declining any government assistance except for their swords and pistols; they rode their own horses and provided their own saddlery and the rest of their equipment. The cost of the uniform alone, with its jacket and waistcoat, breeches and boots, gilt buttons, sash and sword-knot, and the great crested helmet with gilt chains, amounted to the equivalent of almost £1,000 in today's values.[4]

Ingram, who must have been a competent horseman, was left to enjoy his unusual position as a Royal Navy captain and lieutenant of irregular cavalry for three further years, while the Ranger officers also played a prominent role in the preparations for evacuating and laying waste the Dorset coastal strip in the event of a French landing. Then, in the spring of 1798, the Admiralty appointed Ingram to a command in the Sea Fencibles, which had been created by an Order in Council of 14 March.

St Mary's, Burton Bradstock, where Ingram is buried – and from whose tower
the first bells in England were heard celebrating the victory of the Battle of Trafalgar.
(Author collection)

The Sea Fencibles were defined as being 'for the protection of the coast, either onshore or afloat; comprising all fishermen and other persons occupied in the ports and on the coast, who, from their occupations are not liable to be impressed'.[5]

In April 1798, Ingram was appointed to command the Sea Fencibles in the Weymouth and Portland area. Captain Augustus Brine commanded the eastern section and Commander Daniel Folliott the western end. This was not an altogether satisfactory arrangement, especially as the length of the Dorset coast – a little over seventy miles – and the terrain made it necessary to divide it into thirteen subdivisions. Running from east to west, these were Poole, Swanage, Kingston, Lulworth, Weymouth, Portland, Langton Herring, Abbotsbury, Pucknowle, Swyre, Burton Bradstock, Bridport and Lyme. Seeing the need for a co-ordinating hand, the Admiralty decided that while Brine and Folliott should remain in post, the whole of the county's coast should be under a unified command, and on 7 April 1798, appointed Ingram 'to command all such men as may from time to time enrol themselves under the Denomination of Sea Fencibles for the Defence of the Coast of the County of Dorset.' At the same time, the officers of the Impress were directed to place themselves under his command 'and to follow any orders he may judge necessary to give you for His Majesty's service.'[6]

At first, Ingram seems to have been unsure whether this order included Poole, the largest town and port in the county, and he wrote asking for clarification. The Secretary's reply of 16 April was clear: 'I am to acquaint you that you are to consider Poole as within your command and the Regulating Officer there is directed to follow your orders'.[7] When Captain James Hewett, the regulating officer at Poole, died in July and was replaced by Captain John Boyle, an officer three years senior to Ingram in the list of post-captains, Boyle was unhappy. He wrote to the Admiralty on 14 July suggesting that perhaps his senior lieutenant could be responsible for the Sea Fencibles, an arrangement which would 'obviate any irregularity' in matters of seniority. But the orders stood.[8]

When the Sea Fencibles came into being, the captains placed in command received a set of *Instructions for Officers*.[9] The commanding officer was to inform the local mayor regarding his duties in recruiting the new force, 'and to consult with him on the most expeditious and efficacious mode of communicating the same to the inhabitants of the town and its environs'. The captain was also to assemble the local inhabitants (quite how this was to be done was not made clear) and explain what the Sea Fencibles were to do, and to encourage as many as possible to enrol.[10] Ingram decided that one way at least of getting his message across would be by way of a poster. Taking those parts of the Admiralty *Instructions* relating to duties and conditions of service, he had a poster printed in Weymouth headed 'Conditions of Enrollment of Sea Fencibles For the County of Dorset Under the Command of Captain Nicholas Ingram'.[11]

This document aimed to give basic information about the nature of the service, and to calm the anxieties which the maritime community was known to have. The duties of the men who enrolled were simple enough: to train one day a week in the use of pikes and 'great guns' – the coastal artillery. They would be paid a shilling for every day's exercise, and for any other day when called out on duty. Pikes would be supplied, and men were to be responsible for returning them when training was over, or be liable for the cost. (The pikes in question were not the kind issued to some of the infantry volunteers, but long naval boarding pikes.) At times of special danger they would be needed to watch the beaches, and in the event of an

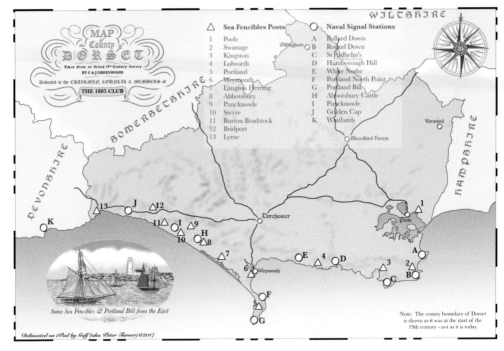

The Sea Fencible posts and signal stations of Dorset. (© Galf)

enemy ship being sighted, be ready to serve aboard any gunboat or armed vessel. Ingram was well aware that his potential recruits were, like the men in the local infantry volunteers, intensely local in outlook. He therefore offered assurance that men would not be required to leave their own part of the coast except in the case of actual invasion, and that if service afloat was required, men would be returned to their own district. He also made it clear that men who did enrol, and whose occupations required them to leave their immediate area, would be given a ticket of leave against impressment. This was a particular fear, and the poster stated 'that their being enrolled and serving in Boats shall not render any man liable to be impressed who was not liable to it before'.[12]

How effective this notice may have been is open to question, since a high proportion of the men who did answer Ingram's call were unable to sign for their pay, and had to make their mark. In 1801, for example, 44 per cent of the men from Burton Bradstock, Ingram's own village, had to make their cross, while 65 per cent of the Swyre men and 64 per cent of the Bridport contingent were also unable to write their names. Ingram, however, was not the man to leave any stone unturned.[13]

The Admiralty had also decided that the naval signal stations which had already been erected along the south coast should be under the command of the newly appointed Sea Fencible officers. The Dorset section of the chain of signal stations had been constructed early in 1794. From east to west, these stations were situated at Ballard Down to the north of Swanage, and Round Down to the south of the town, at St Alban's (or Aldhelm's) Head, Hamborough Hill near Lulworth (now Hambury Tout), Portland Bill and Pucknowle. The ones at Portland and St Alban's were designated 'principal stations' as markers for fixing the position of both British and French vessels. The station at Whitlands, between Lyme and Seaton, which was actually in Devon, also came under Dorset command.[14] However, after a survey of the defences of the southwest coast was made by Captain James Bradby in 1796, he reported that the Whitlands station was too far from Pucknowle for relaying signals. There was however 'a hill called Golden Cup [Cap] between Pucknowle and White Land eligible for a signal post'. This was duly added to the chain.[15]

Ingram, so recently kicking his heels, now had a great deal to occupy his attention. The Admiralty instructions required officers to observe whether the signal stations 'are placed in the most advantageous situations for conveying intelligence along the coast.' He quickly realised that some of them were not. Even with the construction of the Golden Cap station, the layout of the original line remained unsatisfactory. There were gaps in the chain and signals could not always be seen and repeated. He saw that an additional station was required on Portland, at North Point (now the Verne), because the signal mast at the Bill could not be seen from some other parts of the coast. The work was put in hand, though on 30 July 1798, Ingram wrote to Evan Nepean, First Secretary to the Admiralty, explaining that the weather was interfering with the construction, but that he hoped to have it functioning in a few days in order to repeat signals.[16] By 1800, Ingram had become concerned that the signal station at Pucknowle was too far from Portland for the efficient transmission of signals, and he had the lieutenant at Pucknowle, Henry Rosher, burn a blue light at night to test its visibility. Consequently, he recommended to the Admiralty that the station should be resited at Abbotsbury Castle, an Iron Age site further to the east, which was higher and where the signal mast would be clear against the sky, and would make a more effective link with the Portland and Golden Cap stations.[17] The new station was not fully operational until 1803.

It is interesting to note that the Admiralty was prepared to give Ingram a free hand in these arrangements, despite being parsimonious in many other respects. The signal station lieutenants, for example, were allowed a generous 9d a mile to reach their posts, but Their Lordships anxiously demanded a sworn affidavit from each officer certifying that the shortest possible route had been taken.[18]

The Admiralty was also reluctant to finance even the basic requirement for the signal stations on the waterless Dorset headlands to have a water supply. In May 1803, Lieutenant Young at Round Down and Lieutenant Leaver at St Alban's were allowed to have a water butt,[19] and in November 1807, Lieutenant George Pace at Ballard Down was allowed 2s 6d a week for 'procuring water'.[20] But when, in the summer of 1803, Ingram decided that the lie of the land prevented the officer at St Alban's Head from reading the signals made at Hamborough Hill, the Admiralty accepted that 'it would be very much better placed on the high land which is called White Nothe', and the move was carried out without official objections.[21]

There does not appear to have been much initial enthusiasm for joining the Dorset Sea Fencibles. This is perhaps not surprising when it is remembered that at the eastern end of the Channel even Nelson was having difficulties in encouraging recruitment. On 6 August 1801, he was exhorting the captains on the Kent coast that it was essential 'that all good men should come forward on this momentous occasion to oppose the Enemy, and more particularly the Sea-Fencibles … that the horrors of war may not reach the peaceful abodes of our families.' The following day, writing to St Vincent, he had to admit that few men were prepared to go far from their homes or serve afloat. 'This, my dear Lord, we must take for granted is the situation of all other Sea-Fencibles: when we cannot do all we wish, we must do as well as we can.'[22] Ingram would no doubt have agreed with that wholeheartedly.

What sort of men was Ingram actually able to recruit? The Admiralty was not concerned with the age or occupation of men joining the Sea Fencibles, and this information was not entered in the pay lists. In January 1803, however, when making his weekly returns, Ingram decided to include some of this information, whether Their Lordships required it or not. This seems simply to have been a matter of intellectual curiosity, and it does enable us to gain some insight into the composition of the companies under his command.

In the case of the Abbotsbury unit, seventy-five of the eighty-one men on the strength were fishermen. One was listed as a seafarer, two were shoemakers and three combined fishing with rope- or shoemaking. At Lulworth, on the other hand, the picture was more varied, and rather surprisingly, only five of the ninety-six men listed were fishermen. The great majority – sixty-nine – were agricultural labourers. The remaining twenty-two came from non-nautical occupations including a carpenter, a lime-burner, several cordwainers, a butcher, a blacksmith and an innkeeper. On Portland, of the 116 men on the roll, the quarrymen outnumbered the fishermen fifty-six to fifty-three, with the remainder being made up of several trades, two pilots and a lighthouse keeper. In Weymouth, although there were a couple of customs officers, most of the men followed the sea – twenty-four fishermen, fourteen masters or mates and sixteen pilots.[23] This mixed picture was confirmed in August 1805, when Admiral Sir George Cranfield Berkeley, Inspector of Sea Fencibles, visited the south coast. At Poole he found that most of the men were masters, mates, pilots and fishermen. At Swanage and Kingston on the other hand, they were almost entirely labourers and quarrymen.[24]

Given the disparate make-up of his widely dispersed units, and the fact that a significant proportion of the men were landsmen who would have been of very little use at sea, the problem facing Ingram and his officers was how to weld them into a useful defensive force. The *Instructions* seem to have envisaged the Sea Fencibles acting like infantry. They were to be drawn up in whatever numbers were available, and 'to be taught to charge the enemy, or receive the charge of horse or foot; to storm batteries, and to defend them'. As they had no firelocks, Ingram must have regarded these instructions as impractical, and would probably have agreed with W M Hardy, an early historian of Swanage, describing the defensive preparations on Purbeck at a later date, who believed that the Sea Fencibles were to use their pikes at the water's edge, or even in the water when an enemy was actually in the act of disembarking.[25] In the autumn of 1803, Ingram was busy inspecting these weapons and trying them out. A few were broken, but most were good, '9 feet long and full stout enough'. It would be simple, he reported, to obtain new shafts, preferably of ash, and have the steel end fixed for 2s each. In October, he also recommended to the Admiralty that his men be issued with cutlasses, in case fighting should come to very close quarters. A sensible suggestion, but one which was not adopted.[26]

While attempting to organise and train the Sea Fencibles, Ingram, having re-established the chain of signal stations to his satisfaction, had also to ensure their efficient running. This dual responsibility, spread over more than seventy miles of country, much of it precipitous, meant that the officers in charge needed to have the mobility which only horses could give. Before the Peace of Amiens, Commander Folliott had indeed written to the

Admiralty pointing out that he had to keep a horse, and requesting that the Admiralty should bear both the expense of the horse and the cost of the horse tax. 'Acquaint him that no charges of this kind can be allowed', Nepean had written across the letter.[27] Ingram, as we have seen, was an excellent horseman, and it seems certain that he must have used the horse, or horses, which he rode with the Rangers.

When inspecting the signal stations, all officers were instructed to check the condition of the telescopes and the signal flags and balls, and to ensure that the secret signals were being kept secure. What probably gave Ingram some cause for concern was the quality of the men at the stations. Each was commanded by a half-pay lieutenant, assisted by a midshipman and two seamen. In some cases, the lieutenants were of an advanced age. Ingram reported that at the Portland Bill station, Lieutenant McKey had been in the service more than fifty years, which must have put him in his late sixties.[28] And in writing to the Admiralty from Round Down in June 1797, Lieutenant Roberts, who seems to have feared his dismissal, described himself rather pathetically as 'far advanced in years' and one who had 'out-liv'd my friends'.[29] Nor were some of the midshipmen likely to have inspired any great confidence. George Moore at Abbotsbury Castle was forty-one, Sam Mitchell at the Verne was forty-six, and at White Nothe, Thomas Flower was forty-seven. They were in fact the sort of middle-aged midshipmen unlikely ever to pass for lieutenant. And Ingram had already pointed out to Their Lordships that four men per station represented a very low level of manning, since one man would often have to be away to carry or collect messages and to bring back provisions. Further, in August 1804, when the fleet's need for seamen was acute, instructions were issued to the Sea Fencible officers that all seamen were to be discharged and sent to the nearest port. Their place was to be taken by locally recruited landsmen.[30] This cannot have made it easy to maintain efficient signalling.

In March 1806, the Admiralty also directed that officers commanding Sea Fencibles should ascertain that none of the signal station lieutenants, isolated as they were, had 'appropriated any part of the wages of the men themselves'.[31] This must have required Ingram to make another tour of inspection. He was able to report that there was no financial irregularity, except at Portland Bill. Here, the elderly McKey had put his daughter down as a midshipman, and had been paying her as such. He had also been keeping a boy whom he paid himself, while making returns for three men instead of the two actually employed. In future, Ingram told the Admiralty, he would attend to matters of payment in person, and was instructing Captain Brine to the west, and Commander Folliott to the east, to do the same. So far as Lieutenant McKey was concerned, Ingram displayed considerable understanding and compassion. McKey, he pointed out, was old, with more than half a century of service, and that as he had always been attentive to his duties, 'I hope the Honourable Board will be as lenient to him as the case will admit'.[32] The board took Ingram's advice, and McKey was left in post.

In addition to being armed with pikes, the Sea Fencibles were to be trained in the use of the 'great guns', that is, the coastal artillery: 'If there be cannon in the district, (permission being obtained from the officer under whose charge they are) the men are to be exercised alternately at them, and at the pike.' There were, in fact, several batteries situated along the Dorset coast (though some of the guns were unserviceable), including at Weymouth and Portland. There was a battery of six 24pdrs at the Nothe, above Weymouth harbour, which, amongst other things, were used to fire salutes when the royal family were enjoying their seaside holidays. This brought Ingram to the attention of the King and Queen. In September 1798, Queen Charlotte wrote to the Prince of Wales describing a visit to the Nothe battery 'to see the Sea Fencibles commanded by a Sea Captain Ingram ... When they had gone through their exercises they fired a Royal Salute'.[33]

It was, of course, necessary to maintain both guns and ammunition in good condition, and in July 1803, and in his usual indefatigable way, Ingram was writing to the Admiralty to complain that some of the ammunition at the Nothe was ruined because the building in which it was kept was in bad repair. He also wanted some of his men to exercise on the Portland guns. He proposed that a master gunner be appointed, and paid for, and requested an instructor from the horse artillery then in Weymouth. Some of the Weymouth men were indeed sent to the Portland batteries, though Ingram's other suggestions seem not to have been acted on.[34] This was unfortunate: in September 1798, one of the Sea Fencibles had had his arms blown off at the Nothe battery, probably as a result of inadequate training. There were other similar accidents, which might have been prevented had Ingram's suggestion been accepted.

The Queen's mention of Captain Ingram is indicative of the fact that he was a well-known and important figure. Nothing could make this clearer than a false alarm which occurred on 1 May 1804. Early that morning, Major Frampton of the Dorset Yeomanry (as the Rangers had been renamed), received an urgent message that the French were landing in thick fog on Portland. The rider bore a written message:

I came here by the Recommendation of Captain Ingram who informed me that Capt. Daniel had called on him and informed him that the French were landed on Portland and Captain Ingram said that our Corps ought to assist in repelling them immediately. Weymouth is entirely in a State of Confusion and Uproar.[35]

Daniel had in fact panicked; the hostile vessels were probably fishing boats glimpsed through the fog. What seems significant is that the officer Daniel reported to, and who decided to alert the yeomanry, was not one of the regular army or local volunteers, but Captain Ingram.

Although Ingram was evidently very busy with his dual responsibilities, he certainly found time to enjoy himself. George III and the royal family spent most of their summer holidays in Weymouth during what we might think of as the invasion years, and south Dorset enjoyed a vivid social life, including of course, balls. And here we have the testimony of two young ladies. On 18 October 1804, Mary Manfield, daughter of a Dorchester alderman, wrote to her brother John, then serving aboard the frigate *Ambuscade* off Toulon: 'I went to the ball and danced with an officer of the Navy to whom Captain Ingram introduced me'.[36] Another young lady, Mary Shirley, at another royal ball in the same month, wrote to her aunt to describe how the King himself had busied around ensuring the young ladies all had partners, and how 'Captain Ingram got me a very famous German, with whom I danced two dances'.[37]

Ingram was not an officer to be shy of adding to his responsibilities when he felt it necessary. In October 1803, for instance, after the war had resumed, he took it upon himself to establish a twenty-four-hour watch at the Nothe battery consisting of three men at a time, because of the temporary absence of the army.[38] Not long afterwards, he was informing Their Lordships that he had given orders 'to take up any suspicious persons that may land on the coast',[39] and when two Frenchmen did arrive at Weymouth aboard the Jersey packet in May 1807, claiming to be pilots, he had them locked up in a public house and sent to London for instructions.[40]

There was, however, one defensive measure in which Ingram, despite his zeal, failed to achieve success: the provision of armed boats. The government's *Plan for a Voluntary Naval Armament for the Protection of the Coast* was issued to the Lords Lieutenant of the coastal counties when the war resumed. The plan called for seaports to 'equip, at their own expense, a certain number of armed vessels and hulks, to be stationed for the better security and protection of such ports, and to be appropriated to, and manned by, Sea Fencibles'.[41] The government would provide the guns and ammunition. The merchants of Poole seemed prepared to support this plan, but to Ingram's frustration, the shipowners of Weymouth were not, and in August 1803, he was complaining to the Admiralty that they 'do not seem inclined to adopt the plan'.[42] He could make no progress at all, and was forced to accept that the scheme may not have been practical, since vessels of all kinds were, in the nature of things, often at sea and not available in harbour. 'It is apprehended', he wrote, 'that merchants and ship owners living in the sea port of Weymouth cannot afford to let their vessels remain stationary'.[43] He therefore changed tack and proposed that if the government could provide some rowboats substantial enough to carry heavy ordnance, 'the sea fencibles might be employed and able to go out and act against an enemy at all times or tide'.[44] Nothing came of this either, and a year later Ingram was still corresponding with the Admiralty on the subject of armed vessels. The question of gunboats was never resolved.

Two months before Trafalgar had rendered invasion a practical impossibility, Buonaparte had broken up his great encampment at Boulogne and launched the Grand Army on the long march which culminated at Austerlitz in December 1805. Fears of invasion slowly receded, and Ingram's duties diminished. On 21 May 1808, however, he was made a superannuated rear-admiral. The Sea Fencibles were stood down in

Memorial in St Mary's, Burton Bradstock, to Rear-Admiral Ingram and his two wives. (© Galf)

February 1810. The signal stations, on the other hand, had a longer life and were kept in action almost until the end of the war. The network was thought to be redundant following Buonaparte's abdication in April 1814, and was closed down in November. With the resumption of the war in the summer of 1815, however, following the Emperor's escape from Elba, the stations were briefly brought back into action. Finally, some of them at least were transferred to the Revenue to assist in the perennial anti-smuggling operations.

Admiral Ingram's first wife, Sarah King, died in March 1810 and he married Elizabeth-Ann Booth of Bristol in July 1811, and lived in what is still named Ingram House until his death, aged seventy-one, on 3 February 1826. He is buried only a few yards away in St Mary's Church, Burton Bradstock.

At the beginning of the war with France, Nichols Ingram had been an experienced but unemployed officer, and like others in his position had certainly been anxious for a command at sea. His determination to be active in the defence of the country had led him, at considerable personal expense, to become a volunteer irregular cavalryman. The Admiralty's decision to appoint him to command the newly raised Sea Fencibles, and later the chain of signal stations, was a godsend to Ingram and a stroke of luck for the county of Dorset. Land-based though they were, Ingram's new responsibilities were both practical and administrative, and called for diplomatic skills in dealing with the local population. They were also spread along the entire coast, a problem not faced by other military officers, either regular or volunteer. In addition to all this, Ingram was ever ready to assume fresh responsibilities and to urge improvements in coastal defence. And still he found time to participate in the vivid social life of Weymouth occasioned by the summer visits of the royal family, dancing at the balls at Gloucester Lodge. Captain Ingram must have been one of the most widely known figures in the county at this time, known to the King and the county gentry, as well as the humble fishermen, labourers and quarrymen who kept the long watch, and as such he emerges as one of the key figures in the defence of Dorset in the period before Trafalgar.

That Matchless Victory: Trafalgar, the Royal Marines and Sea Battle in the Age of Nelson

Britt Zerbe

The Royal Navy was to emerge from the eighteenth century as the strongest naval force in the world. It had taken all of this century to develop the theory and best practices that would lead eventually to one of the greatest, and one of its largest, battles in the age of sail, the Battle of Trafalgar. Commentary and scholarship has examined this battle in almost every detail,[1] from explaining the French and Spanish points of view,[2] British tactics,[3] to overarching campaign studies,[4] and the personalities involved. This extensive historiography, unfortunately, has overlooked one key group who played an important role in the battle, the Royal Marines. When the Royal Marines are mentioned, it is usually only when referencing an officer by name and his death or wounding. Captain Charles William Adair, commanding officer of marines in *Victory*, for example, is mentioned because he was shot a few moments before and quite near Nelson.

There are only three works which have challenged this trend.[5] Of these, only Colonel Cyril Field's book *Britain's Sea-Soldiers* devotes space to marines' specific involvement in this battle. However, Field's book is woefully inadequate and his commentary concerning the battle itself is done in a broad, sweeping overview. This neglect of the Royal Marines is even more problematic, since more than three thousand marines, one-tenth of the entire corps, were with the fleet off Cadiz. The historiographical oversight is greater when it is considered that the battle had strong resonance with many contemporary marines. Lieutenant William Clarke remarked on hearing of the battle, 'our exultation on [hearing about] the glorious event was mingled with great individual mortification at having lost our share in the conflict which was crowned by that matchless victory'.[6] Clarke, who missed the battle because he was in *Prince of Wales* (Nelson had allowed Robert Calder to return in his own ship even though battle was imminent), spoke to a common sentiment. This oversight concerning the marines' duties during battle and their disproportionate casualties is symptomatic of their marginalisation in the history of the age of sail, and has led to an incomplete understanding of how the Royal Navy became mistress of the seas.

Marines are a unique military force, not constrained by a geographical identity: the army's purpose is to fight on land, the navy at sea and the air force in the air. Instead, marines, even in the eighteenth century, were a multi-dimensional force whose operational ethos required them to exist and fight on both land and at sea.[7] Their actions at sea made them important to the Royal Navy.[8] However, there is reason for focusing on Trafalgar, because on all the twenty-seven British ships of the line engaged in the battle, the marine complements came solely from the Royal Marines. Prior to this, due to the rapidly increasing size of the Royal Navy, regiments of infantry had been mobilised to serve as marines on board British ships.

Doctrine and practice

Historian Brian Lavery has suggested that 'a ship of 74 guns, with about 120 marines, used only about a dozen of them as small-arms men in action'. He goes on to state that there is 'no real reason to believe that marines were particularly effective' at their more traditional role in boarding actions.[9] This is a misunderstanding of the changing importance of marines in eighteenth-century sea engagements, and how they used their concentrated small-arms firepower to great effect during 'pistol shot' actions. Their role in boarding parties has also been largely misunderstood, as they were more effective in repulsing enemy boarding attempts and in providing suppression fire for the naval boarders.

The only documents given to a ship's captain regarding fleet tactics and fighting their ships were the fighting instructions, very vague in their tactical principles and many times added to by individual admirals like Hawke, Howe and Nelson before they went to sea or into action.[10] The only guidance the Admiralty issued to individual marine officers for training concerning individual ship tactics was the *Regulations and Instructions relating to Marines serving on board His Majesty's Ships*. These regulations were renewed periodically throughout this period, but only Article IX was specifically concerned with training at sea. Its statement of responsibility was brief: 'Marines are to be exercised by the Marine Officers in the Use of their Arms, as often as possible, to make them expert therein'.[11] This left many issues unanswered; like where marines should be stationed, how they should fight and what their duties during an engagement were.

However, the Admiralty, naval captains and marine officers did understand the importance of training and the time needed to make men fully prepared: all of these orders called for the men to be 'exercised daily'.[12]

There were naval officers who felt this was insufficient and issued yet more detailed instructions or captain's orders to their marines. These orders were concerned with a wide range of issues from discipline to hygiene but they also gave instruction about the practice of the great guns and small-arms drill. The instructions issued in 1799 in HMS *Mars* (74), while longer than the Admiralty's instructions, were still less than two hundred words, the primary concern being the adequate preparation of ammunition before action.[13] The perceived need for these orders arose from the perceived inexperience of young marine officers and the desire to create a cohesive tactical doctrine. One published pamphlet of advice to naval officers highlighted this: 'if the marine officer is a raw lad, and therefore troublesome, as [then] no one can dictate to you what steps you ought to take in carrying on service'. Indeed many newly commissioned marine officers were young, between sixteen and nineteen years old, and the Commanding Marine Officer in Portsmouth, in 1775, was in complete agreement and felt it was vital that these young officers be 'disciplined'.[14] These problems should not be overstated as first to sixth rate ships had at least one senior marine officer on board, either of captain or first lieutenant's rank and, due largely to the slow promotion and gerontocracy of marine officers, with experience at sea.

The loose nature of tactical thought which the official and naval manuals offered did not lead to a complete lack of theory, and marine officers were forced to look to their own resources for ideas. A handful of private manuals had a dramatic impact. One of the first writers was Lieutenant John MacIntire in his 1763 work, *A Military Treatise on the Discipline of the Marine Forces When at Sea*.[15] While this work has been quoted by many historians as a piece on training and theory for amphibious warfare, it was specifically directed at marines, and MacIntire states that it was gathered from various foreign military maxims, and had been thoroughly 'examined, and approved, by many [Marine] Officers of superior Rank and Experience'.[16]

The great guns

MacIntire's section on sea engagements was made up of 'knowledge I have acquired of this subject' and 'is more from theory than practice'.[17] His theories directly influenced marine officers, transforming the way in which marines trained and performed these tactics in battle. At the start of battle, when the ships were well outside of musket range, marines acted as part of the great guns' crews. MacIntire states this not in a manner of theory but of common practice. In his work he matter-of-factly stated that marines were employed 'at the great guns, to assist the Seamen'.[18] Naval officers agreed and repeatedly ordered marines to join in with the seamen to be 'frequently exercised at the cannon'.[19] One of the reasons for using marines to help man the great guns was the smaller size of the crews of British ships, as opposed to their French and Spanish opponents. With marines filling out the gun crews, they could help maintain the rate of fire. Marines, though, were a very small number of the overall gun teams and at the lowest level of the respective gun crew's command structure.

A good example of this occurred in the 74-gun ship of the line HMS *Goliath*: some 85 per cent of marines in *Goliath* served the great guns during the initial stages of an action: there was at least one marine in every six members of an 18pdr gun crew on the main deck, and two or three marines helping to man the 32pdrs on the lower deck.[20] The scene upon these decks during action was described by one marine lieutenant as: 'every man appeared a devil … all were working like horses', as 'in their checked shirts and blue trousers, there was no distinguishing marines and seamen'.[21] Further, one marine private was stationed in front of the fore magazine and passageway to act as a sentinel to prevent anyone from entering the magazine with any flame or ember. Just 15 per cent were assigned to the poop and forecastle, and they consisted of the officers and the majority of the non-commissioned officers and the most experienced marines.

Eventually, marines became so integrated into the workings of the great guns that some of their officers were even proficient enough to give instruction. Marine Lieutenant George Crespin in *Russell* (74) was known to continually be 'on the poop instructing the Marines in the use of the great guns'.[22] Great-gun training was considered so vital to success that some naval officers demanded it continue for marines when stationed on land, the future First Lord of the Admiralty, Charles Middleton, having advocated in 1779: 'it would be of great service to the navy by rendering the corps of marines much more useful, if they were trained to the management of artillery when ashore, as in action it is generally necessary to quarter the greatest part of them to the great guns'.[23]

Small arms

An increasingly common tactic of the British in the eighteenth century was to wait till their targets were within the distance of 'pistol shot' before engaging. Admiral Hawke as early as 1757, and possibly earlier in 1747, specifically ordered his captains to 'on no account to fire until they shall be within pistol shot'.[24] This tactic changed the importance of marines in sea combat from boarders to a targeted fire support and suppression force. Private manuals reveal the growing importance of this role, and as ships moved to within 'pistol shot', marines began to be brought from the lower decks. The targets for their small arms were enemy officers, their upper decks, and also gun crews. A platoon of the best marksmen 'should be picked out, and ordered to take aim, and fire at the enemy's port-holes: two or three expert men killed at a gun may silence it for half an hour'.[25] In contrast, the French and Spanish used marksmen in their fighting tops during action, but this was not a practice adopted by British marines as the fighting tops in action were unwieldy and the sway of the masts made accurate fire difficult. Nelson and others were also against the use of fighting tops because of the risk of setting fire to the ship's own sails.

Instead, British marines were more effective at 'parapet firing' from the solid wooden decks. Parapet firing was when the ship's crew lashed their hammocks to the side of the ship's upper deck in order to act as a barricade, and behind this barricade marines were to form two lines in depth (three on the larger ships); the first line fired then knelt down to reload, then the second line fired and knelt down to reload and the first line stood to start the process all over again.[26] By creating a constant wall of fire, marines could sweep the upper deck of personnel and hamper gun crews by firing through the enemy gun ports. To maintain the great volume of fire necessary to make this tactic useful, marines would lash arms chests to the gratings, and spare arms were brought up to exchange if another became defective in action.[27] Emphasising the importance of concentrated suppression fire, marine officers were instructed that their men 'must never be suffered to fire at random or in a hurry'. Marines were to practise constantly so that they could 'be accustomed to fire frequently with ball on board a ship at a mark, hung for the purpose at the extremity of the fore-yard arm'.[28] Training allowed marines to become accustomed to the motion of the ship when at sea and helped them to direct their fire in order to sweep clear the enemy's decks, or suppress specific parts of the enemy's ship.

With all the officers and nearly all the NCOs stationed on the upper deck from the very onset of the engagement, they were able to co-ordinate the actions of marines coming from below and give them appropriate formation and targeting instructions throughout the battle. The commanding marine officer was to be posted near the captain of the ship, from where 'he may sooner receive his orders' and relay them on for appropriate action. The officers and non-commissioned officers, by being on the upper deck during battle, were, like their naval counterparts, to carry out another function by their very presence in the thick of the action: 'The Officers are to shew a good example, and appear cheerful, it being remarked that the private soldiers [marines], form their notions of the danger, from the outward appearance of their officers: and, according to their looks, apprehend the undertaking to be more or less difficult.'[29]

Marines were to be in a constant state of readiness, made possible by their training schedules. As discussed above, marines at sea were continuously drilled, but this was to be continued even when they were at anchor. St Vincent's standing orders for the Mediterranean fleet of 22 June 1798 clearly set out that when the fleet or ship was at anchor, the 'whole party of marines in the respective ships of the fleet is to be kept constantly at drill or parade under the direction of the commanding officer of marines' and they were not to be 'diverted there from by any of the ordinary duties of the ship.'[30]

All of this drill and practice paid off when marines were called upon to do their duty in action. During a fight in 1759 with the French ship *Souverain* (74), the marines of Admiral Boscawen's fleet were openly commended for their action, Captain John Scaife of *Chesterfield* (60) writing: 'the fire of the English Marines was so hot, they [French] were obliged to fight [from] their lower deck guns only'.[31] John Howe, a marine in *Robust* (74) during another action stated 'we were now drawn up across the [French] A*rdent* (74) to fire with our small-arms into her'.[32] *Robust*'s fire suppression was so great that they were able to fight off two French ships, giving them enough time till Admiral Graves could offer his assistance. In 1795, when *Blanche* (32) was engaged with a French frigate *Pique* (36), the British marines kept up such 'a constant fire of musquetry into her' that they were able to sweep the decks and silence *Pique*'s guns.[33] After the action, the marines' action was further explained: 'The Marines under Lieutenant Richardson keeping so much directed and constant a fire that not a man could appear upon her Forecastle until she struck, when the second Lieutenant and ten men swam on board and took possession of her.'[34]

Trafalgar had other reported cases where this tactic wreaked havoc on enemy ships. William Robinson, in *Revenge* (74), saw one such incident and related it as such: 'our marines with their small arms, and the carronades on the poop, loaded with canister shot swept them [French] off so fast, some into the water, and some on the decks, that they were glad to sheer off'.[35] The effects of this organised covering fire were also summarised by Second-Lieutenant Paul Harris Nicholas in *Belleisle* (74), which, at Trafalgar, was engaged with the Spanish ship *Argonauta* (80): 'I commenced firing on the ship laying on our larboard Quarter ... we now ceased firing and turned the hands up to clear the ship. We lent the Master and a boats crew to take possession of the Spanish 80 gun Ship'.[36] Meanwhile Nicholas's marines continued their watchful eye over *Belleisle*'s boat as they approached *Argonauta*, ready to open fire should their support be needed again. These are just a few examples of how the theories in private manuals and drills were to be put into great effect by the marines in action.

Boarding – defence and attack

Boardings during the eighteenth century were a rare occurrence; most battles saw ships slug it out with their main guns until one ship struck its colours. However, French tactics had begun to change by the Revolutionary Wars, and another area of marine training was centred on counter-boarding. Since the French revolutionaries were indifferent to the sacrifice of life, and refused to surrender when their position was hopeless, British officers had to learn to board an undefeated enemy. It became necessary for officers, sometimes even senior officers, to lead boarding parties in person.[37]

There were few boardings at the Battle of Trafalgar, with only about a half-dozen ships on each side succumbing to this method of attack. Marine Lieutenant Lewis Rotely's[38] account about one occurring between *Victory* (100) and the French *Redoutable* (74) is probably the most famous from this battle. The attempt began at 1.20pm, when *Redoutable* (74) was on fire and 'rubbing sides with her [*Victory*]'. Rotely continues, 'this was a critical time as it threaten[ed] immediate destruction to our own Ship. The enemy was [about] to board us in the midst of Flames'.[39] However, the French attempt to board *Victory* (100) was decimated by carronading from *Temeraire* (98), stopping a 200-strong boarding party as they were amassing on the deck of *Redoutable*. This allowed *Victory*'s marines and armed seamen time to collect from the lower decks to repulse the French attempt. Captain Charles William Adair, commanding *Victory*'s marines, and eighteen other men were killed and twenty more wounded in this attempt, Adair meeting his fate with a musket ball to the back of the neck.

One of the best descriptions of British boarding parties is outlined in the watch book of *Indefatigable*, a razéed 38, from 1812.[40] Even though this watch book was seven years after Trafalgar, it seems to be indicative of common practice. The boarding party was separated into four, each consisting of different men and weapons. The first boarding party consisted of fifty-two seamen and officers, thirty-five of whom were men rated as able seamen or petty officers. In other words, 62 per cent of the first boarding parties were made up of highly experienced seamen with years of sea service and who could sail the ship if it was captured. Over the next three boarding parties, the number of experienced seamen decreased to 26 per cent (second boarding party), 20 per cent (third), and 13 per cent (fourth). 'A detachment of marines may be ordered to assist' the first and second parties, but it was not until the fourth and final boarding party that the bulk of the marines were to be committed.

The examination of the boarding parties' weapons is also telling. The first boarding party was armed with swords and was drawn from men of the upper deck. The second party was armed with a mixture of swords and pikes, with these men coming from the remainder of the upper deck (with swords) and the other from men on the middle deck (pikes). The third party, again half from the middle and half from the lower deck, carried a mix of pikes and tomahawks. The final party, and the one marines were attached to, were armed part with tomahawks and part with small arms (all marines were armed with muskets and bayonets). Evidently, it was more effective to have marines continue a withering fire upon the enemy from their own ship and thus be able to give supporting fire for the seamen of the boarding parties.

Another duty of the marines was to repulse their 'assailants upon the points of his [marine] bayonets' during boarding attempts.[41] To prepare marines for this duty they practised bayonet drill daily in conjunction with their small-arms drill. The men forming up on the poop deck, they fired one shot then charged with their bayonets; when they reached the end they halted in order to recover their arms, then followed the same procedure on the quarterdeck, and finally again on the forecastle. Bayonet drill was considered to be a marker of professionalism: 'The bayonet, in the hands of men who can be cool and considerate amidst scenes of confusion and horror, is by far more safe to those who use it, as well as more destructive to those against whom it is used, than powder and ball.'[42] By the later Napoleonic period, one army officer, writing in the 3 May 1811 *Edinburgh Annual Register*, commented: 'The Royal Marines, however, frequently called upon to board enemy ships or to repel boarders, had long been noted for close attention they paid to bayonet exercises, and had developed by experiment a more individual style.'[43]

One marine officer called upon to do more than his regular duty during Trafalgar was Captain James Wemyss, of the 71st Portsmouth Company of Marines and commander of the seventy-nine marines in *Bellerophon* (74). He was wounded eight times, and eventually had his arm amputated in Gibraltar hospital.[44] One of his lieutenants, Luke Higgins, was also wounded in the left arm earlier in the action, but he still volunteered to lead the boarding party against the Spanish *Bahama* (74), where he was wounded again, this time in the foot.[45]

The success of the marines in action demonstrates their growing theorisation and training. Marines were able to work in close co-ordination with their naval counterparts throughout every stage of battle, from the operation of the great guns to supporting naval boarding party attempts. Through skill at the great guns and their ability in small arms, marines were an ever increasingly important aspect of the eighteenth-century Royal Navy's ability to fight and win at sea.

Casualties

The Royal Marines were to pay dearly for these new tactics as the casualties at Trafalgar demonstrate. *Victory* alone would sustain the largest number of marine casualties, twenty-three. One observer described the scene after the battle: 'about 4 o'clock the smoke cleared away and [we] discovered the *Victory* completely cut to pieces'.[46] One reason for the large marine casualties in *Victory* may have been that the order to seamen and marines on the upper deck to lie down as they approached the French and Spanish ships was not given, and in the first few minutes of the battle, a double-headed shot killed eight marines as they stood at the ready on the poop deck.[47] Nelson quickly ordered Adair to disperse his men round the ship, 'so that they might not suffer so much from being together'.[48]

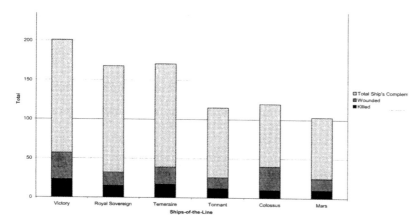

Table 1.[49] Five largest marine casualties at Trafalgar.

Colossus (74), heavily and continuously engaged throughout the action, suffered the largest percentage of casualties at Trafalgar, 50 per cent of marines being wounded or killed.[50] Strangely, the marine officers survived

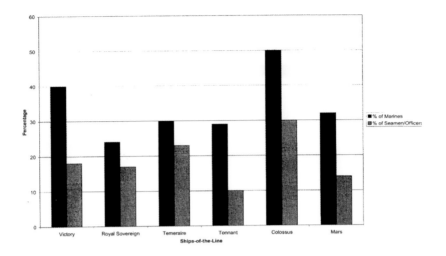

Table 2. Percentage of casualties at Trafalgar.

relatively unscathed, only one of the three being injured.[51] The ship's captain, James Morris, in this journal entry for 21 October 1805 drily appraised the situation as thus: 'Our sails and rigging very much cut, and quite unmanageable. 4 of the starboard lower deck ports knocked off while alongside the enemy. Received fire from the enemy while passing to

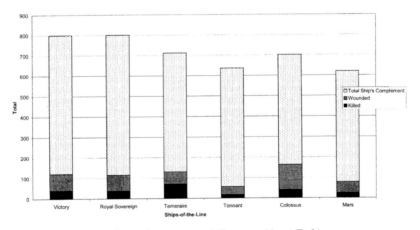

Table 3. Five largest seamen/officer casualties at Trafalgar.

windward. The *Agamemnon* took us in tow'.[52] Even after all of these casualties and damage, *Colossus* still took the surrender of the French *Swiftsure* (74) and the Spanish *Bahama* (74).[53]

The majority of the naval and marine casualties at Trafalgar were in only about half of the twenty-seven ships of the line which were engaged in the battle. The marines, who made up some 17 per cent of the manpower of the British fleet, suffered a higher percentage of casualties in each of the heavily engaged ships on the day of battle: 25 per cent of the dead and 13 per cent of total casualties. Other battles show similar losses, for example at the Battle of the Nile in 1798.[54] Perhaps no losses were as severe as occurred in *Robust* (74) at the Battle of Chesapeake in 1781 when John Howe recounted: 'I was stationed on the forecastle with twelve private[s] 2 corporal[s] 1 sergeant and one Lieutenant of Marines and at this time they were all killed [*sic*] and wounded'.[55]

Conclusion

Marines had been working on methods and practices throughout the eighteenth century. Theorisation and training allowed marines to develop a capable fire suppression and support tactic to wreak havoc upon the enemy's upper and lower decks in action. Royal Marines' training and abilities ensured that whilst the battle was raging they had the discipline to come up from the lower decks to replace casualties on the exposed upper decks, whether to assist boarding parties or to repel enemy boarders. By trickling the marines up from the lower decks as casualties increased, this allowed British ships to fight longer and more effectively than their enemies.

The Royal Marines paid a price for these tactics in action as their casualty rates demonstrated. Casualty figures reaffirm how deadly the upper decks of ships of the line were in the smoke of action: marines proportionally received some of the highest casualties on those ships in the heat of the action. The British ships were lighter manned than their enemies and this might have had devastating effect during prolonged fighting, like that at Trafalgar, if it had not been for the professionalism and ability of the Royal Marines. The Royal Marines increased the lethality of the fleet; they also enhanced the Royal Navy's fighting capability and successes.

Map of the Bay of Cadiz, see colour plate 7
Death of Nelson, see colour plate 10

Loyal Au Mort:
The Adairs at the Battle of Trafalgar

Allan Adair

Brothers Captain Charles William Adair and Master's Mate William Robert Adair both fought at the Battle of Trafalgar. Charles William commanded the marines onboard *Victory* (104) and was killed by a musket ball in the neck as he led his men in repelling boarders from the French *Redoutable* (74). His younger brother, William Robert, was a fourteen-year-old master's mate in *Sirius* (36), under the command of their uncle, Captain William Prowse. William Robert survived, but he was to die six months later in action against the French off the Tiber. This article brings together what is known about the Adairs at Trafalgar.

Adair origins

The Adairs are of Irish origin, but settled in Scotland in the late fourteenth century in what is now Galloway; the family is first mentioned in 1380. They established themselves at Dunskey Castle, set on a cliff-top promontory jutting into the Irish Sea near Portpatrick, and owned the surrounding lands, known as Kinhilt. Dunskey was rebuilt in about 1510,[1] but is now in ruins. It was used as the location of the 1951 film *Kidnapped*, based on Robert Louis Stevenson's novel.

In 1610, during the reign of King James I and the Plantation of Ireland, William Adair of Kinhilt (?–1626) returned to Ireland when he exchanged Dunskey Castle for Ballymena in Ulster, although the family retained land in Galloway until 1736. William's eldest son, Sir Robert Adair (1603–1655), built Ballymena Castle as a centre for his Irish estates as the family became increasingly based in Northern Ireland. Members of this senior branch of the family were called the Ballymena Adairs and held lands at Heatherton in Somerset, Colehayes in Devon and in London; they were later Baronets of Flixton, Suffolk. Sir Robert's grandson, also Sir Robert Adair (1659–1745) raised a regiment for King William III and was knighted by him on the battlefield at the Battle of the Boyne in 1690; family lore is that he was the last Knight Banneret ever created.[2] The last baronet was Major-General Sir Allan Adair Bt GCVO CB DSO MC DL, who commanded the Guards

Armoured Division during the Second World War; the current clan chief is the author. The family motto is 'Loyal au Mort'.

William Adair of Kinhilt had a younger brother, James Adair of Corgie (also in Galloway). From James Adair descended Captain James Adair (?–1686), an army captain, who later settled in Loughanmore, in Donegore, Ulster. Charles William and William Robert were the great-great-grandsons of James Adair of Loughanmore.

Charles's and Robert's father was Benjamin Adair (1738–1794), a younger brother of the head of this branch, Charles Adair of Loughanmore (1737–1810). In classic eighteenth- and nineteenth-century tradition, the eldest son ran the estate; the younger brothers joined the army, the navy or the Marines. With no estates to run, between 1770 and the end of the First World War, all sixteen male descendants of Benjamin Adair (who survived to adulthood) fought for their country. In about 1775, Benjamin married Susannah Prowse, daughter of Richard Prowse and Sarah Serjeant, and it was Susannah's brother William (later Rear-Admiral William Prowse) who commanded *Sirius* at Trafalgar.

Miniature of Lieutenant-Colonel Benjamin Adair. (RMM)

Miniature of Sarah Serjeant. (RMM)

Benjamin was commissioned into the Marines in 1755 and rose to become a brevet lieutenant-colonel. He is first recorded in the Army List in 1779 as a captain in the Marines, seniority 18 April 1771. He was promoted major on 7 June 1782, but in 1787 he is recorded as a captain in the Marines

Portrait of Lieutenant-Colonel Benjamin Adair. (RMM)

with his old seniority; in 1792 both ranks were recorded, but this may be because, at that time, a major in the army equated to a captain in the Marines. In the 1794 Army List, he is recorded as being a lieutenant-colonel with seniority 12 October 1793 (but still a captain in the Marines). He died at sea onboard *Ganges* (74) in 1794, but no records have been found to describe the circumstances surrounding his death.

In May 1781, following his disastrous expedition into Nicaragua, Nelson was in London to convalesce. He had suffered a succession of relapses, the most worrying symptoms being the occasional partial paralysis of his left arm and leg. He sought the advice of a distant cousin of the Ballymena Adairs: Robert Adair, Surgeon-General to the King. Robert Adair told him that he must be patient: his illness would cure itself in time.[3]

Captain Charles William Adair and his family
Benjamin and Susannah had seven children: three sons and four daughters. Charles William, born in County Antrim in 1776, was the eldest.[4] *The Globe and Laurel*, writing 100 years after the Battle of Trafalgar, reported that he

obtained his commission on 31 December 1782 'at the early age of six' which, even by eighteenth-century standards, seems very young.[5] Since most young officers were from the gentry or had family serving in sailing ships, many used their connections to have their sons placed on a ship's books. The practice, known as false muster, was common, even though it was illegal and frowned upon. Adair's first proper appointment seems to have been as a second-lieutenant on 1 July 1791; thereafter he served in Chatham, Plymouth and Portsmouth Divisions, was promoted first-lieutenant 14 November 1793, captain-lieutenant on 3 October 1800 and captain on 1 July 1804.[6]

The Trafalgar Roll notes that he was adjutant of a battalion of 300 marines who landed and captured the Cape of Good Hope in August 1795 and, as well as being senior marine officer in *Victory*, was also inspecting officer for recruiting in the Mediterranean. It adds that he 'behaved with great gallantry in the fight'. Adair joined *Victory* in 1803 and was present at the pursuit of the combined fleets to the West Indies and back, so Nelson would have known him well.

The artist Joseph Turner (1775–1851) records in his *Notes on Officers and Men of the 'Victory' 1805*, held in the Tate Gallery, that Mr Adair was 'broad, rather tall and dark. 5ft 10ins'.[7] Adair appears in Thomas Davidson's famous painting *Nelson's Last Signal at Trafalgar*, although in colour reproductions of the painting, he is often wrongly shown wearing a blue jacket.[8] He is standing on deck calmly with his arms folded and appears to be the only person in the picture not actually doing anything!

Battle begins

If one brings together everything that was written about Adair during the battle, a rather confusing picture emerges. When Secretary Scott was struck down by cannon fire, with the help of a sailor, Adair hauled his shattered remains over the side. Nelson asked Adair, 'Is that poor Scott that is down?' and when Adair confirmed that it was, Nelson muttered, 'Poor fellow'.[9]

One of the key witnesses to Adair's own fate was Second-Lieutenant Lewis Rotely, thirty years old and the most junior marine officer onboard.[10] Many years after the battle, in an undated letter to the editor of *The Times*, refuting French claims that they had boarded *Victory* during the battle, he wrote that:

at the commencement of the battle, 40 prime marksmen, selected from the detachment of Marines, formed the small-arms party. These men were stationed on the poop under the immediate orders of Captain Adair

Charles William Adair as a young man. (Royal Marines Museum)

... From my elevated situation, [I] had the opportunity of hearing every order given from the Quarter Deck and seeing as much as any individual could see of what was going on.[11]

Though it seems that in many ships the marines and bluejackets had been ordered to lie down until the time came to return the enemy's fire, this precaution does not seem to have been adopted onboard the flagship. Rotely records that 'had such orders been given, many a life would have been saved as not a man was hit below the waist'.[12] When a double-headed shot from *Santisima Trinidad* (140) killed eight marines as they stood on the poop, it:

became a slaughterhouse and soon after the commencement the two senior Lieutenants of Marines and half the original 40 were placed *hors de combat* [before the *Victory* had even fired a shot] ... Captain Adair ordered me to bring up a reinforcement of Marines from the great guns ... The reinforcement arrived at a most critical moment. Captain Adair's party was reduced to 10 men, himself wounded by splinters yet still using his musket with effect. One of his last orders to me [was] 'Rotely, fire away as fast as you can' when a ball struck him on the back of the neck and he was a corpse in a moment'.

Rotely also records a slightly different last exchange with Captain Adair in an incomplete and undated draft letter to the editor of *The Cambrian* (Rotely lived in Wales, where *The Cambrian* was published). While trying to find a serviceable musket:

I was told by Adair 'if you go to the poop you will find plenty [before the battle, the Marines had deposited a stand of 80 arms on the poop to be ready in case they were needed by reinforcements from the great guns]; stay with the party there and I will follow you immediately'. These were the last words we exchanged. In passing along the gangway soon after, he was struck by a musket ball on the back of the neck and died instantly.[13]

Drawing on multiple sources, *Britain's Sea Sailors* records that when the eight marines fell on the poop, 'Lord Nelson ... ordered Captain Adair ... to abandon the usual close formation, and to distribute his men around the ship under cover of the hammock nettings'.[14] At about this time, Adair was hit (presumably by splinters) and he withdrew the remaining marines to take up a less exposed position on the starboard gangway. Adair was then hit a second time, shot in the back of the neck, which killed him instantly.[15] He fell as he stood in the gangway encouraging his men as they repelled a desperate attempt of *Redoubtable* to board.[16] This is the account most frequently met with and quoted by Second-Lieutenant P H Nicholas of the marines in *Belleisle* (74). Another version is that, seeing the eight marines fall, Nelson ordered their officer to lead some of his men aloft in order that they might open fire from the tops. 'Come along shouted Adair to his men, and I'll make sailors of you!' He jumped upon the ratlines and 'before he got a fathom aloft, he fell down dead upon the deck at Nelson's feet with 18 musket balls in his body'.[17] The Royal Marine Museum database records that Adair was killed 'from a cannon shot', but this is clearly incorrect. Many witnesses died in the battle, and it will never be known exactly how Adair was killed, but the most likely theory seems to be that he was shot in the neck by a sniper from the tops of *Redoutable*.

It has been widely recorded, most recently in Iain Ballantyne and Jonathan Eastland's *HMS Victory* (Barnsley, 2005), citing the Rotely papers,[18] that Nelson's last words before being hit himself were 'There goes poor Adair, I may be next to follow him'. The standard works on Nelson do not appear to mention this utterance and, despite thorough scrutiny of the papers, the author has been unable to find it.

An anecdote in *The Naval Chronicle* records that, following Adair's death, one of the marine corporals had his arm taken off by a cannon ball: 'Determined not to leave the deck, he picked up Captain Adair's sash, bound it round the stump, collected a party to board the ship and was the first on the enemy's deck'.[19]

In Benjamin West's allegorical painting *The Death of Nelson*, which includes many of the individual events that occurred onboard *Victory* throughout the battle, but condensed into one image, Adair's body is shown lying near the admiral's feet.[20] J R L Turner recorded that 'an unnamed Officer was carried down at about the same time Nelson was struck by a fatal bullet; this could mean Captain Adair, but is more likely to mean the Signal Lieutenant, John Pasco, who was wounded in the arm'.[21]

There is no record of what happened to Adair's corpse. The custom at the time was to leave bodies where they lay during the heat of the battle and, when there was a pause in action, they would be cast over the side without ceremony.[22] Second-Lieutenant Nicholas's account, onboard the dismasted *Belleisle*, states that some of the dead were taken to the gunroom 'lying beside each other … preparatory to their being committed to the deep; and here many met to take a last look at their departed friends, whose remains soon followed the promiscuous multitude, without distinction of either rank or nation, to their wide ocean grave'.[23] So it must be assumed that Charles William Adair's body was thrown into the Atlantic without ceremony.

Aftermath of battle

In a letter to his father dated 4 December 1805, Lieutenant Rotely wrote in sadness: 'Captain Adair, a truly brave man, was shot about the middle of the action and instantly expired. This death will be instantly lamented by all that knew him'.[24] An anonymous anecdote, published in *The Gentleman's Magazine* just after the battle, includes the following touching tribute:

At an early age Captain Adair obtained a commission in the Marines and, from the commencement of his military career, he has been actively engaged in the cause of his country. Endeared by many excellent qualities to a numerous and respectable acquaintance, he will long live in their remembrance. The propriety with which he discharged the various duties of life was exemplarily conspicuous, uniformly displaying the most amiable deportment and instructive example. In his professional capacity he was zealous, assiduous and exact. As a son, a husband, a parent, friend and master, he was beloved and respected in each walk of life. His mind was cheerful, his manners gentle and his heart benevolent: he possessed that happy disposition which the wise man ranks among the great blessings, and which retains little of that baneful inheritance which is supposed to be derived from our first parents. Few men have by their death occasioned a more general impression of regret and sorrow, as he was universally esteemed, so is he universally lamented; it may be said he has left the world without an enemy. To his country and his friends his loss is great indeed; but alas! how much greater to his poor afflicted widow, whose only consolation will be the remembrance of his virtues. This sketch of his character, drawn by one who esteemed him and loved him, is presented as a tribute no less due to justice and truth, than to the memory of departed friendship and worth.[25]

Adair's pocket pistol was later found by Lieutenant Elliot of the Marines, between the beams in the marine officers' cabin. 'It had been so long in its hiding place that, upon its removal, the stock crumbled into dust'. It was restocked in *Victory* oak and in 1846 was presented as a retirement gift to Rear-Admiral John Pasco, *Victory*'s signal lieutenant at the battle. An Australian descendant donated the pistol to the Officers' Mess, Portsmouth Division in 1945,[26] and it is now on display in the Royal Marines Museum.

Charles William's wife, Ann Adair

Charles William had married Ann Eaton in Stoke Damerel, near Devonport, Devon, on 11 September 1800.[27] Ann was the widow of Captain Eaton of the Royal Navy. It is safe to assume that this was thirty-two-year-old Captain John Eaton who, on Monday, 3 July 1797, whilst trying unsuccessfully to see Vice-Admiral Lord Hugh Seymour, MP for Portsmouth and a Lord of the Admiralty, committed suicide by stabbing himself in the belly in the lieutenants' waiting room at the Admiralty.[28] A contemporary press report announced that:

a very melancholy circumstance occurred this afternoon at the Admiralty. Captain Eaton of the Navy, who had lately been appointed to the command of the *Marlborough* (74), refused to accept the ship, and in consequence of some difference of opinion between him and the Lords of the Admiralty, he stabbed himself in such a manner that his life is despaired of.[29]

The union of Charles and Ann produced a daughter Ann Nelson Adair, born on 11 or 15 July 1801 (both dates are recorded);[30] she was baptised at St Margaret's Church in Rochester, Kent, on 12 August 1801.[31] She died, presumably unmarried, in the October quarter of 1850 at Bodmin. She is recorded in the 1841 census as aged forty, living on her own means, in Pool Street, Bodmin, together with (amongst others) her aunts Jane Prowse (eighty) and Maria Prowse (sixty-five), Rear-Admiral William Prowse's sisters, both of whom were mentioned in his will.

Charles William had made his will on 24 May 1803 onboard *Victory* at sea, witnessed by John Bunce, Lieutenant, Royal Marines and Jas Godwin Peake, Lieutenant, Royal Marines.[32] Bunce left *Victory* before the Battle of Trafalgar, but Peake remained (he was Adair's deputy). Charles William left his entire estate to his 'dearly beloved wife', Ann Adair, who at the time resided at Brompton, near Chatham, Kent. He appointed George Kempster of 20 Great Marlborough Street, London, and the Rev William Chafoy, curate of the parish of Gillingham, Kent, as his executors. He asked that his body should be committed to the earth or the sea 'as it shall please God'. The will was proved in London on 7 February 1806. Brompton was then a small village between Chatham Dockyard and Gillingham where some officers had their quarters. George Kempster was probably the family solicitor; the address, in the heart of Soho, still exists today and is the Courthouse Hotel. Presumably Rev Chafoy was the local vicar in Gillingham.

Lloyd's Patriotic Fund, set up in 1803 to provide relief for men wounded in military action (in both the army and the navy), to support the widows and dependants of men killed, and to grant honorary awards in recognition of bravery, was generous in responding to applications for assistance made by officers or clergymen on behalf of disabled seamen and marines, or the dependants of men killed in action. On the recommendation of *Victory*'s captain, Thomas Masterman Hardy, the fund awarded Ann an annuity of £25 for life, to be inherited by her child (or children)[33] after her death. Another application was received from Mr George Sergeant of Stapleton near Bristol on behalf of Charles William's mother, Susannah, also a widow, living in Tamerton Foliot near Plymouth, and she was awarded an annuity of £20 for life. Ann also received her husband's prize money for Trafalgar (£65 11s) and his share of the additional parliamentary award of £161.[34]

William Robert Adair

At Trafalgar, Charles William's youngest brother, William Robert Adair (1790–1806), born at Stonehouse, was a master's mate in *Sirius*, under the command of his uncle Captain William Prowse (1753–1826), the brother of Charles's and William's mother Susannah. On 19 October 1805, *Sirius* was the closest inshore ship to Cadiz and Prowse had the honour to signal to Henry Blackwood, commander of the British frigate squadron, that the Combined Fleet had hoisted topsails and was coming out of port. In light airs, it was not until the next day that the enemy fleet cleared Cadiz and *Sirius* had to sail smartly away to avoid being taken: her captain's log records that 'one of the enemy's squadron fired a broadside at us'.[35]

There is some debate as to William Prowse's origins, but he was born in Stonehouse, Plymouth, and his lieutenant's passing certificate shows that he joined *Dublin* (74) in November 1771.[36] One source says that he was raised as a child on a trading vessel and it is implied that he was of humble birth.[37]

As a frigate at the Battle of Trafalgar, *Sirius* was stationed on the windward side of the weather column, where she was expected to repeat signals and to assist ships in distress. In the approach to battle, Prowse and the other frigate commanders waited onboard *Victory* until shot began to pass over her, when Nelson sent them back to their ships. Thus Prowse was 'one of the last persons with whom that great commander ever conversed, being with him on board the *Victory* for several hours previous to the commencement of the battle of Trafalgar, and remaining by his side until within gunshot of the enemy's line'.[38]

Prowse, however, claimed that he was delayed in *Victory* and did not return to *Sirius* until the battle was over,[39] and in Thomas Davidson's picture, he is seen standing just forward of his nephew, Captain Adair, gazing at his own ship through his telescope. Following the battle, *Sirius* took the crippled *Temeraire* (98) in tow.[40] As she did so there was still firing from the tops of the French *Redoutable*. In a letter written by *Sirius*'s master, William Wilkinson, to his uncle in Dublin, Wilkinson claimed that the sharpshooter who mortally wounded Nelson was shot by the marines of *Temeraire*:

We [*Sirius*] towed the *Temeraire* out from between two French line of battle ships that had struck to her. One of them, the *Redoutable*, was engaged some time by the *Victory*, and it was one of the villains on board her that shot Lord Nelson from out of her Top. And when alongside of the *Temeraire* they threw a stink pot on board her which was near blowing up the three ships. The [French] officers called out for Quarters and desired the men in the Top to cease firing, but they killed several of the *Temeraire*'s men notwithstanding but when they surrendered the Marines shot everyone as they came down from the Tops and among them the villain that shot Lord Nelson.[41]

Wilkinson might well have added that they also shot the villain who had shot their captain's nephew.

William Robert Adair survived the battle, and was awarded £44 5s 6d prize money and a parliamentary award of £108 12s, but he did not live long enough to collect his money and the proceeds went to Greenwich Hospital. His mother Susannah was paid the money on 24 May 1808; she also applied for a Royal Bounty of £30 19s 2d.[42] Susannah died on 24 November 1826 at East Stonehouse.

Six months later, on 17 April 1806, when William Robert was still only fifteen years old, *Sirius* fought a French flotilla and captured *Bergère* (18) off the Tiber (Civita Vecchia).[43] The tragic early end to his short life is told in William Prowse's fulsome obituary in *The Gentleman's Magazine*:[44]

[Prowse] was subsequently employed in the Mediterranean under the orders of Lord Collingwood, to whose favourable notice he recommended himself by his exertion and zeal on many occasions, but particularly by the gallantry evinced by him, April 17, 1806, in attacking a very formidable flotilla of the enemy off the mouth of the Tiber, and compelling the French Commodore to surrender. The flotilla consisted of one ship, three brigs, and five heavy gun vessels, mounting on the whole 76 long guns, and 21 carronades (2 of which were 68 pounders). These vessels, when attacked by Captain Prowse, were lying to in compact order of battle, within two leagues of the mouth of the river, and near a dangerous shoal. The action was commenced within pistol shot, and continued with great vigour on both sides for two hours, when the ship struck her colours. It being now 9 p.m. and the *Sirius* much crippled, owing to the smoothness of the water having enabled the enemy to use their guns with the greatest effect, Captain Prowse was prevented from pursuing the others, a circumstance much regretted by him, as several were greatly disabled previous to their sheering off, and had it been day-light would most probably have shared the fate of their leader. The prize proved to be *La Bergère*, of 18 long twelve pounders, 1 thirty-pounder carronade, and 189 men; a remarkably fine vessel, commanded by Chancy Duolvis, a Capitaine de Frègate, Commodore of Flotilla, and Member of the Legion of Honour. The loss sustained by the *Sirius* in this dashing affair, amounted to 9 killed and 20 wounded. Among the former was her Commander's nephew, Mr. William Adair, Master's Mate.

In his despatch to Lord Collingwood from Malta on 29 April 1806, Prowse wrote, 'I have deeply to lament the loss of my nephew, the only officer'.[45] No details are known of the circumstances of William's death.

Charles William Adair's siblings and their descendants

Charles William had one other brother, Major-General Thomas Benjamin Adair CB (1780–1849), who married Sarah Bratton, and three sisters: Maria (c1778–1848), who never married; Amelia Sophia Leonora (c1782–1864), who married her first cousin and heir to the head of their branch of the family, Thomas Benjamin Adair of Loughanmore (1776–1855);[46] Ann Jane Millicent (c1782–c1871), who married William Michell; and Elizabeth (c1792–c1852), of whom little is known.

There are memorials to the Loughanmore Adairs in the porch of St John's, Donegore, and also in St Coleman's, Derrykeighan. To acknowledge the family's connection with the Royal Marines, Adair Road can be found close to the gates of Eastney Barracks. Five family portraits, and all the orders and decorations are displayed in the Royal Marines Museum. When the Commandant-General Royal Marines set up his headquarters in Portsmouth in 1993, he moved into what had been called Spithead House in The Parade. In view of the Adair family's long association with the corps, CGRM had considered naming his new residence Adair House, but eventually settled on Mountbatten House. [47]

Afterthought

Since the Adairs settled in Ulster in 1610, as well as the many Loughanmore Adairs already mentioned in this article, no fewer than twenty-three of the main Ballymena branch have also served in the army, the Royal Navy or the Royal Marines. Of these, one was present at the Siege of Gibraltar, another died at Waterloo, and many served with distinction in both world wars and Korea, gathering three DSOs and two MCs. The author has three adult sons and for the first time for twelve generations, not one of the siblings has joined the services. He is often asked whether he is disappointed by this. His reply is: not one bit, the world moves on …

West's Death of Nelson, see colour plates 2 & 3
Nelson's last signal, see colour plate 12

Geoff Hunt

Plate 1. Geoff has generously allowed The 1805 Club to reproduce the image opposite in the *Trafalgar Chronicle* to celebrate this edition dedicated to the Royal Marines and to the United States Marine in the age of sail. Entitled Lobsters, writes Geoff, it was painted in 1995 and was a working title which he was given with the manuscript of one of David Donachie's books.

Earlier in 2017, marine artist Geoff Hunt held an exhibition of his works in Mayfair, the art and antiques heart of London. Geoff has been painting for nearly thirty years and the exhibition at Marine Artists in Duke Street, St James, was the largest ever of his paintings displayed together. Three rooms were filled with a feast of his work, including four large, new works, and exhibited also many smaller oils, watercolours and drawings from the artist's studio.

Some one hundred pictures portraying American and British naval history in the Age of Nelson, many of HMS Victory herself, were on diplay. Geoff is well-known for his attention to detail and meticulous research into logbooks, diaries, plans and models. Once when a client asked whether the sea in a painting could be roughed up a little, Geoff is rumoured to have replied, 'No, because that's how it was at the time when the logbooks recorded only a gentle breeze.' Another artist, the internationally famous Christer Hägg, says of Geoff: 'He is surely a shining star on the marine painters' canopy. I admire him a lot, especially for his research and detail when he makes his ship's portraits and historical scenes.'

Even readers who are not art collectors, or who have no room on their walls for more pictures, probably own a Hunt, because Geoff has worked with some of the leading authors of maritime fiction and has illustrated the covers of books by Dudley Pope and Patrick O'Brian, and also the early covers of Julian Stockwin's novels. Several of the covers for O'Brian's novels, which normally greet visitors to the RN Museum in Portsmouth, were brought to London for the occasion.

Every painting by Geoff is brought to life by his extraordinary and exquisite technique, the rigging taut and finely painted, and the sail stirring in the breeze or flapping, the sea and skies just as seamen would expect. This is great art which stirs the soul, captures historic moments and brings fiction-writing to life.

Plates 2 and 3. In 1770, the Anglo-American Benjamin West painted *The Death of General Wolfe*, and when in 1801, Horatio Nelson met West, Nelson asked why West had not produced any more similar paintings. West told him that it was because he had found no subject of comparable notability,

and Nelson expressed the desire that he would be the subject. West's *Death of Nelson* is not an accurate representation of the event, but an idealisation which includes people who were not even present at the event. Nevertheless, individuals within the picture were drawn from life, the uniforms are accurate and it includes, for example, the only known representation of Lieutenant Lewis Roteley RM. (Portrait: Sim Comfort Associates; key: National Portrait Gallery)

Plate 4. The Battle of Bunker Hill, 17 June 1775, by John Trumbull (1756–1843). The painting shows the death of James Warren – the American major-general who served as a private in the battle – and to the right the mortally wounded Major John Pitcairn, who commanded the Marines. (Yale University Art Gallery)

Plate 5. Fighting Tops, 29 May 1781: US marines firing rifles from the fighting top of the Continental frigate Alliance in a battle with the British, by Colonel Charles Waterhouse. (US Marine Corps Art collection)

Plate 6. The assault on Derna, Tripoli, 27 April 1805: US Marine Lieutenant Presley N O'Bannon leading his marines in a charge, by Colonel Charles Waterhouse. (US Marine Corps Art Collection)

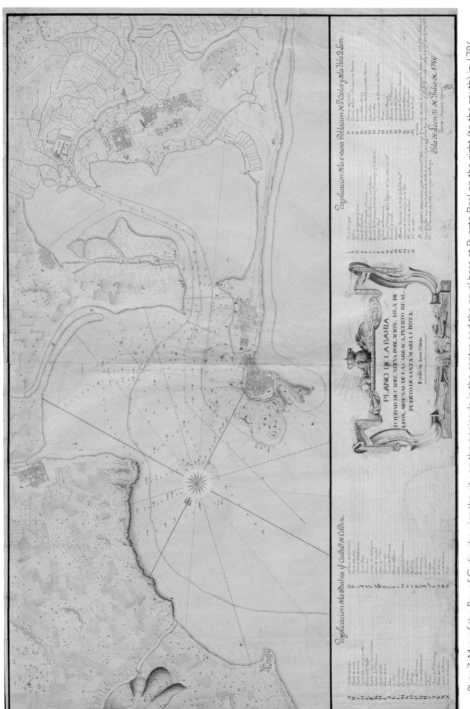

Plate 7. Map of the Bay of Cadiz, showing the city on the peninsula in the centre and the naval base at Puerto Real on the right (to the south) in 1786. (Museo Naval de Madrid)

Plate 8. Marines at the great guns, off Tripoli, 3 August 1804, by Colonel Charles Waterhouse. (US Marine Corps Art Collection)

Plate 9. US marines manning their guns at Bladensburg, Maryland, in defence of Washington DC against the British on 24 August 1814, by Colonel Charles Waterhouse. (US Marine Corps Art Collection)

Plate 10. An alternative 'Death of Nelson' with the fallen hero surrounded by Royal Marines, including Sergeant Seeker who took charge of the party which carried the dying admiral below. (Adair collection from *Britain's Sea Soldiers: A History of the Royal Marines Their Predecessors & of Their Services in Action, Ashore & Afloat, & Upon Sundry Other Occasions,* Cyril Field, 1924)

Plate 11. Changing back to green: in 1833 President Andrew Jackson ordered that the uniforms worn during the Revolutionary War should be restored to the US Marine Corps, and new uniforms arrived onboard the frigate uss *Brandywine* off Valparaiso in May 1845; by Colonel Charles Waterhouse. (US Marine Corps Art Collection)

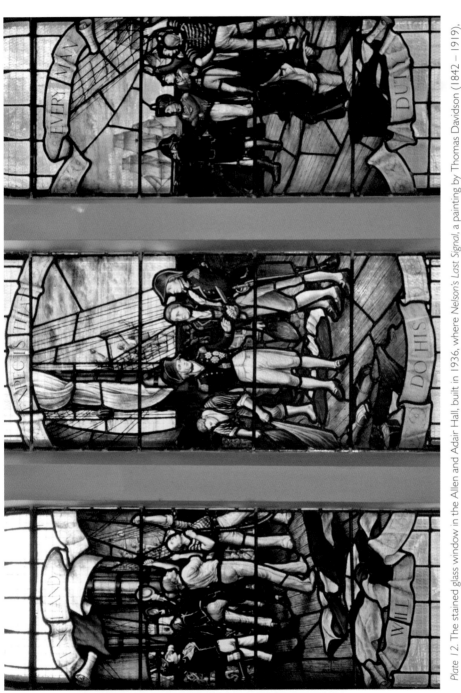

Plate 12. The stained glass window in the Allen and Adair Hall, built in 1936, where *Nelson's Last Signal*, a painting by Thomas Davidson (1842 – 1919), is reproduced. Captain Charles Adair RM stands on the right, in a red coat, chatting with his kinsman, Captain William Prowse of the frigate HMS *Sirius*, who is looking towards the enemy through his telescope. (Courtesy the Rev John Anderson, photo by Penney Johnston)

Marine Stephen Humphries 1786–1865

By Himself

Stephen Humphries was baptised on 31 December 1786 in the parish of Stottesdon and Farrow in Shropshire: his father was also called Stephen and his mother was Nancy (Ann), née Tolley. According to family legend, young Stephen's first attempt in Ludlow to enlist in the Royal Marines was refused because he was only 5ft 3½in tall. However, the Marine Description Book[1] shows that he was a labourer and 5ft 7in (1.70m) tall, with light hair, grey eyes and fair complexion when he was recruited on 25 February 1805, and that he joined the 126th Company of the Plymouth Division of Royal Marines. Humphries' memoir of his service in the Royal Marines 1805–27 is probably unique.

His sons, John (1822–1902) and George (1828–77), emigrated to New South Wales in the 1850s, and Stephen died in June 1865 in Acton Round, Bridgnorth. It is likely that it was his daughter Susannah (1833–1909), who followed her brothers to Australia, who took with her her father's memoirs. The original copy of the diary is still with the family and there are two manuscript copies: this version is based on a copy made by a grandson 1889. The story is told in Humphries' own words without alteration.

I enlisted into the Plymouth Division of the Royal Marines on April 10th, 1805. I was at that time 19 years of age, having been born in the year 1786.[2] We lay in the barracks at Plymouth until 7th June following, when I embarked on board the *Achilles* Man of War of 74 guns and sailed on the 28th of the same month for Cadiz to watch the French and Spanish combined fleets.[3]

The *Achilles* was commanded by Sir Richard King, Bart. We cruised off and on Cadiz till the 21st October 1805. In the meantime we had been joined by four sail of the line commanded by Lord Collingwood. It was on the ever memorable 21st October 1805 that we had the surprise and satisfaction of discovering the combined fleets of France and Spain at break of day standing out of the Bay of Cadiz in two lines, apparently prepared for battle, and expecting the English fleet commanded by Lord Nelson, to engage them. Nothing could have been more gratifying to Lord Nelson and the brave men under his command than this opportunity of striking a great blow for the honour of England, and the more so as we had begun to be weary of cruising about and waiting for them so long. I fancy I can even now, 47 years after the battle, see the satisfaction with which every man went to his post when Lord Nelson made the signal for us to make all sail and to prepare to give battle to the enemy.

There being but a light wind, the English fleet did not come up with the enemy until one o'clock, noon. Then began the glorious fight at Trafalgar. For about half an hour the shot of the enemy fell short of us. But when their shot began to tell with effect upon the *Achilles*, we received command to open fire on them. And very soon our captain laid us alongside an enemy's line of battleship. The battle raged awfully for fully five hours, and numbers were killed and wounded in the English fleet. But the slaughter on the side of the enemy was vastly greater as they had considerably more than a thousand men on board on each ship. In the midst of the fight our beloved Nelson fell, being picked off by the enemy's marksmen, of whom great numbers were distributed about the masts and rigging of the ships of the combined fleets.

It is well known to every Englishman that Nelson gained a complete victory, but with a gale of wind coming on, the English could not take their prizes into Gibraltar, but were obliged to destroy them after taking out their prisoners. And it was not until after buffeting the gale nine days that we got into Gibraltar, when after landing the most badly wounded of the crew and putting them in hospital, we sailed for England, our ships being crowded with prisoners.

In this great naval battle the enemy had 33 sail of the line and the English 27 engaged. From some of the prisoners we heard that the French Admiral had boasted to the people in Cadiz that he would bring in all the English to their prisons in four hours after leaving the harbour.

In the midst of the battle, especially of such a tremendous battle as Trafalgar was, it is impossible for anyone actively engaged to make observations on what was passing. Our brave Nelson had signalled 'England expects every man to do his duty' and I verily believe every man under him felt as if victory would depend on his own single exertions, and was therefore so intent on doing his duty that he was heedless of the slaughter going on around him and of everything except his own occupation. I however recollect two incidents, one of which concerned myself only, while the other made a great impression on the whole of the crew of the *Achilles*. Of the first which concerns myself, I must explain that I was very young and but newly enlisted, and this awful fight was the first I had seen. I was, though a marine, engaged at a great gun as a sponger, and it was while so engaged that I took an opportunity to turn my head to see what the Frenchmen were doing, who were then lying within fifty yards of us. Just at that moment they loosed a broadside at us, and to the day of my death I shall remember the awful and grand sight that it appeared to me. However it was for but a moment for we lost no time in returning their salute.[4]

With regard to the other occurrence, it took place just after the crew had finished their breakfast of boiled rice. After all had finished their allowance there was still some left in the copper. Some of the crew asked the cook's leave to eat the remainder, which was granted. There was some little scrambling amongst those behind to get to the copper, and one impatient man in particular made use of such dreadful curses and bad wishes towards those who had the good fortune to be nearest the copper, as to stagger even sailors. Now it happened afterwards that the first roundshot of the enemy; that told among our crew struck this man on the side of the head smashing it to pieces, and his tongue was dashed against the still hot copper to which it stuck, and so remained for some hours. This was talked of by the sailors for many a day afterwards as a judgement against him.

The *Achilles* arrived at Plymouth from Gibraltar in November succeeding the battle of Trafalgar, and after refitting, sailed to join the channel fleet.[5] Two months after we were sent to cruise off Cherbourg, when our ship's crew cut two vessels out of the harbour with the loss of four men. Shortly after, we in company with four other English ships, took five frigates off Rochfort [Rochefort].[6] We then received orders to embark troops in England for the siege of Flushing, and nine or ten days having been spent there after landing the troops, we took them on board again and also many prisoners and returned to Dover. Two days after we sailed for Cadiz and I was one of the volunteers who stormed and took possession of a fort from the French, which was situated on a small rocky island commanding a portion of Cadiz at the upper part of the harbour. Having destroyed the fortifications we sailed direct to the Gulf of Venice, where we stayed nine months in company with the *Eagle*, 74 guns. At about the end of this time drafts of about sixty men were sent on shore from each ship to collect cattle, sheep or any other kind of provisions. I went with one company as Bugleman. I was sent with a corporal to the top of a hill to watch the country and give notice of the approach of any force which was likely to come against us. It seemed the enemy had got notice of our landing, for the corporal and myself had not marched more than half a mile when we were pounced upon by fifteen men in our rear who had been concealed in some bushes, and we had passed without discovering them. They had therefore cut off our retreat to our comrades. At the first discharge I put the bugle to my mouth to sound the advance to my comrades, but before I could finish the notes the bugle was shot from my mouth by a second volley, and the notes being thus cut short, my comrades who had heard the first four notes thought I was killed, for they distinctly heard the volley from the enemy. Our foes now advanced and took us both prisoners and dragged us along in great haste, as many pulling at us as could get hold at one time. After taking us to what they thought a safe distance from the coast they gave us in charge of five horsemen who marched us at a rate of about twenty miles a day and gave us nothing to eat or drink until the end of each day's march, and then only some black bread.

In this manner we reached Trieste and were taken before the French General who offered us sixty dollars and promised us great promotion if we would join the French army, and he threatened at the same time to feed us very badly if we refused. We answered him that we would sooner live on brick dust and oil than desert our colours. Upon this we were marched to prison and from bad living and dirty straw to lie upon and with the confinement, we felt sick after six weeks and were sent to the hospital. From the hospital we prepared to make our escape by the advice of an Irishman who had deserted from the English fleet. We had cut our sheets into strips for this purpose when we were detected and brought before the officers and doctor of the hospital and examined as if for a Court Martial. Upon saying it was by the advice of the Irish deserter who had promised to help us through we were sent to prison again and the Irishman was flogged through the town, and he richly deserved his punishment for he had first advised us to escape and had then betrayed us expecting some reward.

We lay in prison two months after leaving hospital, when an officer told us an order had arrived for our exchange. He asked us if we had shoes and shirts, to which we replied that we had shoes but no shirts, so he gave us a shirt each. We were then entrusted to two gendarmes who had orders to march us to Ravenna. After having marched for a few miles our guards asked if we had any food with us, telling us we ought to have brought two days provisions with us. We said we had none. Consequently we had to march that day and part of the next without having a mouthful of anything. We were lodged in a small prison while they fed their horses, when the corporal and I cast lots which was to sell his shirt for bread. It fell to my lot, so I took off my shirt and calling a little boy I made him understand that I wanted to see his father. The father came and I gave him my shirt through the bars of the prison, for which he gave me two pisterenes, worth about tenpence each English money. I asked him to go and buy us some bread with it which he did, and we very soon ate it, and we then continued our march till night, when we had bread sufficient given us for the two following days. We were marched back an entirely different way to the one we came, and were thirty days going from Trieste to Ravenna, sometimes even marching by moonlight, on which occasions I had to lead my comrade the corporal who was moonblind and was also very weak, until at length he was taken very ill and could no longer walk. At this time we met a miller on the road carrying a batch in a bag on his horse. The gendarmes without ceremony threw the batch from the horses and mounted my comrade upon it, and in this way after three days we reached Ravenna. I was now so reduced and the corporal so ill, that the commandant was ashamed to present us in our then condition to the English. He therefore ordered us into the hospital, where we were clothed and supplied with anything we wanted to eat and drink.

After lying in the hospital seven days, we were conveyed to the island of Lysea [Lissa or modern Vis] where the 35th regiment of Britain's Infantry lay at that time, and very soon after we had the happiness to rejoin our messmates on board the *Achilles*, who had given us up for dead, and were very glad to see us again. From them also we learned that we had been exchanged for five prisoners they had taken in a prize.

The *Achilles* was under orders to return to England at the time we went on board. On our arrival there I and my comrade were sent into hospital in Portsmouth. We were from our late hardships in a very weak state, in fact the poor corporal soon died, never having rallied after his late sufferings, but I recovered in three weeks.[7]

The second American war having then broken out, I volunteered to join a Marine Battalion as Bugleman. The Battalion was forming at Portsmouth and was commanded by Major Lewis. After a stay of three weeks we sailed for the Bermudas. After staying there a fortnight we sailed to the River Chesapeake and remained in the neighbourhood about two months, every day engaged in destroying the shipping and stores of the enemy. Being joined by two regiments of Infantry and a company of Artillery, the whole commanded by General Ross, we marched towards Washington. We came to a bridge leading to a town called Blazenburg [Bladensburg], which bridge was commanded by the field pieces of the enemy. Our field pieces and rocket brigade having been brought up a sharp encounter between the artillery on both sides continued for some time, which ended by the enemy retreating and our companies crossing the bridge. We then came upon the troops of the enemy drawn up in line of battle and so sharp was the engagement that followed that many scores of dead and wounded were lying about in a very short time. In two hours the enemy retreated and after resting an hour we followed them to the city of Washington from which they also fled. This was in August 1814. On entering the city some shots were fired from a large house, one of which killed a general's horse under him within three yards of where I stood. A party of men were ordered to set fire to the house. We were engaged all that night in spiking cannon, destroying magazines and disabling the enemy as much as possible. We also burned all the shipping in the docks.

General Ross having been informed that twenty thousand of the enemy were marching upon us from Baltimore, ordered a retreat to the shipping, and the troops having been embarked we sailed to Baltimore.

We landed at the most convenient place and were advancing on Baltimore when we fell in with the enemy about five thousand strong, and for about an hour the engagement was very hot. General Ross being shot dead in the middle of it. The enemy being beaten retreated to Baltimore, and from information gained from deserters our commander thought it best for us to return to our ships which we did at daybreak next morning.

In this engagement one of the enemy made a thrust at me with his bayonet as I was half turned round looking to my officer for command. The bayonet passed between my clothes and my body, and at that moment my comrade thrust his bayonet through my antagonist and he fell dead. It was also while we were up the river at Baltimore that a party of us were in danger of being all slain or made prisoners. A foraging party of fifty to which I was attached as usual to give warning with my bugle, were landed. We had to pass through a wood to reach the open country, which having done in as good order as possible we came to a strong post and rail fence which divided the wood from the fields. We got over the railing and had proceeded about halfway across the field when we saw about a hundred of the enemy's cavalry at the other end of the field and partly concealed by the trees, preparing to make a dash at us. Our officer in command ordered me to sound the retreat and our party made the best of their way into the wood in any way they could, when however we soon got into order and faced about, feeling sure they could not have it all their own way, if ever they leapt the rails. In the meantime as it was my job to sound the retreat, I was the last to run, and so close were the horsemen to me that, seeing that I would certainly not have time to clamber over the rails I tumbled myself over it without stopping an instant. My head was barely below the top rail when the heavy blow of a trooper's sword fell upon the rail, and at the same time my well-meaning trooper and several of his comrades fell from a well directed fire from our party at the side of the wood. Part of the cavalry then galloped to the end of the wood where the fence terminated, but there they were stopped by some broken ground of which they seemed to be ignorant, for several of them plunged in and were obliged to quit their horses and take to their heels, and the party of them soon gained some high ground at a respectful distance. I now examined the rail at the spot where the sword fell intended for my head, and I saw that the steel had entered between two and three inches into the wood. I then went and looked at the dead trooper, and took from him a handsome pistol which I afterwards gave to the officer who had the command of our foraging party. My comrades having shot the horses that were entangled in the bog, we all made the best of our way to the boats which we reached none too soon, for the enemy marched a strong force of infantry down to the beach before the boats were quite out of reach of musketry, but although they fired a few parting salutes we all escaped without injury.

From Baltimore we sailed for Point Peter, where all the marines and other troops were disembarked. On being informed by a man of colour that some factories about fifty miles up a certain river might easily be destroyed, fifty men volunteered, I with my bugle one of them, to do the destruction. After rowing towards the place all one day and a night, we were fired upon from bushes by the Indians and had four men killed and seven wounded. Having returned their fire with a cannonade and musketry from the boats, but without being able to see our foes, we retreated to the main army at Point

View of the quarterdeck of HMS *Queen Charlotte* at Algiers, 1816, watercolour painted by Captain John Sandford, Royal Marines. (Sim Comfort collection)

103

Peter, finding the whole country alarmed. Nine days after this two American officers came to us with news of peace being proclaimed between the two countries. Shortly after, we embarked for England and soon arrived once more at Portsmouth. In a few days after, orders were given to disembody the battalion of marines into which I and others had volunteered for service in America and for every man to rejoin his own division.

My division being then in Plymouth I proceeded there and joined it, remaining in barracks for a few months, until volunteers were called for an expedition against Algiers from each division of marines, when I again volunteered and sailed a few days after with the rest of the expedition.

I was on board the *Impregnable*, and at Gibraltar the fleet was joined by six Dutch men of war, and the whole put under the command of Lord Exmouth. In August 1815[8] we sighted Algiers, when a range of batteries one above the other, and stretching along the shore for a considerable distance, presented to us a formidable enemy such as but few of us had ever before seen. Lord Exmouth signalled every captain to take his post opposite a battery which he pointed out to each.

In this dreadful battle the *Impregnable* by an accident to the anchor

**GIVE THANKS FOR
STEPHEN HUMPHRIES, 1786-1865,
A ROYAL MARINE WHO TOOK PART IN
THE BATTLE OF TRAFALGAR**

**A HUSBAND KIND, A FATHER DEAR,
A WARRIOR BRAVE LIES SLEEPING NEAR**

This plaque on the wall of St Mary the Virgin repeats the words on Stephen Humphries' grave outside which was rediscovered under brambles and restored by his Australian descendants in 2005. (Author collection)

104

tackling was unable to cast anchor at the exact place appointed, and so from the force of the tide and other causes she was driven, not only so near to the batteries she had to fight as to be within point blank musket shot, but also into a position from which her guns could not tell with full effect.

Thus in the *Impregnable* the slaughter was terrific, she having over five hundred killed and wounded aboard her and she received upward of 300 heavy shot in her side opposite the battery.[9] A shot from the enemy also exploded some powder on her deck, killing many of our men. The enemy did great execution among our crew with their small arms owing to our lying so near their battery. And they being protected by good breastworks were able to pick off our men as easily as a gunner may shoot rooks. From this cause our guns were repeatedly swept of their men. Three times in succession, and all within a few minutes were eight men killed at once at the gun to which I was attached, and each time I escaped without injury. One cannon ball entered the side of the ship in a direct line with my body, but did not quite pass through the good old English Oak, yet it made such a dent that I could see the light both above and, below the shot. I could not help exclaiming 'Well done old fellow, stop there'. At length the men getting short we were obliged to allow part of the guns to remain silent to get a sufficient number to work the others with some of the officers even working with the men to keep the guns firing.

At a late hour in the evening Lord Exmouth signalled for all to weigh anchor and stand off until morning. But the brave admiral on board our ship was obliged to signal for assistance to weigh anchor, so roughly had our crew been treated. We anchored at a distance for the night, and on the following morning Lord Exmouth made signal to weigh anchor and renew the action.

On the Governor of the place observing this signal he came on board Lord Exmouth's ship, the *Queen Charlotte*, and delivered his sword into Lord Exmouth's hand, and made an offer to come to any terms.

We remained a few days repairing our battered rigging, we then proceeded to Gibraltar where we left our wounded and sailed thence to England, where I lay six months in barracks. We then embarked on board the *Ephegene* [*Iphigenia*] which ship was engaged to convey some of Buonaparte's officers to Malta as prisoners, and at this time I had the pleasure of seeing the great and mighty Buonaparte himself, on board the *Bellerophon*.[10]

From Malta I returned to England and after taking in fresh water we were ordered to the West Indies. Here in six months we lost 106 men by fever, of whom eleven were officers. Every man in the ship except myself and four others took the fever. Owing to this loss we were ordered home and I went into barracks again where I remained eighteen months.[11]

I was then ordered aboard the *Thetis* commanded by Sir John Phillimore under whom I served three years on the West Coast of Africa being several times engaged in fighting the Ashantees at Cape Coast Castle.

I then returned in the *Thetis* to England and went into Barracks, and in the year 1827 was discharged with a small pension, after serving my king and my country from April 10th 1805 to February 15th 1827, nearly 22 year.

I have received two honourable medals, one for Trafalgar and one for Algiers, and am now in the year 1856, in my 71st year.[12]

US marines at Bladensburg, Maryland, see colour plate 9

The Royal Marines Battalions
in the War of 1812

Alexander Craig

The Naval Discipline Act of 1749 had exempted land forces serving as marines in HM ships from being liable to be tried by a naval court martial, giving rise to discontent by naval officers until on 3 November 1795, the Admiralty sent an order to the commander-in-chief at Portsmouth, ordering all army troops to be disembarked and replaced by regular marines. The navy would still be required to transport land forces across the seas, and an exception was made for the Royal Artillery detachments, who were needed to serve in bomb vessels.

There followed an increase in the recruitment of new marines and the retention of experienced men. The marines were all volunteers, never pressed, and raised throughout Britain with the promise of action, adventure and prize money, and in wartime a bounty was paid. In 1794, when the marines numbered 15,000, the bounty was 8 guineas per recruit, raised in 1801 to £26. Later in the Great War 1792–1815, foreigners, including Dutch, German, Polish and Swiss were also recruited, some from prison hulks, and a recruiting station was opened in the Caribbean where free blacks were taken into the colours. In 1802, the marines became a Royal Corps, and by 1805 the Royal Marines were 30,000 strong.

However, when in 1804 three bombs, *Aetna*, *Acheron* and *Thunder*, were sent to the Mediterranean fleet under Lord Nelson, the Royal Artillery subalterns in charge of the mortars objected to having their men ordered 'to do duty as marines, keep watch at night, help to wash decks, and in harbour act as sentinels, without asking the artillery officer to allow his men to do so.' Nelson called the three officers to his ship where he reprimanded them personally, and sent letters to each commander of the bomb vessels with a copy of the 'Act of Parliament for the regulation of His Majesty's Ships, Vessels, and Forces by Sea' to be given to each RA officer so that 'none could claim ignorance to the Act'. Nelson then wrote to William Marsden, Second Secretary to the Admiralty, on 29 May 1804: 'If these continued attacks upon the Navy are to be carried on every two or three years, it would be much better for the Navy to have its own Corps of Artillery'.[1]

On 18 August 1804, an Order in Council was duly approved, forming a company of Royal Marine Artillery at Chatham, Portsmouth and Plymouth, and a fourth company of RMA was latter added from Woolwich. Officers and men were drawn from the existing Royal Marines, an Admiralty letter stating they were: 'to be selected from the most intelligent and experienced officers and men of the respective divisions.' A permanent instructor provided the theoretical training of officers, 'it being found necessary for Artillery Officers to possess a certain amount of scientific knowledge' and in the 'theory of projectiles.'[2] The pay was the same as that of the RA, and the ranks of bombardiers and gunners were to be used in place of corporals and privates. Captain Richard Williams,[3] who was recognised as the most competent officer in the new companies, and who advocated the widening of the role of the RMA into field artillery, was made senior officer and promoted to lieutenant-colonel in January 1805. The RMA took over the bomb vessels, and the new corps saw their baptism of fire off the French 'Iron Coast' of 130 batteries.[4]

However, when the Admiralty placed an order for six field guns with the Board of Ordnance, the board after a year objected stating: 'field guns are not necessary stores for naval service.'[5] When the Admiralty persisted, a single 6pdr gun was sent to Chatham and the RMA was obliged to borrow field guns from local militia companies for training. Only in 1810 were more guns at last supplied on loan. Meanwhile, the new RMA experimented on devices such as Fulton's torpedoes (ie mines) and Congreve's rockets. When Admiral Duckworth's fleet forced the Dardanelles in 1807, the RMA were present in the bomb vessels *Meteor* and *Lucifer*. Perhaps the first RMA casualty was Lieutenant George Elliot Balchild,[6] who in April 1804 was one of the first directly commissioned RMA officers, and who was severely wounded while engaging Turkish batteries and forts, which employed fifteenth-century siege guns firing 800lb stone cannon balls.

Mr Madison's war – the War of 1812

In 1803, the USA made the Louisiana Purchase from France for $15 million, funds used to finance much of Buonaparte's invasions in Europe. By 1812, the British forces in Spain were in difficulty, while Buonaparte was leading his armies triumphantly towards Moscow, when on 11 May the British prime minister was assassinated. At this point the USA joined the war, declaring war on the British on 18 June.

By 1813, after successful service in the Peninsular War, the 1st Battalion RM was quartered at Plymouth and the 2nd was at Berry Head, Torbay, when both battalions were increased by an additional rocket corps of fifty

RMA under Lieutenants Balchild and Stevens,[7] while the main artillery armament was upgraded to four light 6pdrs, two light 5.5in howitzers, two 10in mortars, and two brass 8in howitzers. The *Hampshire Telegraph* recorded: 'The *Diomede, Fox* and *Romulus* are to sail for Torbay, to take on board the Battalion of Marines which is in the barracks at Berry Head. Three other ships will receive the battalion which is at Plymouth. They consist of about 1,700 men, including the two companies of RMA, and are in as high state of discipline and efficiency as any troops in H.M. Service.'[8]

At Bermuda the 1st Battalion was brigaded with the 2nd Independent Company of Chasseurs Britanniques or Canadian Chasseurs commanded by Lieutenant-Colonel Williams, while the 2nd Battalion was brigaded with the 102nd Regiment and the 1st Independent Company Chasseurs Britanniques, commanded by Lieutenant-Colonel Charles Napier of the 102nd, and all under the command of Colonel Sir Thomas Beckwith RA. The independent companies or chasseurs were, in fact, not Canadians, but formed of French prisoners of war who had been enlisted for service against the Americans. By May 1813, the British naval blockade extended from New York to New Orleans, when the British fleet off Lynnhaven, Virginia, was joined by the vessels and troops from Bermuda. The British naval commander-in-chief Admiral Sir John Borlase Warren, Napier and Beckwith discussed the impending amphibious assault without any input from Colonel Williams or Major Malcolm. The target chosen was the naval base at Norfolk, and when the British blockaded the mouth of Chesapeake Bay, the Americans landed the guns of USS *Constellation* to protect the approaches to the arsenal and Gosport navy yard, and the militia's defences were reinforced by 150 sailors and marines from *Constellation*.

The most obvious point of attack was at Craney Island, where after dark on 22 June a boat flotilla of British boats grounded on the shallows, and was bombarded by grape and case shot at short range. Fifteen boats were severely damaged, and three more sunk, including the barge *Centipede*. The British lost eighty-one dead, with numerous others wounded, and at least thirty chasseurs defected to the Americans. When the situation was reassessed, Rear-Admiral Sir George Cockburn was placed in charge of amphibious operations.

Cockburn's chosen target was the town of Hampton on the Virginia shore of Chesapeake Bay, to cut the road to Richmond and cause the Americans to shift troops to protect that city. Early on 25 June, boats carrying both brigades landed three miles west of Hampton, and circled around to attack from the rear, while another flotilla of armed launches carried Balchild's rocket company close inshore towards the town. 'A

The burning of Washington forms the background to this portrait of Rear-Admiral (later Admiral of the Fleet Sir) George Cockburn. *Rear-Admiral George Cockburn* (1772–1853) by John James Halls. (BHC2619, Royal Museums Greenwich)

noisy demonstration' was made by firing cannon, salvos of rockets, and continuous musketry, diverting the defenders' attention to the shore line, while Napier's regiment, two companies of chasseurs, and Parke's RMA with three field guns formed one column, and Williams led another column with both RM battalions and two field guns. The British advanced for a mile through a wooded area to the rear of Hampton, where the Americans had a battery of two 6pdr guns and infantry. When the British emerged from a wood and formed up in a ploughed field, under fire from the American guns but before return fire could be given, the American infantry bolted.

The battle ended with the capture by 1st Battalion RM of seven American field guns and the colours of the 85th US Infantry, and the 68th James City Light Infantry were captured. The guns and their ammunition were destroyed, but the colours were presented to Warren onboard his flagship, *San Domingo* (74). British losses were five killed and thirty-three wounded and the American losses were approximately thirty. The battle, however, posted a black mark on the British forces: the French mercenaries had run amok after the battle, pillaging and murdering, and after an enquiry, all foreign chasseurs were shipped back to Bermuda.[9]

The American authorities were informed that British forces would:

Land without offering molestation to the un-opposing inhabitants, either in their persons or properties, to capture or destroy all articles of merchandise and munitions of war, to be allowed to take off, upon paying the full market price, all such cattle and supplies as the British squadron might require, but, should resistance be offered, or menaces held out, to consider the town a fortified post, and the male inhabitants as soldiers, the one to be destroyed, the other, with their cattle and stock to be captured.[10]

Thus started the British blockade of Chesapeake Bay, a 'year of depravations' for the states of Virginia and Maryland. Over the next few months, the British captured American ships and sent them to Bermuda as prizes, and held Baltimore and Annapolis under threat of attack, while the region suffered food shortages and high prices. Kent Island was captured and occupied by the RM battalions, the 102nd, and Parke's artillery company, and became the base for operations until it was abandoned in favour of the smaller island of Tangier.

Canada

When sickness broke out in the fleet, the marines were moved to Halifax, Nova Scotia, where they were inspected by Sir John Sherbrooke on 23 September 1813. The following day dispatches were received requesting a battalion of marines to be sent at once to Lower Canada (Quebec) where an American invasion was feared, and the 2nd Battalion in the transports *Success*, *Fox* and *Nemesis* were sent up the St Lawrence River. Within a week came a more urgent request: a Royal Navy squadron had been lost on Lake Erie, and the 1st Battalion with the artillery and rocket companies were embarked in the transports *Diomede* and *Diadem*. The weather was exceptionally bad, and both flotillas eventually sheltered at Green Island on the south shore of the St Lawrence, where it was decided to move them the last hundred miles to Quebec by a relay of schooners.

They arrived in the city between 6 and 23 October, whence the 2nd Battalion marched out towards Montreal, while the 1st, which had lost much camp and personal equipment when a schooner sank, re-equipped locally. The road to Montreal was nearly impassable and the weather foul, so at Trois Rivières the 2nd switched to water transport. Amongst those vessels was *Swiftsure*, a steam-engine vessel which took the artillery companies and returned to collect 300 marines, the first recorded use of a steam vessel for such purpose.

Montreal was in celebration. The American army had been defeated at the battle of Chrysler's Farm on 11 November, and both battalions took part in a parade on the Champ des Mars under the newly erected Nelson's column. Shortly after arrival, the 1st Battalion was sent to Île aux Noix on the Richelieu River, north of Lake Champlain, and the 2nd Battalion to Fort Wellington in Upper Canada (Ontario): both locations were close to the US border and had been raided by the enemy. There the battalions acclimatised themselves to Canada's snowy conditions, learning about winter warfare from the local militia units and the Indians. Williams commanded the fort at Île aux Noix with elements of the 13th Regiment and 10th Veterans Battalion, along with Canadian militia units, and a flotilla commanded by Commodore Daniel Pring.[11]

On 30 March 1814, the US Army of the North crossed the border and attacked the British fortified post at La Colle Mill. Williams sent as reinforcements the flank companies of the 13th Regiment plus two companies of RM, while Pring sent the sloop *Chubb* with Parke's artillery company, Balchild's rocket half-company and a number of RM infantry onboard. The battle was fought in heavy snow and centred on a stone sawmill. Congreve rockets caused near panic amongst the enemy and when *Chubb*'s long guns were able to engage the light artillery of the Americans, the entire enemy force retired. Six hundred British had engaged and defeated an army of 4,000, and the American general, Wilkinson, was court-martialled and dismissed from service.

By May of 1814, the Royal Navy had won the shipbuilding race on Lake Ontario and the senior British naval officer on the Great Lakes began an offensive against the US Navy's supply chain to further impede their efforts to complete new vessels. An amphibious assault was begun on Fort Ontario and the port of Oswego, led by the two new vessels on Lake Ontario, HMS *Prince Regent* (58) and HMS *Princess Charlotte* (42), carrying the 2nd Battalion Royal Marines, the Swiss mercenary De Wattville Regiment, the

Glengarry Light Infantry (Canadian Fencibles) and the RM Artillery company. On 5 May, the fleet opened a bombardment, but two attempts to land troops were thwarted by American guns. The following morning the British ships closed the shore to pound the fort with cannon and rockets, while the Royal Marines and De Wattevilles landed about 500yds east of the fort and formed up on the beach. When the landing force came under a heavy fire of grape and musketry from the woods, the Glengarry Light Infantry were ordered forward, while the main force advanced on the fort and 200 armed seamen landed at the foot of the fort. The American regulars formed double ranks and fired repeated musket volleys while retiring to a defensive ditch, but the British broke through and raced for the fort's flagpole to capture a fifteen-star flag. Three men were cut down attempting to climb the pole, and when Lieutenant John Hewitt[12] began his climb up the pole, he was hit twice. When a wounded American raised his musket to shoot him again, Hewitt's sergeant killed the American with a bayonet thrust. Hewitt cut down the flag with his sword, slid down the pole and collapsed from loss of blood. The Americans hastily abandoned the fort. The British naval commander wrote: 'Our men had to climb a long and steep hill exposed to a destructive fire, but they gained the top, threw themselves into the ditch and stormed the ramparts. The second Battalion of Royal Marines excited the admiration of all. They were led by the gallant Major Malcolm and suffered severely. Captain Holtaway fell gallantly at the head of his company.'[13]

The British general's report made special mention of Stevens and his rocket company which provided covering fire during the landings. Others mentioned in dispatches were Hewitt and Lieutenant James Lawrie.[14] Once the fort was taken, the town of Oswego was occupied, several schooners were seized, and both USS *Growler* and USS *Penelope* were raised from the harbour and used to remove tons of food, naval munitions and cordage, along with seven heavy cannon previously destined for the US naval base at Sackets Harbour. The fort was blown up.

Notwithstanding their success, when the victorious British returned to Kingston, Ontario, on 7 May, an Admiralty order was waiting to disband the 2nd Battalion Royal Marines for 'naval service on the lakes',[15] while the RMA company was to remain under the army in Upper Canada. The war against Buonaparte was winding down, and Britain was sending an army to replace the Royal Marines. The 1st Battalion at Île aux Noix also received the disbandment order, and Williams's officers drew ballots to determine their future: some remained on Lake Champlain, while the remainder went to Lake Ontario. Captain Alexander Anderson[16] remained as the senior

Lieutenant-Colonel Sir James Malcolm, Royal Marines (1767–1849), born in Dumfriesshire, brother of Admiral Sir Pulteney Malcolm, Major-General Sir John Malcolm, Madras Army, and Vice-Admiral Sir Charles Malcolm: they were known as the 'Four Lairds'. (National Portrait Gallery)

RM officer, but was killed at the Battle of Lake Champlain on 11 September 1814, when the British lost four major vessels. Williams with his cadre returned to Halifax.

Britons strike home!

On 25 January 1814, Vice-Admiral Sir Alexander Cochrane became the British commander-in-chief. This aggressive Scotsman took a firm hand of the naval situation and by April had renewed the blockade of the American shoreline from New England to New Orleans. Cochrane embraced his instructions 'to retaliate upon the Maritime Coast of the United States.'[17]

With those orders came 15,000 troops and four of Wellington's best generals, among them Major-General Robert Ross[18] with 4,500 troops, including the 3rd Battalion Royal Marines under Major George Lewis,[19] who had served in Holland and was sent to Tangier Island in the Chesapeake. Here the 2nd Battalion was reformed under Colonel Malcolm from half of the new arrivals. Each battalion was reinforced by 300 refugee former slaves, trained by the senior sergeant of HMS *Albion*, Sergeant William Hammond,[20] who was promoted to ensign by Admiral Cockburn. They built Fort Albion with barracks on Tangier Island, and Hammond, with officers from the West India Regiment, turned his men into disciplined troops.

Both battalions participated in most of the amphibious actions that took place in the Chesapeake Bay, including the Battle of Bladensburg, the occupation of Washington and the attacks on Baltimore. They also served in the battle of New Orleans and on the Georgia coast.

From April to December 1814, British forces increased pressure on the United States with three separate attacks, one by Cockburn in the Savannah, Georgia region, another by Cochrane on Mobile, Alabama, and an advance towards New Orleans, and in Canada, Major-General Brisbane planned a third, springtime campaign against New York and Vermont. By February 1815, news of the Treaty of Ghent cancelled all these operations. The Royal Navy transported much of the army back to British territory, and the Colonial Marines were disbanded in 1816 and settled as free men with land grants in Trinidad and Tobago.

The First Royal Marine Battalion's Peninsular War 1810–1812

Robert K Sutcliffe

Since 1664 marines had served at sea: the marines complement of a first-rate ship was one captain, three subalterns, four sergeants, four corporals, two drummers and 131 privates, whilst a 28-gun ship would only have one subaltern, one sergeant, one corporal and twenty-one privates.[1] However, in 1810 a permanent battalion of Royal Marines, including a company of Royal Marine Artillery was dispatched to support Wellington's army in Portugal ashore. After recall, it was ordered to the northern coast of Spain to conduct amphibious assaults on French-held coastal defences.[2]

The British army had been driven out of Spain in January 1809, when Sir John Moore's army was evacuated from Corunna. This represented the nadir of British military action on the Peninsula.[3] However, the British still held Lisbon and the Spanish held Cadiz. In April 1809, Wellington[4] was directed to Portugal to take command of a force of 30,000 British and 16,000 Portuguese troops.[5] After initial successes, driving Marshal Soult's force out of Oporto and then a costly victory at Talavera, Wellington's progress began to falter. Napoleon had drafted 90,000 additional troops into the Peninsula. The reinforced French army steadily pushed the British army out of Spain back into Portugal.[6] In October 1810, Wellington was obliged to withdraw his army behind the strategically placed defences of the Torres Vedras lines situated north of Lisbon, stretching westwards to the Atlantic coast and eastwards to the River Tagus, providing a defensive shield around the Lisbon peninsula.[7]

The naval commander-in-chief on the Lisbon station was Vice-Admiral George Cranfield Berkeley (also colonel in the Royal Marines). Wellington depended totally on the effectiveness of Berkeley's fleet to secure the communications and supply routes between England and Portugal and to prevent an attack from the sea.[8] However, the naval contribution to the defence of Lisbon went far beyond this: its seamen and marines played a significant role in its defence and in the subsequent routing of the retreating French army both ashore and on the Tagus.

Even before Wellington's arrival, Berkeley had created a marine brigade of some five hundred men from the various ships' contingents, whom he had garrisoned, exercised and trained in the forts at the entrance to the River Tagus.[9] In mid-May 1809, this force supported the army's preparation for the defence of the Tagus: seamen, marines and gunboats, with heavy cannon, were sent up the river. Subsequently, a flotilla of flatboats ferried heavy guns, equipment and troops upriver, saving considerable time, a six-hour journey by river avoiding several days of marching.[10]

During the next few months, Berkeley was occupied ensuring continuity of supplies and provisions for the army by securing the convoy routes, whilst building and preparing an evacuation fleet. The proposed evacuation point would be St Julian's in the Tagus estuary.[11] Then, as the French advanced on Lisbon in October 1810, the navy aided the army's retreat back down the Tagus, ferrying troops, removing the batteries and destroying the forts on the riverbanks, and burning or capturing country boats to avoid them falling into French hands. Meanwhile, marines and seamen manned

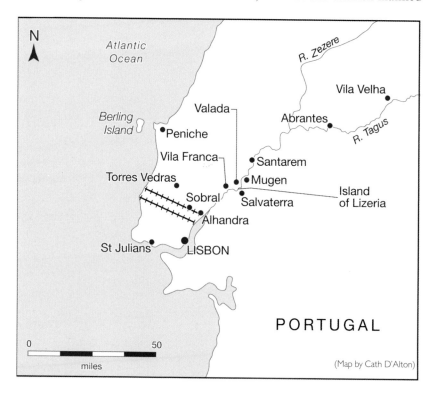

N

Atlantic
Ocean

R. Zezere

Vila Velha

Berling
Island

Valada

Abrantes

R. Tagus

•Peniche

Vila Franca

•Santarem

Torres Vedras

•Mugen

Island
of Lizeria

Sobral

Salvaterra

Alhandra

St Julians

LISBON

PORTUGAL

0   50
miles

(Map by Cath D'Alton)

the telegraph stations on the Torres Vedras lines, because Wellington did not believe that he had time to train the army to use the naval signal regime. They enabled the army to pass messages from one end of the line to the other, a distance of twenty-nine miles, within seven minutes.[12] In addition, gunships were positioned at each end of the lines to discourage enemy advances.[13] On 15 October 1810, marines and seamen in a flotilla of gun boats made an attack on Villa Franca, behind the French lines. The enemy was driven from its posts by cannon fire and pursued inland. Then, on the 20th, a party of 100 marines and fifty seamen with two field pieces erected a battery on Liseria Island in the Tagus (opposite Salvaterra), thus protecting the army's cattle herds that grazed there, and preventing attack upon the rear flank of the British lines, as well as keeping open a bridge and communications to the south bank.[14]

By 14 November 1812, Marshal Massena, commander of the French army of Portugal, which had ground to a halt before the Torres Vedras lines, was forced to retreat to Santarem. His army was starving, it had no meat nor corn, surviving only on polenta (boiled maize and flour).[15] Berkeley ordered Rear-Admiral Sir Thomas Williams (also colonel in the Royal Marines) to lead an armada of 300 armed boats up the river, keeping abreast of the army as it pursued the enemy. A flotilla of gunboats was sent up ahead to clear the French army from the roads on the river banks, and a division of country boats, with pontoons and equipment necessary for constructing flying bridges, brought up its rear. They proceeded some forty miles upriver where they assisted General Hill's division of 16,000 men to cross over to the south bank.[16] The enemy halted its retreat at Santarem and started to build a very strong defensive position; the British combined force was within three miles of it, with Williams's flotilla alongside.[17] His orders were to prevent French troops on the south bank crossing to assist the forces at Santarem and to destroy the stores of boats, timbers, ropes and casks that the enemy had stored for bridge-building. Wellington also requested Berkeley to send forward some Congreve rockets, together with officers and seamen who had experience of using them.[18]

In November 1810, Wellington wanted to establish a force capable of moving quickly to defend against attack, or to act offensively. He asked for a brigade of Berkeley's seamen and a battalion of his marines to occupy the fortified positions to relieve the incumbent regiments, who would join his mobile force.[19] When Berkeley advised Charles Yorke, the First Lord of the Admiralty, of this request he was surprised when advised that 'there was a very fine battalion of marines with a detachment of marine artillery attached which had been prepared for a particular service and prevented from proceeding upon it by untoward circumstances of wind and weather, now at Plymouth ready to go at a moment's notice'.[20] This battalion which consisted of six companies, each of eighty rank and file, and each with a company of marine artillery, embarked at Plymouth on 29 November. Commanded by Major Richard Williams and his second, Major Abernethie, were five captains, nine first-lieutenants, three second-lieutenants, twenty-eight sergeants, eleven drummers, one adjutant, two staff-sergeants and 462 rank and file. The Royal Marine Artillery Company was commanded by Captain C F Burton and his seconds, First-Lieutenants T Lawrence, Richard Jeffries and J J P P Bisset, with three sergeants, two corporals, three bombardiers and ten gunners. They arrived at Lisbon on 8 December 1810, about four weeks after Massena began his withdrawal.[21]

Berkeley intended to base this battalion, supplemented with marines from the ships of the squadron, in the forts defending the Tagus estuary and in positions near the city. The ships' marines would be stationed such that they could be returned speedily to the fleet, if required to resist an attack from the sea.[22] On 17 December, the 1st Battalion was reviewed and presented with two colours by the British envoy.[23] On 25 December, Wellington ordered that the 2nd Battalion of the 88th Regiment should be replaced by marines from the squadron and sent to Loures, a town to the

The Fort or Castle of Almada, which for centuries has defended the southern entrance to the Tagus, was garrisoned by the Royal Marines during the Peninsular War. (Alamy stock image)

119

north of Lisbon. On 31 December, the 1st Battalion was sent to join the 88th, but it only remained at Loures until 16 January.[24] It returned to Lisbon to take up duty in the forts, particularly at St Julian, where a third line of defence had been established to protect any urgent evacuation.[25] For most of this period, the Royal Marine Artillery was garrisoned at Fort Almada across the Tagus, overlooking Lisbon. In April 1811, Major Williams requested that the battalion be allowed to march forward to fight alongside the army, but his request was denied.[26] Individual marines also attempted to seek a transfer to a regular army regiment: 'I would prefer dying a volunteer in the brave 95th than to remain here (in a naval ship on the Tagus)'.[27]

The Admiralty had not fully considered the implications of establishing a permanent battalion: Berkeley, however, did recognise the unique situation, and he queried the disciplinary code for such a force, reaching the conclusion that this scenario was not addressed in any of the regulations of the marine forces nor the Admiralty articles. He advised the Admiralty that he had 'endeavoured to obviate any inconvenience which might arise', by ordering the battalion to be borne as supernumeraries on a separate list, without victuals or wages, on the books of *Agincourt* (64), thus bringing the battalion firmly within Admiralty regulations.[28] Later he was utterly astonished when he discovered that the battalion had been dispatched with no money, for pay or other contingencies, with no alternative arrangements established.[29]

In March 1811, Berkeley submitted a report to the Admiralty, as shown in Table 1, demonstrating the disposition of 360 seamen and officers and 1,149 marines and officers serving ashore with the army.

On 8 March, Berkeley advised the Admiralty that the enemy had evacuated from Santarem and the army was in pursuit with gunboats keeping abreast or reconnoitring ahead.[30] Meanwhile, the navy continued to provide defensive support around Lisbon by manning batteries around the estuary and on the islands of the Tagus, and helped to build additional jetties at Fort St Julian's as well as supporting Wellington's advance. Marshal Beresford requested boats to build a bridge over the Guadiana river on the Portuguese-Spanish border, just south of Badajoz. This was only possible by conveying the flatboats by land from the Tagus, a very challenging task given their bulk and weight. It required a large force of seamen and marines and almost two hundred oxen to drag them over rocky and mountainous terrain, and to Beresford's astonishment twelve flatboats arrived by this overland journey of nearly eighty miles, facilitating the construction of the bridge, thus enabling his army to advance over the

Lisbon, 7 March 1811.

A Return of the Officers and Men belonging to His Majesty's Squadron under Admiral the Honourable George C Berkeley employed on Shore with the Army and up the Tagus.

Seamen	Lieutenants	Midshipmen	Men
At the Telegraphs on the Lines of Defence (Torres Vedras)	1	8	16
At the Signal Post at St Julians Castle at the entrance of the Tagus		2	4
Up the River in Gun Boats with the division of the Army on the South side of the Tagus.	1	8	92
Officers and Seamen of the transport Service employed in the Gun Boats, Battering Ships, Bridge Boats and conveying Stores and Provisions up the River.	3		225
Total number of Naval Officers and Seamen	5	18	337

Royal Marines and Royal Marine Artillery	Majors	Captains	Subalterns	Staff	Sergeants, Rank and File
At Fort St Julians of the RMA		1	2	1	47
Sea battalion landed from the ships at Fort St Julians, Passa De Arcos and the Entrenchments for covering the Embarkation at Belem and the Citadel.		7	11	2	546
Marine Battalion In the Citadel and Guards at Lisbon and Belem.		5	14	2	509
Total number of RMs and RM Artillery		12	27	5	1,102
Total number of officers and men					1,509

The Heavy Guns and Mortar Boats with the Ships Launches under the Command of two Captains of the Navy and Lieutenants and Midshipmen proportioned to their numbers were withdrawn when the Army advanced but are ready to return to their posts at a moment's notice, if necessary.

Source: NMM, YOR/2, direct copy of the original return.

river.[31] Similarly, a few weeks later, Wellington requested that a bridge be built over the Tagus at Vila Vehla, fifty-two miles northeast of Abrantes. The river passage was exceedingly difficult: it took six days and each boat required fifty men with 7in hawsers to drag them over the twenty-three falls. The remaining seven were shipped by road, requiring several hundred oxen: this took nine days.[32]

After several recalls, all resisted by Wellington, the 1st Battalion, which had increased to eight companies of seventy rank and file, together with the artillery company, was withdrawn. It left the Tagus on 17 February 1812. On return to England, the battalion was not broken up to return to the various divisions, as would have been customary; instead it was sent to Portsea, where it underwent several months of drills and exercises, and was fully equipped for field service.

In April 1812, Wellington captured Badajoz. He was anxious that General Caffarelli's French army of northern Spain, which was bogged down in its attempts to suppress the northern Spanish guerrilla armies, remained distracted and unable to strengthen Marmont's defence of Salamanca, his next target.[33] The Admiralty, keen to support this, ordered Captain Sir Home Popham to be attached to Admiral Lord Keith's Channel Fleet. He was instructed to blockade the northern Spanish coast from Gijon to the French frontier, secure a safe anchorage on that coast, and assist the Spaniards to harass and annoy the enemy, keeping them sufficiently distracted from the main theatre of war further south.[34] To support this endeavour, the 1st Battalion of Royal Marines, still commanded by Major Williams, was ordered to accompany Popham. It re-embarked 694-strong on the transport ship *Diadem* (455 tons) and sailed, accompanied by Popham's *Venerable* (74), on 6 June 1812. After calling at Corunna, Popham arrived off Bermeo on 23 June. On the 23rd and 24th, the marines of the fleet and the battalion made several amphibious assaults at Bermeo and on the banks of the river leading to Bilbao. During that two-day rampage, thirty-one 18pdr guns in seven batteries and four 24pdrs in two batteries were destroyed, as well as the attendant magazines and guard houses.[35]

On 1 July, Popham sailed for Guetaria, which was about twelve miles west of San Sebastian, to support an attack by a local guerrilla group. However, Popham found that negotiating joint actions with the Spanish guerrilla leaders was not straightforward: their immediate goals and priorities did not always coincide with British plans. Although well-intentioned, they were not always reliable partners.[36] Major Williams landed at Guetaria with 200 marines, but the non-arrival of the guerrillas and the reappearance of a French column obliged Popham to call off the

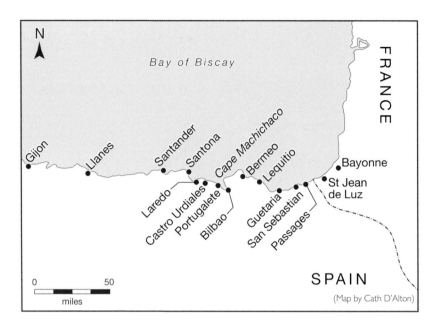

N

Bay of Biscay

FRANCE

Gijon

Llanes

Santander

Santona

Cape Machichaco

Bermeo

Lequitio

Bayonne

St Jean
de Luz

Laredo

Castro Urdiales

Portugalete

Bilbao

Guetaria

San Sebastian

Passages

0   50
miles

SPAIN

(Map by Cath D'Alton)

attack. The squadron sailed for Castro Urdiales. On 6 July, the marines landed with two guns and began to fire on the defending fort. Once again, the appearance of French troops sent to relieve the local garrison forced the marines to abandon their position, leaving the guns behind. Next morning, the guns of the squadron opened fire on the town, forcing the enemy to withdraw from the batteries; the guerrilla force managed to drive French relief troops out of the town into the surrounding hills. A party of 300 marines were landed to seize the town and battery and turn the guns on the fort. *Medusa* (38) bombarded the road into town to prevent the French troops returning without facing 'the most destructive fire'. After sustained bombardment of the fort from the squadron's guns, carronades and rocket ships, the garrison of 150 men finally surrendered after running low on provisions and ammunition, at five in the morning of the 8th. The ordnance captured included two brass 12pdrs, eighteen iron 24pdrs and five iron 6pdrs.

On the 10th, leaving a party of marines and Spanish artillery to hold the fort for as long as possible, the squadron sailed to its next target, Portugalete, west of Bilbao.[37] Three warships were positioned as close to the harbour entrance as possible. Captain Sir George Collier took charge of the gun launches, barges and pinnaces, which were manned by 150 marines, together with the ships' boats which were intended for chasing, cutting off escape, and storming the batteries on the east side. Two 8pdr field pieces and some arms were to be landed for the guerrillas, together with a howitzer which was to be placed under the command of Lieutenant Lawrence RMA and a party of artillerymen. The battalion was readied to land from *Diadem* once possession of Portugalete was confirmed, but at 11pm the Spanish guerrilla leader Jacobo Alvarez came on board to report that enemy reinforcements were approaching from every direction. At daybreak on the 11th, the inshore squadron opened up a constant fire, preventing the enemy from manning the batteries, whilst Collier's carronade launches were close inshore annoying the enemy intensely, and the remaining ships maintained fire to prevent enemy troop movements. The marines took to their boats with a field piece and a howitzer to capture the quay battery and to destroy the guns in the other batteries.[38] At noon, Popham received news that the enemy had received significant reinforcements; he immediately ordered the withdrawal of the British force. The enemy troops entered the town and began firing on the squadron as it pulled out to sea, heading for Castro.[39] On the next day, Popham ordered the marine battalion to land at Castro to reinforce the squadron marines in the garrison there.

On 15 July 1812, he received a note from the guerrilla leader Gaspar de Zaureque, advising that he would take his force to Guetaria for another attempt to take the town, if Popham would do likewise. On arrival, Popham landed two 24pdrs and a howitzer, with some marines and marine artillery men. These guns and the ships' guns laid down a heavy volley of fire, but 'the wind was directly on the battery and the smoke so great that it was impossible to see our own shot, indeed we were obliged to stop firing three times to let the smoke clear away so that the men might take aim and during that time we were very exposed if the enemy had been able to stand by their guns'.[40] A sudden squall halted the attack, and again approaching French reinforcements forced a speedy re-embarkation; the howitzer was saved, but not the 24pdr guns. Whilst at Guetaria, Popham received the news of Wellington's success at Salamanca, and from intercepted dispatches, he had also learned that Caffarelli had been unable to send troops to assist Marmont.[41]

Popham then planned to attack Santander in support of guerrillas led by Porlier, to prevent the 1,600-strong garrison retreating to Santona as was suggested by intelligence received.[42] By 26 July, the squadron had managed to set up a battery of four cannon and a mortar on the island of Mouro, in a good position to bombard the castle which defended the entrance to

Santander's bay. The guerrilla force cut off the landward approach to the town. As the squadron entered the harbour, the French evacuated the castle, but they fought strongly to defend the town and forced the British to re-embark, with Collier, another captain and thirty-one others wounded and twenty-seven dead. The squadron stood off, but on the night of 2nd/3rd the French evacuated Santander and the British and Spanish guerrillas took possession, establishing a safe sheltered anchorage on that coast. A subsequent raid on Bilbao was successful because the French garrison had also withdrawn. This meant that only San Sebastian, Guetaria and Santona were still in French hands: the Admiralty was very keen to take Guetaria and, in August 1812, sent out the 2nd Battalion Royal Marines under Major James Malcolm (and a further 300 marines in early November). However, neither Popham nor Wellington had sufficient confidence in the Spanish troops and guerrillas to believe that this was achievable, so Santoña became the priority. [43]

So on 28 October, Popham, believing that that Spanish troops would be arriving in the neighbourhood to support an attack on Santona, ordered Williams to take the 1st Battalion ashore to await the Spanish force, but it did not materialise; intelligence of an approaching formidable French force persuaded Williams to withdraw.[44] Popham was becoming exasperated with the guerrilla leaders, finding it increasingly difficult to engage with them. Eventually, the Admiralty's enthusiasm began to wane. Popham was ordered home, *Venerable* sailed on 21 December 1812, and the two battalions of marines sailed for England on 12 January 1813. Popham had clearly demonstrated his squadron's ability to move speedily backwards and forwards on the coast, thus driving the French forces to distraction. No sooner had they sent off a force to relieve one of their beleaguered garrisons than the guerrillas, aided by Popham's squadron and the Marine Battalion, was threatening another. Wellington genuinely believed that this ad hoc activity had prevented Caffarelli dispatching a significant number of his force to support Marmont in his defence of Salamanca.

The first, permanent, Royal Marine battalion was a break from the traditional ad hoc formation of battalions of marines from available ships' companies. At Lisbon, the 1st Battalion played a defensive role releasing regular troops to be sent forward to the front lines, whilst the marines from the ships' companies played a more active role on the Tagus. On the north coast of Spain, the 1st, later joined by the 2nd Battalion, together with early Royal Marine Artillery corps, played a very active role in the onshore-raiding parties which became the hallmark of Popham's command on that station.

The 'Blue Colonels' of Marines: Sinecure and Shaping the Royal Marine Identity

John D Bolt

In 1803, Marine First-Lieutenant Alexander Gillespie penned what is considered to be the first-ever written comprehensive history of the Royal Marines by a member of the corps. Through the patronage of the Duke of Clarence, to whom Gillespie dedicated his work, the Corps of Marines had only recently acquired the honorific of a Royal Regiment in 1802. Marines would now claim the title by which they are known today: the Royal Marines. In this first corps history, Gillespie aimed to chronicle the numerous honours and personalities which shaped the corps from the earliest maritime regiments of Britain. There was, however, another purpose to this history. Gillespie felt a duty to his service to highlight to readers what must have been to him and his fellow marine officers a grave injustice: the continued practice by the Admiralty of bestowing sinecure ranks in the Marines to senior naval officers.

This practice, which instated admirals as generals, and post-captains as colonels within the marine divisions of Portsmouth, Plymouth and Chatham, was also known as the 'blue colonels' system. The term as such did not imply any connection to the blue uniforms attributed to the artillery of the time, and later to the blue coats of the Royal Marine Artillery, known as the 'Blue Marines'. Instead, it reflected the connection of the officer to the Royal Navy and his blue naval uniform in contrast to that of the Marines' red coat. While holding no particular operational function, these positions provided a considerable stipend to these select few. In his history, Gillespie cited his disdain for this practice as follows:

> Disclaiming every prejudice, I am led to ask how far either policy or justice can sanction the transmission of such an institution to posterity? They were originally the benevolent grants of a grateful Monarch, to distinguished individuals. As such indeed they have continued to be; but experience has shewn, that Field Officers are the very life of discipline, and that if so respectable an addition were unalienated from the active members of the Corps, this principle would be still more animated. A

man who suppresses his feelings upon any that demands them is unworthy of the name. How is the thought, that the Marine Veteran, who ascends by the rules of slow gradation, can never reach the summit of his profession![1]

This denunciation of a long-standing grievance against the Admiralty by serving marine officers punctuates Gillespie's narrative, and calls sympathetic readers to the plight of career officers. To marines, the naval officers that were granted these promotions within the marine hierarchy were an affront to many whose prospects for advancement were consequently dim. While the systematic awarding of sinecure ranks to senior naval officers was discontinued in 1833, its tenure proved most troubling to the development of the Royal Marines as a military body. What follows will describe how this practice of sinecure roles in the Royal Marines came about, and what this meant to a service which was intent on establishing its own unique identity.

In 1755, with the imminent spectre of a new war on the Continent, Parliament voted on the establishment of five thousand marines to be formed into fifty companies. The new Marine Corps would be framed on a structure of three divisions, where one would be based in each of the Royal Dockyards of Portsmouth, Plymouth and Chatham.[2] In no way did the marine divisions equate to the army fighting formation of the same name. The function of the division was administrative in nature, providing depots in the dockyards from which detachments could be sent to sea. In these early years, on very rare occasions, marines could be organised as a task force under battalion structures, such as in the American colony at Boston in 1775.[3] Up until this time, maritime regiments or those regiments belonging to the army, would be raised in time of war and then disbanded at its conclusion. This re-establishment of the Marines was a sign that the services and value of retaining such a military body had not gone unnoticed. The divisions were to be, for the next two hundred years, the only permanent units of the corps. This organisational pattern was to remain a recognisable structure of the corps up until the late twentieth century.

Under Lord Anson as First Lord of the Admiralty, the corps would be directly subordinated to the Admiralty with its own Marine Department and Pay Office consistent with naval practices. Each division was given a full colonel, with the title of colonel-commandant, along with two lieutenant-colonels and two majors. Captains would lead companies which, at first, would include two lieutenants. The divisional structure also allowed for further administrative roles for officers, to include adjutants and division quartermasters. No commandant-general existed, but a 'colonel-in-town' was posted in London at the Admiralty as the nominal commander of all the marine divisions.[4] Officers for the new Corps of Marines would come primarily from the army, many from the half-pay list from disbanded marine regiments from the recent War of Austrian Succession. Under the Admiralty, the Marines were not subject to the long-standing purchase system of officer commissions in the army; many other officers would later choose the Marines as they simply had no money for a commission in the army. This started, as some former serving marines have noted, the reputation of the Marines at one time as the 'poor man's regiment'.[5]

While at sea and aboard ship in marine detachments, marines naturally served under the direct command of more senior naval officers. Detachments for sea service would be organised from these companies, sometimes as few as twenty marines, with the merging of at least two companies for service on larger ships of the line. Back on land, naval officers were still never far from the organisational structure of the marine divisions. In 1760, an Admiralty Order in Council proposed the method which ushered in the new practice sinecure roles for naval officers:

And if Your Majesty shall be pleased to appoint Officers of the Rank and Authority of Colonels. We also beg leave to suggest, that it appears from the ancient Establishment of Marine Forces, and particularly from certain Regulations made in Council soon after the Revolution, that the Colonels but none of the other Officers might be Sea Commanders. We therefore humbly submit to Your Majesty whither it may not be for the Advantage of your Maritime Service, and likewise a just and well timed Encouragement to Your Sea Officers, so far to revive the ancient Establishment as to appoint Three Captains in Your Majesty's Navy to be Colonels of Marines at the before mentioned established head-quarters, and that whenever the said three Captains, or either of them, maybe promoted to the Rank of Flag Officers, other Captains in Your Navy be appointed Colonels of Marines in their Room, and the said Flag Officers not to be permitted to continue in their Station after such their Promotion; but to act in their superior Rank of Admirals.[6]

Captains serving ashore or at sea, waiting promotion to flag rank, would be made colonels of marines with an annual salary of £700 per year or £2 per day. At first two, and later three, flag admirals would be granted general ranks within the Marines as major-general, lieutenant-general, and later general of marines. These 'blue' colonels and generals in waiting were not or ever had been marines themselves, but were selected on the basis of a recognition by the Admiralty of their being naval officers of distinction with meritorious service in their own right.[7]

In June 1795, Captain Horatio Nelson was gazetted colonel of the Chatham Division.[8] Nelson was, however, far from Kent at this time, being based in Genoa and engaged in confounding the French in the Mediterranean. Few of these naval captains ever visited their divisions, let alone took any active part in the discipline or training of their marines. One exception included then Captain Richard Howe, who sent a letter to his division in June 1760, stating that upon his return from an absence in Bath, he wanted the division on parade with a full accounting of all the men.[9] The rank, and role, was designed as a sinecure, to which no duties or command authority were assigned. The Corps of Marines were not structured for deployment in the field as a cohesive unit, and neither would a division ever expect to do so. Instead of creating further opportunities for marines to rise within their own divisions, even to the pinnacle of their own corps, the Admiralty instead institutionalised a practice of bestowing honorific ranks to deserving naval officers at the expense of the Marines.[10] This practice proved a troubling development and problematic for those career-minded marines who were confident in the development of their corps' unique service culture and identity.

Slow promotion was, however, a harsh reality for marines. Generations of marines would be plagued with infrequent promotion, or simply no opportunity to advance. Gillespie, the author of the early Royal Marines history, was himself at the time of writing his history still a first-lieutenant with over twenty-four years of service.[11] In August 1805, Lt Lewis Rotely, upon passing out of the Royal Naval Academy at Portsmouth, wrote to his father:

> If you will look into the monthly Navy list you will find in the Marine list upwards of 280 Second [Lieuts] all to be made First [Lts] before it comes to my turn as they are all promoted by seniority. I am particularly fortunate in joining the Division at this time as there is an augmentation going to take place consequently upwards of an Hundred Second [Lts] will be made Firsts which will put me a great ways up on the lists provided I am entered upon the Admiralty lists from the time [I passed].[12]

Within two months of joining the Portsmouth Division, Rotely would find himself aboard *Victory* (104) as the fourth marine lieutenant in his detachment, and serve at Trafalgar. He would survive unscathed and dine out on his tale of the epic battle for the rest of his days, but his time in the corps was a perpetual struggle of subsistence on meagre pay and the hope of prize money.[13] Before his death in 1861, Rotely had achieved the rank of major in the Foreign Service, but only managed a first-lieutenant's pension from the Royal Marines.[14]

Slow ascent through the officer ranks, despite efficacy and loyal service, was of particular consternation to marine officers. Despite the renewed commitment by the nation to a dedicated body of amphibious soldiers, the Marines were largely a marginalised entity within the larger construct of the Royal Navy. Despite this, marines since their renewed inception had begun to cultivate their own unique culture within their organisation – they had begun to see themselves as a thing apart.

Besides the disaffected voices of marine officers, few championed the cause for restitution. In 1777, officers of the corps forwarded to the Lord Commissioners of the Admiralty their displeasure as to the injury of placing naval officers over them, all to no effect.[15] Unsurprisingly, marine voices raged in the newspapers of the day:

> The impossibility of rising in the Marine service was cruel, as it must be to see a general officer with only the pay of Lieutenant Colonel of marines, while three Captains of the navy have 40s a day as Colonels, though the eldest was not born when he was supposed to be made an officer.[16]

The Marines would find few other friends in government, though some would recognise how such a practice of naval sinecures would provide a demoralising effect on the loyal and faithful body of serving marine officers. One such voice calling for change was Christopher Hely-Hutchinson, the Member of Parliament for Cork City and fifth son of Irish statesman John Hely-Hutchinson. A veteran of battle on the continent against Napoleon, Hely-Hutchinson feuded in Parliament with, among others, Charles Philip Yorke, then Lord of the Admiralty, over recognition for the Marines. In a February session of Parliament in 1812, Hely-Hutchinson proposed a motion to remedy to a litany of injustices to the Royal Marines, specifically calling out the injustice of naval sinecures stating:

> He had felt himself impelled by an imperious duty to call the attention of the Admiralty to the degraded military state of the Marine Corps, and to the [supercession] in rank of the officers of that corps, by which they

were not allowed to share in the garrison duty, which, he conceived, was a great slur on the corps.[17]

Hely-Hutchinson commented further on the injustices of slow promotions, stating that:

If the marines were compared with the line or artillery, they were excluded from the staff; they had no adequate proportion of field officers, and that the promotion was most dishearteningly slow.[18]

Lobbying for action, Hely-Hutchinson implored Parliament:

To remedy these grievances without delay: the corps should be increased, the situation of its commandant improved, promotion accelerated – all of which might be done without any addition to the public burthens.[19]

The Member of Parliament for East Looe, Admiral Sir Edward Buller, summed up the dismissive sentiment in Parliament at this time stating that he 'never heard it insinuated that the Marine Corps had any peculiar ground of complaint'.[20]

Further dissident voices did, however, appear with some frequency in the newspapers of the day, and continued to denounce the injustice of the system. One such writer to the *Hampshire Telegraph and Sussex Chronicle* in 1830 stated:

The Officers of the Marines only ask that they may be placed on a level in point of promotion with the Artillery and Engineers, who like themselves rise by seniority; in short they only ask for justice, they require nothing more, yet strange to say even this is denied them, and I cannot better prove the truth of this assertion, than by stating that many of the Captains actually serving, have been more than 34 years; the First Lieutenants more than 25 years; and the Second Lieutenants more than 18 years in the service.[21]

The author, signing simply as 'A Friend to The Marine Corps', concluded with a brief meditation on what the morale of the marine officer corps would be concerning their predicament:

What zeal can an Officer have, I would ask, who after more than a quarter of a century spent in defence of his King and country still remains a Subaltern? What must be his feelings at the neglect he has experienced, conscious of having merited treatment, very far different.[22]

The sinecure naval roles would be struck down in a session of Parliament in 1833. Intriguingly, this time there were fewer impassioned speeches about the injustices against the corps, but instead motivated by the blunter instrument of fiscal reform. On 14 February 1833, Parliament closed the day's session with a motion for the stoppage of sinecures and pensions, to which the Member of Parliament for Middlesex, Sir Joseph Hume, a frequent sceptic of the naval estimates brought before Parliament and a champion of reform, opened the discussion saying that:

> The state of the country loudly demanded the most rigorous economy on the part of the Government; and the Parliament were bound to relieve the country from its present burthens.[23]

The pensions and sinecure roles of the army and navy were, in fact, a principal target for this motion. Sir James Graham was First Lord of the Admiralty appointed by the prime minister, Charles, Earl Grey. Sir James stated that for the Admiralty sinecure roles were:

> Narrowed to the propriety of continuing to have two Generals of Marines, four Colonels of Marines, a Vice-admiral, and a Rear-admiral of England. The whole amount of salary received by the whole of these officers was [£4,740].[24]

However small the sum, Sir James stated that, if called for, it was the duty of the House to strike this sum from the Admiralty books. Perhaps aware of the naval legacy that was about to be shelved, Sir James called the House to remember that:

> As to the propriety of retaining the office of General and Colonel of Marines, he would merely state, that Lord Nelson and Lord Collingwood had both been Generals of Marines, and that in the list of Colonels of Marines were to be found the names of some of the most gallant officers that had ever graced the British navy. The emoluments of these officers were small, but the stimulus which they afforded for gallant deeds, and heroic exertions, was incalculable.

132

Graham read out further names from annals of naval history who had also once held these roles, many all too familiar to the House. Hume retorted, citing the case against all the sinecure roles delivered to the House, stating that 'not one of them hardly was a resident at the place where his office was, and every such office was a complete sinecure.'[25] As for the Marines, Hume cited the case of Admiral Sir George Cockburn, who was now on his way to the West Indies, and who was a major-general of marines. 'Could anything be a more complete sinecure than that?' said Hume.[26] The House divided, the ayes came to 232, the noes 138. A majority vote of 94 put to an end the long honours tradition of naval sinecure roles in the Royal Marines.[27] The sinecure roles of the 'blue colonels' system would finally be struck down, in part, as a fiscal concern.

While the system was finally discontinued in 1833, the incumbents retained their ranks into retirement until their death; the last four naval captains who served as colonels did so until 1837. By 1833, when the system came to an end, a total of eighty-three naval captains had been colonels of marines. A total of ten admirals had served as generals of Royal Marines, nine more were lieutenant-generals, and a further five others as major-generals. Some captains who had held colonelcies in the Marines would later become generals a couple of years after their promotion to flag rank.[28] Admiral George Cockburn, cited in the parliamentary debates, was made a colonel in 1811, and later a major-general in 1821, which ranking he held until his death in 1853. Admiral Samuel Barrington was a colonel, lieutenant-general and, in 1799, was made general of marines until his death in 1800. Admiral Sir Richard Bickerton manage to hold all three generals' ranks available at one time or another. Admiral Lord Nelson only ever held the rank of colonel in the Marines for the Chatham Division, and that for only two years from 1795 to 1797.

While the sinecure system of the 'blue colonels' did come to an end, the problems faced by the Royal Marines continued. As naval technology shifted from sail to steam and with the new technologies of gunnery and communications, what future role a marine corps who traditionally served at sea with the navy might have was in doubt. While the corps continued to serve with distinction in the many campaigns of the nineteenth century that saw the rapid expansion of the British Empire, their relevance was often called into question. Promotion prospects, even with the abolition of sinecure posts, did not improve much more for senior officers. In 1919, General Sir George Grey Aston, in his published memoirs, offered a reflection of service in the corps at sea and what the wardroom mess might appear to the marine officer. A first tour might find the marine officer among naval officer peers, lieutenants and junior officers. On later tours, Aston reflected:

133

> When a Marine Officer goes to sea for the second time he finds his contemporaries in the Navy have all passed over his head in the Service, and he must resign himself to these conditions, but he still finds many of them serving in the messes. A senior Marine officer going for the third time finds that they have become Captains of their own ships, possibly Rear-Admirals, and no longer to be met in wardrooms.[29]

Of the prospects for promotion where marines were subordinated within the Admiralty, Aston concluded:

> A Marine ... has no prospects whatever in the Naval Service when he gets beyond a certain rank, because, with the best of intentions in the world, the Admiralty have no suitable responsible work to give him.[30]

Not without a little humour, Aston closed his memoirs with a succinct observation on at least one superlative trait of service in the Marines:

> There's one advantage about the Marine service that is not nearly enough appreciated. It effectively cures the vice of personal ambition. Lucifer might still have been in heaven if he had been a Marine officer.[31]

The early story of the Marines is one of frequent incarnations and dissolutions, predicated by the needs of the nation in time of war. By the twentieth century, in 1947, the Royal Marines experienced a nearly complete transformation. General Julian Thompson has argued that although the current corps is the direct descendant of its pre-1941 ancestors, those marines would hardly recognise the Royal Marine Commandos of the latter twentieth century in the years following the Second World War.[32] With over 350 years of history, the lineage of the Royal Marines has been at times precarious. Certainly, the Royal Marines have had to adapt to changing times, at home as well as on campaign, for the nation's battles. If the system of sinecure roles in their organisation signified another instance to the Marines of the hold the Admiralty held on them, ultimately what enabled the Royal Marines to develop and thrive was their own sense of a unique identity apart.

List of the naval sinecure roles in the Royal Marines

Name	Naval Rank	Seniority	Marine Rank	Seniority
Hon Edward Boscawen	Admiral	7 February 1758	General	10 Nov 1759
Hon John Forbes	Admiral (Blue)	5 February 1758	General	1 May 1763
Richard Howe, 1st Earl Howe	Admiral of the Fleet	12 March 1796	General	12 March 1796
	Captain	10 April 1746	Colonel	4 February 1760
Hon Samuel Barrington	Admiral (Blue)	24 September 1787	General	20 August 1779
	Vice-Admiral (Blue)	29 March 1779	Lieutenant-General	26 January 1786
	Captain	29 May 1747	Colonel	13 October 1770
John Jervis, 1st Earl of St Vincent	Admiral of the Fleet	19 July 1821	General	11 May 1814
	Admiral (Blue)	1 June 1795	Lieutenant-General	26 August 1800
Alexander Arthur Hood, 1st Viscount Bridport	Admiral (White)	12 April 1794	Lieutenant-General	19 August 1799
William, Duke of Clarence (later King William IV)	Admiral of the Fleet	24 December 1811	General	17 March 1823
Sir William Johnstone Hope	Rear-Admiral (Red)	4 June 1814	Major-General	5 January 1818
	Captain	7 January 1794	Colonel	1 August 1811
Sir Richard G Keats	Vice-Admiral (White)	4 June 1814	Major-General	7 May 1818
	Captain	24 June 1789	Colonel	9 November 1805
Sir Richard H Bickerton, Baronet	Admiral (Red)	12 August 1819	General	28 June 1830
	Admiral (Blue)	31 July 1810	Lieutenant-General	5 June 1818
	Vice-Admiral (Red)	25 August 1809	Major-General	20 April 1810
James Saumarez, 1st Baron de Saumarez	Admiral (Blue)	4 June 1814	General	13 February 1832
	Captain	7 February 1782	Colonel	14 February 1799

Name	Naval rank	Date	Army rank	Date
Sir Charles Saunders	Vice-Admiral (Blue)	14 February 1759	Lieutenant-General	10 November 1759
Sir Hugh Palliser	Admiral (Blue)	25 September 1787	Lieutenant-General	8 December 1775
Sir Thomas Pye	Admiral (White)	29 June 1778	Lieutenant-General	26 September 1780
Sir Richard Onslow	Admiral (Red)	9 November 1805	Lieutenant-General	7 May 1814
	Captain	14 April 1762	Colonel	21 September 1790
Sir William Sydney Smith	Admiral (Blue)	19 July 1821	Lieutenant-General	28 June 1830
	Captain	7 May 1783	Colonel	23 April 1804
Sir Alan Gardner, 1st Baron Gardner	Rear Admiral	12 April 1794	Major-General	28 June 1794
Lord Cuthbert Collingwood, 1st Baron Collingwood	Vice-Admiral (Red)	9 November 1805	Major-General	4 January 1809
Sir Richard Goodwin Keats	Vice-Admiral (White)	4 June 1814	Major-General	7 May 1818
	Captain	24 June 1789	Colonel	9 November 1805
Sir George Cockburn, 10th Baronet	Admiral (Blue)	10 January 1837	Major-General	5 April 1821
	Captain	20 February 1794	Colonel	1 August 1811
Sir Peircy Brett	Captain	30 September 1743	Colonel	2 February 1760
Augustus Keppel	Captain	11 December 1744	Colonel	2 February 1760
Sir Thomas Stanhope	Captain	12 July 1745	Colonel	21 October 1762
Augustus J Hervey	Captain	15 January 1747	Colonel	21 October 1762
Sir Hugh Pigot	Captain	22 April 1746	Colonel	12 March 1770
Thomas Graves	Captain	8 July 1755	Colonel	31 March 1775
Robert Digby	Captain	9 August 1755	Colonel	3 April 1775
Joshua Rowley	Captain	14 December 1753	Colonel	23 January 1778
Robert Boyle-Walsingham	Captain	15 Jun 1757	Colonel	19 March 1779
John Elliott	Captain	5 April 1757	Colonel	19 March 1779

Name	Rank	Date	Rank	Date
William Hotham	Captain	17 August 1757	Colonel	19 March 1779
Sir John Lindsay	Captain	28 September 1757	Colonel	21 June 1781
Phillips Cosby	Captain	19 May 1761	Colonel	24 September 1787
George Bowyer	Captain	28 October 1762	Colonel	24 September 1787
Sir William Cornwallis	Captain	20 April 1765	Colonel	24 September 1787
George Murray	Captain	26 May 1768	Colonel	1 February 1793
Robert Linzee	Captain	3 October 1770	Colonel	1 February 1793
Sir James Wallace	Captain	10 January 1771	Colonel	1 February 1793
Horatio Nelson	Captain	11 June 1779	Colonel	1 June 1795
Sir Thomas Pakenham	Captain	2 March 1780	Colonel	1 June 1795
Sir George C Berkeley	Captain	15 September 1780	Colonel	1 June 1795
John T Duckworth	Captain	16 June 1780	Colonel	8 June 1797
Edward Thornborough	Captain	24 September 1782	Colonel	14 February 1799
Sir William G Fairfax	Captain	12 January 1782	Colonel	14 February 1799
Sir Edward Pellew	Captain	25 May 1782	Colonel	1 January 1801
William Domett	Captain	9 September 1782	Colonel	1 January 1801
Sir Thomas Troubridge	Captain	1 January 1783	Colonel	1 January 1801
Sir Samuel Hood	Captain	24 May 1788	Colonel	15 August 1805
Edward Buller	Captain	19 July 1790	Colonel	9 November 1805
Robert Stopford	Captain	12 August 1790	Colonel	9 November 1805
George Martin	Captain	17 March 1783	Colonel	23 April 1804
Sir Richard J Strachan	Captain	26 April 1783	Colonel	23 April 1804
William Lechmere	Captain	21 September 1790	Colonel	2 October 1807
Thomas Foley	Captain	21 September 1790	Colonel	2 October 1807
Charles Boyle	Captain	22 November 1790	Colonel	28 April 1808

Name	Rank	Date	Rank	Date
Sir Thomas Williams	Captain	22 November 1790	Colonel	28 April 1808
William Hargood	Captain	22 November 1790	Colonel	28 April 1808
Robert Moorsom	Captain	22 November 1790	Colonel	28 April 1808
Sir Charles Hamilton	Captain	22 November 1790	Colonel	25 October 1809
Henry Curzon	Captain	22 November 1790	Colonel	25 October 1809
Benjamin Hallowell	Captain	30 August 1793	Colonel	31 July 1810
George J Hope	Captain	13 September 1793	Colonel	31 July 1810
Lord Amelius Beauclerk	Captain	16 September 1793	Colonel	31 July 1810
James Nicoll Morris	Captain	7 October 1793	Colonel	31 July 1810
Samuel H Linzee	Captain	8 March 1794	Colonel	1 August 1811
Lord Henry Paulet	Captain	9 January 1794	Colonel	1 August 1811
Charles Elphinstone Fleming	Captain	7 October 1794	Colonel	12 August 1812
Charles V Penrose	Captain	7 October 1794	Colonel	12 August 1812
James Bissett	Captain	24 October 1794	Colonel	12 August 1812
Pulteney Malcolm	Captain	22 October 1794	Colonel	12 August 1812
Sir Henry Hotham	Captain	13 January 1795	Colonel	4 December 1813
George Burlton	Captain	16 March 1795	Colonel	4 December 1813
Sir Josias Rowley	Captain	6 April 1795	Colonel	4 December 1813
Edward Codrington	Captain	6 April 1795	Colonel	4 December 1813
Willoughby T Lake	Captain	4 January 1796	Colonel	4 June 1814
Sir William Charles Fahie	Captain	2 February 1796	Colonel	4 June 1814
Sir George Eyre	Captain	6 February 1796	Colonel	4 June 1814
John Talbot	Captain	27 August 1796	Colonel	4 June 1814
William Robert Broughton	Captain	28 January 1797	Colonel	17 August 1819
Sir Edward Berry	Captain	6 March 1797	Colonel	17 August 1819

William Prowse	Captain	6 March 1797		Colonel	17 August 1819
Thomas Baker	Captain	13 June 1797		Colonel	17 August 1819
Aiskew Paffard Hollis	Captain	5 February 1798		Colonel	19 July 1821
Sir Edward W C R Owen	Captain	23 April 1798		Colonel	19 July 1821
Sir George Scott	Captain	15 June 1798		Colonel	19 July 1821
Sir Thomas M Hardy, 1st Baronet	Captain	2 October 1798		Colonel	19 July 1821
Lucius Hardyman	Captain	27 January 1800		Colonel	27 May 1825
Edward Brace	Captain	22 April 1800		Colonel	27 May 1825
Sir Jahleel Brenton, 1st Baronet	Captain	25 April 1800		Colonel	27 May 1825
Sir Francis William Austen	Captain	13 May 1800		Colonel	27 May 1825
William Skipsey	Captain	18 March 1802		Colonel	22 July 1830
Hon Frederick Paul Irby	Captain	14 April 1802		Colonel	22 July 1830
Sir Christopher Cole	Captain	20 April 1802		Colonel	22 July 1830
Hon D Pleydell-Bouverie	Captain	28 April 1802		Colonel	22 July 1830

139

The Royal Marine Uniform Sword
by Blake, London,

Provenanced to Captain Richard Welchman, Royal Marines

Sim Comfort

An excerpt from Sim Comfort's *Naval Swords and Dirks* 2 vols (Sim Comfort Associates, 2008), pp186–8, and *Boarders Away with Steel* by William Gilkerson (Andrew Mowbray, 1991), p122.

The sword is a bronze gilt mounted stirrup hilt fighting sword with langets depicting a fouled anchor within a wreath of laurel. The lion head pommel has a flattened tang. The grey sharkskin grip is spirally bound with triple gilt wire that makes seven turns and the gilt ferrule is banded. The top of the knuckle guard has a rectangular slot for securing a sword knot. The slightly curved single-edged blade has no fuller and is half blued and gilt. The decoration comprises the Royal Marine insignia of a globe and anchor supported by flora wreaths on the obverse and a nautical stand of arms with floral swags on the reverse. The back-edge is signed: BLAKE, LONDON. The black leather scabbard is fitted with three gilt mounts that provide two rings and a frog stud for suspension. Overall length: 84cm/33 inches. Blade length: 71cm/28 inches. Condition: The hilt, blade and scabbard are all in very fine condition with much original gilt to the mounts and no rust to the blade.

A clipping from the *Morning Post*, circa 1912, tells us:

In an old red wallet, such as all officers carried about the time of the French wars a hundred years ago, which belonged to Captain [Richard] Welchman, serving in the Royal Marines at that date, I have found a package of highly interesting documents ... Captain Welchman was appointed Lieutenant on July 26, 1803, and was given the commission of Captain in 1810. He was Captain of Marines on board his Majesty's ship *Lion*, Captain Heathcote in command, at the time of the Java expedition.

The scene now changes to the late 1980s when I met a dealer who had the red wallet which contained a *Morning Post* newspaper article about

Welchman, but all of the original documents had been already sold. From him also came the Royal Marine gorget that belonged to Welchman and a number of gilt Royal Marine buttons of the period. Everything having come from 'an old trunk'. Not long after this I was offered the Royal Marine service sword, which appeared to have come from the same source and provenanced to Captain Richard Welchman and as such is the earliest identifiable Royal Marine service sword in existence.

From William Gilkerson, we then find the wonderful story of Captain Welchman, his mounted horse marines, and their success on the island of Java, when on 4 September 1811, Captain Welchman was landed in command of a naval brigade of fifty sailors and 190 marines, his mission was to challenge the French occupation of Java. Soon after landing at Sheribon (modern Cirebon, a port on the north coast of Java, some two hundred miles east of modern Jakarta) Welchman's party met and captured a French general and a colonel from whom they learned of a retreating column of several hundred hostile troops in their vicinity. Finding sufficient horses and saddlery for the entire force at his disposal, Welchman ordered his sailors and marines to mount up, and they rode off inland in pursuit of the enemy, at one point having to hew their way through heavy brush with cutlasses. Regaining the road, his sailors on horseback and his horse marines captured some five hundred enemy troops.

'My party was so small', Welchman later wrote, 'I could not take charge of the prisoners, nor even their arms, the latter I destroyed and gave the people their liberty.'

When Welchman arrived at Bongos (a fortified post), its garrison fled, leaving the town to the naval cavalry, and also twenty-three chests of gold, the treasure of the French army on the island. Passing only long enough to send the fortune back to the fleet under guard, the enterprising Welchman arranged for a relay of horses and pressed on with the remainder of his force toward the next garrison town, Carang Sambang, where a much larger force reputedly awaited them. On the road, Welchman was met by a French officer under a flag of truce who had ridden to offer the surrender of the 400-man garrison.

Welchman thereby occupied his objective and took stock. Suffering no casualties, he had captured nearly a thousand enemy troops, including one general, two lieutenant-colonels, one major, eleven captains and forty-two lieutenants: he had secured an untold fortune, and he had possession of Carang Sambang's defences and rich warehouses. However, his improbable raiding party was exhausted and saddle-sore after its forced, thirty-seven-mile ride; he was deep in enemy country, surrounded by disarmed prisoners whom he couldn't guard, and somewhere nearby was the main strength of the French army. Under the circumstances Welchman prudently consolidated his gains and made contact with the fleet. By one o'clock of the morning of 11 September he had re-embarked his sailors and marines, weary but without loss.

As noted, the maker of the sword is signed Blake, who could have been George (fl1806–1807) or Ann who ran the business at Old Wapping Stairs from 1808 to 1816 and continued as a sword maker to 1823. As Welchman was promoted to Captain Royal Marine in 1810, it appears that the sword was made by Ann Blake.

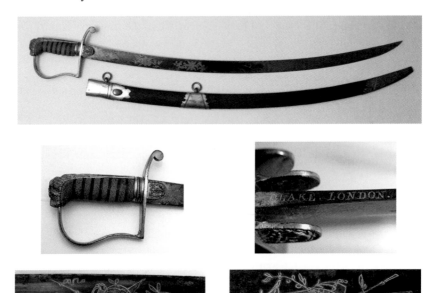

Details of Welchman's sword, pouch and epaulette. (Sim Comfort Associates)

142

Captain Philip Gidley King, Royal Navy, Third Governor of New South Wales

Tom Fremantle

On 3 September 1808, a Royal Navy captain aged forty-nine years died at Tooting in south London. He was neither rich nor famous, but his thirty-six years of service in the Royal Navy had been full of remarkable courage and achievement, and he had been commended by ministers of the government. If he had died at a time when the government was not preoccupied with war in Europe, he might have been recognised more, and rewarded properly for his lifetime's achievement. The story of his life

Captain Philip Gidley King RN (1758–1808), the third governor of New South Wales.
(National Library of Australia)

provides an extraordinary example of unstinting service to the benefit of the nation to the detriment of his own health, with none of the rewards so often provided to others. It underlines the difficulty of managing a transglobal operation at the end of the eighteenth century, when communication halfway round the world, uncertain as it was, might take between six and nine months, and the government in London was struggling with war and potential invasion from France.

Early years
Philip Gidley King was born on 23 April 1758, just two months after Nelson, in Launceston, Cornwall. His father came from a long line of drapers in the town and his mother was from a family of attorneys in Exeter. At the age of seven he was sent away to Bailey's School at Yarmouth in the Isle of Wight, where education appears to have been most focused on the Christian religion and maritime studies. As was quite normal at the time, aged twelve in 1770, he secured a berth aboard the sloop *Swallow* (14) as servant to Captain Shirley, deployed to protect the lucrative East India trade. By 1775, he was serving as midshipman aboard *Prudent* (64) under Captain Gideon Johnston, who wrote a very glowing report on him to Mrs King, describing him 'as one of the most promising young men I have ever met in my 23 years' service'.[1] Later the same year, he seems to have joined *Liverpool* (24), Captain Henry Bellew, which was despatched to help suppress the newly independent American colonies, and in April 1777, he passed for lieutenant.[2] Standard texts say *Liverpool* was wrecked in Jamaica Bay, Long Island, without mention of enemy action,[3] but King's biography tells a very different story of how *Liverpool* was trapped by the French fleet in the Delaware River and fought valiantly, although massively outnumbered, until she was set afire and sunk.[4] King swam away from the wreck and was picked up by *Princess Royal* (98).

Evidently, the young King had an opportunity, like so many others, to demonstrate his courage and skill off the coast of America, though his movements immediately after this incident are unclear. It appears that he joined *Renown* (98), which was cruising in the West Indies, as a lieutenant under Captain George Dawson. Whilst in *Renown* he was placed in charge of a prize for which he independently and without his captain's approval appointed a prize agent.[5] This appears to have led to his court martial, a reprimand, and being dismissed the ship. Precise dates are unclear and require further research. *Renown* returned home in 1780 for refit and in the same year it is reported that King was aboard the *Kite* cutter in the Channel.

King's father must have died at some time in 1781, and his mother decided to sell the draper's shop which had, in any case, been tenanted for several years. King spent time ashore, perhaps in early January 1782, when the sale was completed. But before January was out, he experienced his life-changing stroke of luck. He was appointed to *Ariadne* (20), Captain Arthur Phillip, and when Phillip transferred only eleven months later to *Europe* (64), he insisted on taking King with him. King's biographer suggests that the two men were attracted to each other, despite the twenty-year age difference, because they both tended to enjoy quiet and contemplative conversation rather than boisterous activities; both enjoyed strong religious conviction and unswerving faith in the monarchy and empire. Their time together in *Europe* was cut short by peace after a single troop-carrying voyage to India, and they were placed on half-pay. Phillip returned to farming in Hampshire, whilst King returned to Launceston with his mother and, given the disposal of the shop, may have tried his hand at some farming.

Convict voyage

The British government had been in the habit of exporting as many as a thousand convicts a year to the American colonies until the War of Independence. Africa was considered as an option, but appeared not to answer, so by the early 1780s, England's gaols were becoming desperately overcrowded, despite the use of prison hulks in the major ports. Joseph Banks, who with Captain Cook had visited the eastern seaboard of Australia, then known as New Holland, recommended Botany Bay as an ideal site for the establishment of a new penal colony. However, it took a major prison riot in Portsmouth to spur the government into action, and in March 1786, Lord Sydney issued an order for 750 convicts to be carried to Botany Bay. In August of that year, Captain Arthur Phillip was appointed to lead the project and to be the first governor of the new colony.

From the start the great adventure was mired in difficulties, and Phillip had to fight hard to secure the level of stores necessary for his fleet and the convicts to survive for two years without additional support. It took almost nine months for the expedition to be brought together, with eleven ships ranging in size from *Sirius* to the 150-ton *Supply* (8) which King described as 'much too small for so long a voyage ... and ... a very improper vessel for this service.'[6] Phillip's flagship *Sirius* was a converted supply ship, formerly *Berwick*, fitted with 20 guns. The first lieutenant, William Bradley, who was already serving when the conversion was ordered, was an accomplished surveyor and artist and kept a meticulous journal,[7] and as his second lieutenant, Phillip chose King, whose own journal is an important source of information about the years 1787 to 1790.

One interesting appointment was Lieutenant William Dawes of the Marines, who was also an expert in navigation and mathematics, recommended by Sir Joseph Banks and put in charge of the Kendall timekeeper allocated to Phillip. On delivery to Portsmouth, it had spent three days in the hands of the headmaster of Portsmouth Academy who rated it before delivering it onboard. There were strict instructions that the officer of the watch was not to hand the watch to his successor until both had sighted it, it was to be wound daily at noon, and the marine sentinel was instructed to remain in post without relief until he had seen the watch being wound.[8]

Phillip's fleet was finally ready and on 'The 14th [May] at day break we weighed & ran thro' the Needles & by Noon got a good Offing with the Wind at E.S.E'.[9] Amongst the 1,500 souls onboard about half were convicts, with around 150 marines to guard them. The fleet sailed first to Santa Cruz, Tenerife, where they arrived on 4 June. Diplomatic courtesies were exchanged and King, who attended the Spanish governor, the Marquis of Branceforte's dinner, was clearly impressed. They were shown around Santa Cruz and made a day trip to the city of Laguna, a town which he described as lying in a former marsh, drained, but 'not sufficiently to exclude very obnoxious damps & Fogs particularly in the Winter which renders this a very unwholesome place.'[10] His journal is full of detailed observations about the town and the countryside including comment on the ease of defence, which might have been useful to Admiral Nelson when he attempted to take Santa Cruz ten years later.

The First Fleet off Santa Cruz, by Lieutenant W Bradley. (Author collection)

Having passed close to the Cape Verde Islands, where King had commented about the appearance of the islands and described reefs and sea conditions, the fleet reached Rio de Janeiro, making a formal entrance with the exchange of appropriate salutes on 6 August. Phillip and his officers called upon the 'Vice King', and King commented: 'The Hospitality & attention to every person in our fleet by the inhabitants of this place of all Ranks, merits the warmest gratitude on our parts.'[11] King's journal makes more, detailed comments this time about the approaches to Rio: 'Ships bound in should leave no opportunity of getting in, as it often happens that the Sea breeze does not come in for days together tho' in general the Land & Sea winds are tolerable regular'.[12] There is also plentiful comment about the economy of Rio, with details of the level of exports of sugar, rice and indigo.

Having watered the ships and restocked with fresh supplies, the fleet sailed on 5 September 1787, meeting some very mixed weather. The journal tells of the birds which have been seen: 'Albatrosses & Pintada birds, the last we first saw in Lattde 32°.10 & Longitude 25°.25' Wt nor did they forsake us till our arrival at the Cape of Good Hope, The Albatrosses were not so attentive yet scarce a day past without seeing one or two of them, among which some were very large'.[13] They anchored in Table Bay on 13 October, when King tells of his call on the governor, Monsieur van der Graaf, who declared that he would provide every assistance. However, it shortly transpired that although cattle and wine could be supplied in

HMS Sirius and her convoy enter Botany Bay, by Lieutenant W Bradley.
(Author collection)

147

quantity, flour and bread were extremely short due to three years of famine: 'Every article of refreshment is to be got here in the greatest plenty but very dear', and King gave details of prices.[14] He noted that they arrived without any sickness aboard their ships and that not one person had to be hospitalised. Finally, after just a month, with livestock embarked, including four mares and a stallion, they left Cape Town and set off on 13 November for the final stage of their voyage.

A few days out from Cape Town, on 23 November 1787, Phillip decided to allow *Supply* to go ahead with some of the faster sailers, aiming to reach Botany Bay and establish a base by the time the others caught up. Accordingly, he, with King and Dawes transferred to *Supply* and the fleet divided into two.[15]

Arrival at Botany Bay

Supply soon forged ahead and left the slower part of the fleet out of sight. The weather was heavy with a big sea and, though steering ESE, they found themselves being set northwards from the 39th parallel upon which they aimed to keep. 'The brig labours much and is very uncomfortable. It must be acknowledged that ease and convenience were not our errand on board this vessel'.[16] On 4 December, King noted a sudden shift of wind to the SSE, which brought severe cold, and he noted 'the man at the helm, John Breedon, was affected with a kind of stupor'. They continued to experience heavy weather and gales: King's midday fixes showed the distance run, generally around 160 miles, and he comments on the bird life accompanying the ships. On 3 January 1788, they are 'satisfied with seeing Van Diemen's Land.'

Ten days later they had worked up the east coast in strong but variable winds, frequently experiencing a southerly current, and came in sight of some landmarks identified by Captain Cook. It took a further five days of reefing and setting sails, as the wind blew hard and kept changing direction, before they felt confident enough to close the shore and identify the entrance to Botany Bay. At 2pm on 18 January 1788, *Supply* anchored in the northern part of the bay, boats were hoisted out, and Phillip, King and some other officers prepared to go ashore. They were greeted by the Aborigines with menacing gestures, but were directed, through signs, to a good freshwater stream.[17] Phillip proceeded to soften relations by offering beads and looking glasses, and King commented that they 'seemed quite astonished at ye figure we cut in being cloathed [*sic*] & I think it is very easy to conceive ye ridiculous figure we must appear to those poor creatures who were perfectly naked'. During the next few days they began a thorough exploration of the bay, looking for a spot which might be suitable to set up the colony. Whilst every move must have been a step into the unknown, with the potential for attack by Aborigines at any time, King's comments make it appear rather like a relaxed picnic: 'here we went onshore & eat our salt beff & in a glass of Porter drank ye healths of our friends in England'.[18]

On 20 January, King told in detail of his exploration of the south side of the bay. Initially he met with hostility from the Aborigines, but after withdrawing and later returning with Phillip and more men, friendly relations were established and King began to make notes of the language. With due consideration to the feelings of potential readers of his journal, he described how the Aborigines became interested in knowing the sex of the visitors, given that none of them was bearded. King 'ordered one of the people to undeceive them in this particular', whereupon many women appeared and offered themselves. King 'declined their mark of hospitality', but produced a handkerchief and called over one of the women who 'suffered me to Apply the handkerchief where Eve did ye Fig leaf'.[19] It was a long day and they had twelve miles' pull back to the ship, where they arrived at midnight. Over the following two days, Phillip and a small team sailed north to explore the future Port Jackson and as soon as they returned on the 23rd, orders were given to prepare to sail. *Supply* anchored in Port Jackson on the evening of the 25th, and at daybreak on the 26th, the English colours were displayed onshore and the land claimed for His Majesty with a *feu de joie* and the drinking of His Majesty's health.[20]

Convict colony

Having established a base, there was clearly much to be done to prepare facilities ashore for the convicts so that their security could be assured and they could begin to support the work of clearing, planting and building. Things seemed to move very quickly and the convicts were all landed, clearing accomplished, and some planting begun within two or three days. On 1 February, Phillip informed King that he was to go to Norfolk Island and establish an outpost there, with the intention of cultivating and harvesting flax, which Captain Cook had observed growing there. As *Supply* was prepared and loaded with the necessary stores, Phillip ordered King, with Lieutenant Dawes, to return to Botany Bay and call on Jean François de Galaup, Comte de La Pérouse, the French explorer and navigator who arrived there as Phillip's fleet left. King provided a detailed account of La Pérouse's ships and some of his exploration during previous months, in what must have been the last contact La Pérouse's expedition had with Europeans, because shortly afterwards both ships and men disappeared without trace. King's narrative told of how La Pérouse had

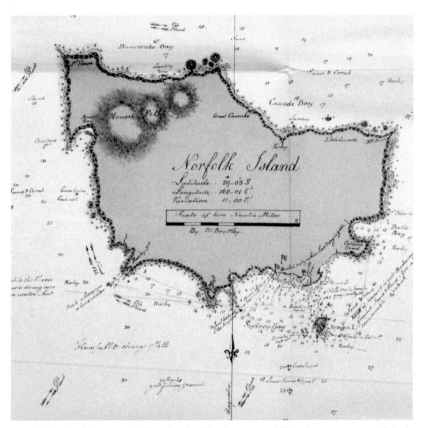

Norfolk Island by Lieutenant William Bradley. First lieutenant of *Sirius*, he was an accomplished surveyor and artist and kept a meticulous journal. (Author collection)

lost Captain de Langle, eight officers, four men and a boy when he and a watering party were attacked on the island of Maouna (one of the Isles des Navigateurs), Samoa, echoing closely the circumstances of Captain Cook's death in Tahiti. The reception King experienced from La Pérouse also leaves one in no doubt that the French had no territorial ambitions in New Holland – the motivation was clearly scientific.[21]

Norfolk Island

Supply sailed from Sydney 'with a very fine breeze' on 15 February 1788, with King's team of settlers which consisted of Mr James Cunningham, master's mate, Mr Thos Jamieson, surgeon's mate, Mr Roger Morley, 'an

Adventurer' who had been a master weaver, two marines (Charles Heritage and John Bachelor) and one seaman (the carpenter William Westbrook) belonging to *Sirius*, nine male and six female convicts – a total of twenty-two people, including King himself. They had planned for the stores and equipment to be enough to enable them to survive for six months without support, although within that time they hoped and expected to begin to provide some food for themselves. After passing Lord Howe Island and making observations about its position and appearance, they arrived off Norfolk Island on 28 February. Over the next five days, King and his officers made exploratory trips ashore to assess the best landing place and to choose a site suitable for a settlement. He landed in Cascade Bay on the northeast of the island and spent one day exploring around Mount Pitt, the highest point of the island, hacking a way through thick undergrowth amongst tall trees, and then scrambling back down to the shore along the course of a dried-up waterfall. When he had almost despaired of finding any landing place suitable for the settlement, the wind shifted, so that the surf on the south side of the island allowed him to find a way through the reefs and shoals, within what became known as Sydney Bay. On 6 March, the whole party was ashore and the colours hoisted; in the evening, 'before the Colours were hauled down, I assembled all y^e settlement & Lieut Ball

HM Ships Sirius and Supply off the reefs, Lieutenant W Bradley. (Author collection)

present I took possession of y^e Isle drinking "His Majesty" "the Queen" "Prince of Wales" "Governor Phillip & success to y^e Colony" after which three Cheers were given'.[22]

The following two years saw the little settlement at Norfolk Island grow under King's benign rule. He was driven by a strong and idealistic philosophy based on profound religious belief, which he and Phillip must have discussed at length. On Norfolk Island he had a chance to establish a community rooted in Christian love, where everyone worked willingly to provide for themselves and for their neighbours, allowing the more hard-working to become a little wealthier, but preventing anyone from exploiting the less capable. Authority was maintained by two marines, although the number gradually increased with each new arrival of convicts from Sydney, but King never felt the need to impose a military style of discipline. Early in 1790, Phillip ordered King to return to England to plead with the government for more supplies to keep the colony alive. In the meantime, Major Ross, the marine commander from Sydney and lieutenant-governor, who made no secret of the fact that he did not wish to be there, arrived to relieve King and immediately imposed martial law; with more compulsion, productivity fell significantly.

The greatest challenge to the resilience of the settlers was the continual attacks on their crops – rats, grubs, caterpillars, perroquets [sic], and a hurricane which King compared to those of the West Indies, all took their toll. There was one attempt to overthrow the government of the island by kidnapping King and luring a visiting ship into the island to be captured. King was warned and was able to take preventive measures and arrest the suspects. When found guilty by the island's magistrates, most were sentenced, but then pardoned by King in honour of the King's birthday.

Plea for support

Meanwhile, the main part of the new colony in Port Jackson had experienced its own setbacks, and provisions were reaching a critical level, with starvation beckoning. Phillip believed it essential that more support should be sent from England, and, to tackle the immediate shortage, that *Supply* should make the voyage to Batavia to purchase food there. King was ordered by Phillip to take passage in *Supply* and from Batavia to secure a passage to England, taking despatches and a personal plea to Lord Grenville, Secretary of State for the Colonies, and the government urgently to send a well-provisioned new fleet. *Supply* sailed from Port Jackson on 17 April, but it took some four weeks of negotiations with the Dutch authorities in Batavia before food and medical supplies could be acquired to take back to Sydney, and a vessel found to take King to England. Fearing the potential ravages of deadly fever which was rampant in Batavia, King left as quickly as possible aboard the packet *Snelheid* on 4 August 1790. After five or six days at sea, 'the captain, and his two mates, and all the sailors except four, were incapable of getting out of their beds.' King took essential measures for self-preservation and determined that neither he nor the four still healthy sailors would go below. The fit men were given 'three large glasses of port wine a day, and two tea spoons full of bark in each glass.' They were made to wash frequently with vinegar and 'fill their noses with tobacco', and he made a form of tent on the quarterdeck. Most of the sailors and officers were dying, 'carried off by a most malignant putrid fever'.[23] On 29 August, they anchored off Mauritius, the captain and three sailors dying as they were carried ashore. In the next three weeks at Mauritius, King arranged for a new crew to be entered and the vessel sailed for England on 21 September. Happily, the remainder of the voyage was uneventful and they reached London on 20 December 1790.

In his first few days back home, King met Lord Grenville and Evan Nepean, Admiralty Undersecretary, who were complimentary and supportive, promising a fleet with further supplies as quickly as possible. His promotion to commander was confirmed, as was his appointment as lieutenant-governor. He married on 11 March 1791, and he and his bride

The wreck of the Sirius, by Lieutenant W Bradley. (Author collection)

embarked four days later aboard *Gorgon* to return to Norfolk Island, where they arrived after a brief stop in Port Jackson in November 1791. This was the start of a second and longer tour[24] to develop Norfolk Island into a secure and reliable source of additional food for Port Jackson, and a 'prison' for some of the more intractable transportees. When Governor Phillip left for home, his interim successor, Major Grose, made clear his disdain for the way in which King was running Norfolk Island, and found an excuse to reprimand him formally for diverting for ten days a ship which was effectively being used to enrich Grose's fellow officers in Sydney. King had used the ship to return two Maoris to their tribe, after they had revealed what they knew of flax growing and processing.

The governor

By 1796, King's heath had deteriorated as his family had grown, and he asked to return to England, thinking that if he returned to fitness he might rejoin his colleagues in the fleet fighting the French, and thus secure his future. However, as his health recovered, he recognised that this was not realistic, as he had already fallen well behind his fighting colleagues, and his only prospect for future recognition was to press for the support of Sir Joseph Banks and his former boss Phillip, now an admiral, to return to New South Wales as governor. With the British government preoccupied with war with the French and Spaniards, it is hardly surprising that the administration of a new, faraway colony received little attention, and although King was given a 'dormant commission' as governor in May 1798, the vessel which was being specially prepared for service out there proved to be wholly unfit for sea in the English Channel, let alone in the Indian and Pacific Oceans, and was scrapped.

Eventually, King, his wife and one of his children arrived in Sydney with a letter dismissing Governor Hunter and with his own commission. Hunter was extremely resentful of King and refused to relinquish his post for some six months, whilst King carried out a review of the colony and discovered the situation had worsened considerably during his absence. The army was controlling the rum trade, and had been very successful in lining the pockets of many of its officers, at the expense not only of many individual settlers, but also the colony. Productivity was low and morale at rock bottom. King knew that he must act and that in doing so he would make enemies. He controlled the price of rum by forbidding its sale by any officer, resulting in the price dropping from £8 to £1 per gallon inside a year.[25] He enforced controls on other goods by limiting the mark-up to 100 per cent instead of the 500 per cent officers had been taking. These and other measures led to continual aggravation between him and the army, although gradually he gained the upper hand, and productivity in the colony grew to a point where it was almost capable of feeding itself without outside help. He expelled Captain John Macarthur, the charismatic, rich and successful, though junior, army officer, for duelling with, and almost killing, his superior officer. He dealt firmly with an uprising led by some Irish transportees, by acting swiftly and decisively in the middle of the night, preventing the rebels from establishing a strong base from which to terrorise the whole colony. The economy was flourishing with new enterprise, encouraged by King, and could boast shipbuilding, sandalwood, whaling and sealing, milling, salt-making, tanning, flax and rope-making, textiles, brewing and coal extraction.

After three years his health was again beginning to deteriorate and King asked to be relieved. It took two years for the government in London to appoint Captain William Bligh, and another six months before he arrived. King at once passed the responsibility to Bligh,[26] but he was too ill to board the vessel to take him home. Finally, in February 1807, he could embark and he arrived in London, somewhat recovered in strength, towards the end of the year. His final days were spent pleading passionately for a level of pension which matched his commitment and service to his country over the previous forty years. He died just a year later, having received no recognition from the post-Pitt government, leaving his wife with very little to live on.[27] Clearly, the value placed upon the creation and establishment of a new colony was at the time far lower than the financial and social rewards for sinking enemy ships.

Captain James Cottell:
The Pictorial Life of a Trafalgar Veteran

John Rawlinson

James Cottell was born in Barnstaple on 16 August 1781 and spent much of his life in the Marines. He was a prolific amateur artist who recorded many of the events he witnessed in sketches and watercolour, often using the smallest fragments of paper or card on which to draw. He must have spent much of his spare time painting.

As well as painting the events he had seen, James also copied others; this picture of *Victory* during the Battle of Cape St Vincent was painted from Richard Dodd's engraving.
(James Cottell, © National Museum of the Royal Navy)

Cottell's father William was a local solicitor who was mayor of Barnstaple in 1784. The family traced its ancestry to the Norman family of Cothele and the Champneys of Yarnscombe. Cottell's father died when he was seven; however, the family remained wealthy and were able to send him

The marines on the left show officer's uniforms in 1797, the year James joined the corps. The centre depicts the uniforms of the Trafalgar period and on the right are the uniforms of the 1840s. (James Cottell, © National Museum of the Royal Navy)

For many years a plaque on Barnstaple bridge recorded that James's father, William Cottell, was mayor when repairs were commissioned in 1784. (James Cottell, © National Museum of the Royal Navy)

away to school. He went first to Mr Turner's in Exeter and later to Mr Willson's Academy at Cheshunt, where he joined the Warwick militia as an ensign. Cottell's mother also died whilst he was young. His formal education ended when, aged sixteen, he returned to Barnstaple. James transferred into the North Devon militia and served alongside his eldest brother John, now head of the family, who was already a militia lieutenant.

Inscribed on reverse 'This was done 1798—when in the North Devon Militia, Frankford Barracks, Plymouth, James Cottell, The Effects of imagination'. (James Cottell, © National Museum of the Royal Navy)

Cottell's other brother William had joined the Marines in 1793. James was to follow him into the corps and was granted a commission as second-lieutenant in September 1798, when he was just seventeen years old. Only four weeks later William was dead. James recorded the terrible news in his diary:[1] 'rec'd an account of the Death of my brother William, whose memory never be erased from my heart … he died of wounds rec'd on the Robust 74 in taking the Hoche & the Squadron, under Command of J.B. Warren'.[2]

Blockades and battles: 1798–1803
Cottell joined the Plymouth Division of Marines in mid-December 1798; a week later he embarked in *Mars* and was to find himself at sea for most of the next seven years. The war against France was being fought mainly by the navy, with British fleets blockading French ports and individual ships and squadrons protecting trade routes around the globe.

HMS *Eurydice*; in the distance Nelson and a squadron of frigates anchored in the Downs, September 1801. (James Cottell, © National Museum of the Royal Navy)

As the fleet increased in size, so the demand for detachment commanders led to quicker promotion and, on occasion, to the use of second-lieutenants in command of detachments. So Cottell commanded the marines in *Eurydice*, and he was promoted to first-lieutenant while only twenty-three

The location or date of this intriguing image is unrecorded in Cottell's sketchbook, although it may relate to the image above. (James Cottell, © National Museum of the Royal Navy)

years old. Frigates served as the eyes and ears of the navy, and Cottell's diary shows *Eurydice* was no exception; she was employed on a vast range of tasks, sailing as far as Newfoundland and the Cape of Good Hope, with both extremes of weather and the enemy to contend with during his three years on board.

Typical diary entries read:

23rd April 1800 ... took a French brig, 14 guns, Lt Boganvill detained and sent in a Swedish ship ...
9th August 1800 ... joined Earl St Vincent's fleet off Brest, Adml Sir J Warren in the *Renown* was sent with us, anchored off Belleisle on the 15th ...
9th November 1800 ... a perfect hurricane, we drove out but had the good fortune to hold on ... *Havoc*, *Pelican*, *Spiteful* gun brig & two merchant vessels went ashore ...
17th November 1800 ... Sailed and landed spies near St Malo.

After service in the Channel Squadron, *Eurydice* was dispatched to Canada on convoy duty, sailing as far as Quebec. On her return, she was soon on her way to the Indian Ocean, spending the next year patrolling the east coast of the subcontinent. It was here that news of the short-lived Peace of Amiens reached the ship: '18th October 1802 ... fired a salute of

An almost idyllic scene is one of the few images Cottell signed: his initials appear on one of the upturned boats. (James Cottell, © National Museum of the Royal Navy)

Landing from a small warship in a sheltered cove, an inshore vessel looks on.
(James Cottell, © National Museum of the Royal Navy)

twenty-one guns in conformation of Peace'. *Eurydice* returned to Spithead in March 1803. The ship paid off and Cottell returned to barracks and, for the first time in four years, he was allowed leave, spending three weeks at home in Barnstaple.

Food shortages had been common between 1794–1801[3] but by 1803, the date of this painting, there would be little need for a simple food basket to have an armed escort. (James Cottell, © National Museum of the Royal Navy)

161

Tonnant and Trafalgar: 1804–1805

Cottell returned to sea in March 1804 when he joined *Tonnant,* one of the finest ships in the Royal Navy. She was a French-built 80-gun ship, captured at the Battle of the Nile. Cottell spared few words as he records the news that the Franco-Spanish fleet was at sea, the massing of the British fleet, the battle and its aftermath:

> 20th August 1805, HMS *Tonnant* … anchored in front of Gibraltar in consequence of hearing that the combined fleet was at sea and had chased Adml Collingwood off Cadiz
> 23rd August 1805 … we joined Collingwood with 4 sail …
> 30th August 1805 … joined 18 sail … which made us 26 …
> 28th September 1805 … joined Lord Nelson in *Victory* with 2 sail …
> 19th October 1805 … general chase …
> Oct 21st 1805 … about 12 o'clock the memorable Battle action off Trafalgar began … in 4 hours & 5 minutes we found ourselves the Conquerors … Adml Magon in the *Algazares* [*Algésiras*] & a Spaniard struck to the *Tonnant* … we had 26 killed and 50 wounded.

Sadly, it is not known if Cottell depicted the action at Trafalgar: his granddaughter is known to have given individual painting as gifts to family and friends. Two significant images of the aftermath of the battle do survive, and show a battle-scarred fleet making for Gibraltar. (James Cottell, © National Museum of the Royal Navy)

Inscribed on the reverse 'The Victory and Tonnant going for Gibraltar after the Battle of Trafalgar 28th Oct. Prince at anchor, Canopus and Belleisle in the mole.'
(James Cottell, © National Museum of the Royal Navy)

Tonnant was second in line behind *Royal Sovereign*. However, slow sailing meant that she soon gave way to *Belleisle* and *Mars*. Charles Tyler, *Tonnant*'s captain, called to *Belleisle* as she passed: 'A glorious day for old England, we shall have one a piece before night'.[4] *Tonnant*, her band playing 'Britons strike home', was soon engaged with two enemy ships, so close that the crew used her pumps to put out a fire on board the French *Algésiras* which threatened to spread to their own vessel.[5] In a desperate fight, only the steady fire of her guns saved *Tonnant*, eventually her crew boarding and capturing *Algésiras*. Soon her other adversary, the Spanish *Monarca,* also struck her colours to *Tonnant*; however, all her boats had been destroyed and *Tonnant* was unable to claim her prize. In the margin of his diary, Cottell recorded that *Tonnant* used 5 tons, 80–100 barrels, of powder to fire 1,700 18pdr and 1,740 32pdr shells during the battle: he also recorded that *Monarca* had raked *Tonnant* broadside into quarter.[6]

Cottell recorded the aftermath of the battle and *Tonnant's* return to Portsmouth.

28th October 1805 … anchored at Gibraltar, went into the mole …
16th November 1805 … sailed …
30th November 1805 … anchored at Spithead …
19th December 1805 … went into harbour, the troops cheering us, *Belleisle* & *Mars* & *Tonnant* proceeded the *Bellerophon*.

163

Recruiting and raids: 1806–1810

Cottell left *Tonnant* during February 1806. He was to spend the next three years with the recruiting service, based in the east of England, leading recruiting parties at Grantham, Lincoln, Boston, Newark and Leicester.

A Danish warship firing a salute, after an engraving in the *Naval Chronicle*, spring 1807, 'A View of the Sound from above Elsinore, with Cronenburg Castle'.
(James Cottell, © National Museum of the Royal Navy)

On 22 October 1808, Cottell returned to more active duty, joining the frigate *Sirius*, and in February the following year sailed in convoy for India: '2nd March 1809 HMS *Sirius* … took a French schooner headed from Nantes to Senegal', and '14th June 1809 … off the Isle of France [Mauritius] fired at by the battery from Cannonier point, we returned some broadsides … we had two men wounded, one died'.

Cottell's diary continues:

21st Sept 1809 … landed at St Pauls, Isle of Bourbon [Reunion] with 182 men of the 56th Regt, 150 sepoys, 209 R[oya]l. Marines and 100 seamen,

A tiny sketch depicting the squadron action against St Paul's.
(James Cottell, © National Museum of the Royal Navy)

landed about 4 in the morning and at 9 had possession of the place, 130 cannons or more, *Caroline* Frigate, *Streatham* and *Europe* Indiamen, *Grapler* brig, 3 small brigs, several others surrendered.'

Inscribed on reverse 'The spot where Lts Pye and Howden RM were wounded (the latter died on the morning of the 21st Sept 1809) at St Pauls Isle de Bourbon'.
(James Cottell, © National Museum of the Royal Navy)

'In making a push for the Barracks a man was discovered who Lieut Mr Burton recognized as having run away in a prize after murdering the officer. The man was brought to England and was hung at Horse Manger [sic] London. 21st September 1809'.
(James Cottell, © National Museum of the Royal Navy)

Hoisting the British colours on the captured Battery at Isle de Bourbon.
(James Cottell, © National Museum of the Royal Navy)

Cottell was mentioned in the *London Gazette* and the *Naval Chronicle* in recognition of his actions during the capture of the Isle de Bourbon, a fellow officer writing: 'The first battery mounting nine 24 pounders commanding the margin of the bay was stormed and carried by Lieut Cottell and part of *Sirius'* Marines, where the British Colours were first planted in that colony which enabled the squadron to stand in and the troops to move forward.'

In August 1810, the British strategy turned to the capture of Isle de France (Mauritius), where the Royal Navy would suffer one of its biggest defeats of the Napoleonic War. In the difficult and unknown waters of Grand Port, *Sirius* and *Magicienne* were burnt by their crews to avoid capture, *Nereide* was disabled by the French *Bellone*, and *Iphigenia* was forced to surrender. A note by Cottell describes the island as covering a 'surface of 400,000 acres; soil generally of little depth and full of stones':

17th July [1810] Sailed for the Isle of France. 21st Arrived off there ...
23rd July Detained an American ship, *Janus*, from Batavia to Isle of France; in the evening was fired at from Canonnier Point; one shot hit the spanker. Worked round the island; sent the boats to cut out a chaponiere [schooner] found there – too bad ... fired our broadside; the boats returned with the loss of one man killed – Slater, Butcher – one man wounded.'

The night-time assault on the Isle de Passe.
(James Cottell, © National Museum of the Royal Navy)

The next target was an island covering the approaches to the harbour:

August 8th The Boats were sent to attack the Isle de Passe; too much wind; sailed in the evening; found the *Otter* from the Cape ...
13th Took the Isle de Passe; Lt Norman, one seaman & two marines killed and several wounded.

Captain Pym's report on the night attack, written on the following day to his commodore, is more explicit:

The Isle de Passe is in our possession, it completely commands the Grand Port. At Dusk last night I hoisted out my boats and ran down in sight of the rocks; at half past 8 o'clock they pushed off and at eleven o'clock got within hail and completely surprised the Island in the rear; it was stormed and carried in a few minutes ...Our loss has been rather severe, but from the importance of this Post, I think it could not have been [taken] with less. I have to request you particularly recommend as being highly deserving of Promotion Lieuts Chad and Watling, Lieuts Cottell and Bates of the Royal Marines ...

The captain was evidently unaware that such recommendations in respect of Royal Marine subalterns were ineffective; their promotion was governed by seniority. A week later, the squadron entered the port itself, after retaking an East Indiaman and working their way in without sufficient pilots or adequate charts; the result was perhaps predictable:

21st Retook the *Windham*; 22nd In going in to attack the French frigate, got on shore. Joined the *Iphigenia* and *Magician*. In going in got again on shore. The *Nereide* was obliged to strike; the *Magician* was set on fire and blew up in the night ...
25th The *Sirius* was obliged to be sacrificed in the same way ...

In December, a larger British force captured the Isle de France and the prisoners were released.

Marriage, family and France: 1811–1823

After his release, Cottell returned to England on board the captured French frigate *Astrée*. The journey home was to take nine weeks, sailing via St Helena and Ascension: on the way the crew enjoyed an unexpected feast: 'March 5th 1811, Ascension ... 80 turtles were turned by the *Ceylon* & *Nereide*, received five about 400 lbs each.'

A 36-gun fifth rate ship, possibly HMS Sirius, c1808.
(James Cottell, © National Museum of the Royal Navy)

Cottell' s only representation of India. Inscribed on reverse 'Elephant Island
from Butchers Island, Bombay. J Cottell, Oct 25th 1811 Northampton.'
(James Cottell, © National Museum of the Royal Navy)

Cottell had only been back in England for four months, having settled on leave in Northampton when he recorded in his diary: 'August 13th ... left Northampton for Grantham, arrived there in the evening ... on the 16th, my birthday, was married to Elizabeth Hill'. We know very little about Elizabeth: the register at St Wulfram's in Grantham shows she lived in the parish and was twenty-one, eight years younger than Cottell. Cottell's only other mention of his wife was in much later life whilst he was serving away from his family in Portugal during 1833: 'Dreamt of often walking delightfully in arm with my wife's arm'. Their first child was born at Chatham in 1813; Elizabeth Maria was the first of twelve children, nine of whom survived to adulthood.

Inscribed on reverse, 'Jas Cottell, St Servan Oct 1820.' Traces of a second, faint pencil inscription are difficult to read but appear to say 'The Gorge at Plymouth, from passage'. (James Cottell, © National Museum of the Royal Navy)

As the war with France drew to a close, the number of officers and marines needed was greatly reduced. The other ranks were discharged from the service to earn a living as best they could. Many officers were placed on half-pay and in 1814 Cottell was no exception. The family at first stayed in England, but by 1819, Cottell had decided to join many other officers who, seeking to survive on reduced means, went to live abroad. The Cottells settled at St Servan in Brittany.

Inscribed on the reverse 'Jas Cottell, Sept 1815, Bordeaux'.
(James Cottell, © National Museum of the Royal Navy)

Inscribed on the reverse in a later hand 'This is the house and some members of the Cottell family in France', and in a different hand, not James Cottell's, 'St Servan, Brittany'. (James Cottell, © National Museum of the Royal Navy)

171

Beyond attending ceremonies and fetes the family had little to do with the local people, socialising with the other British families in the area. Cottell kept a detailed account book of his expenditure during their time in France: this details the family school fees, the cost of their food, dancing lessons and many other facets of normal life in post-Napoleonic France. However, there was good news: 'May 26th 1823 ... received my appointment to full pay at Chatham', and with this news the Cottells' life in France was over. On 15 July 1823, they sailed for England, returning to Chatham via Jersey, Southampton and London.

Politics and Portugal: 1824–1834

Cottell arrived at Chatham on 26 July 1823, where they were to remain for just over a year before Cottell exchanged divisions with another officer and moved his family back to the West Country. They settled into life in Plymouth, and Cottell soon fell into peacetime barrack life. Most of his interest over the coming years was naturally with his growing family. Four more children were born between 1824 and 1830, Cottell recording the tragically short life of his last child in two entries:

> March 17th 1830 ... Emily Jane born at No5 Buckingham Place, Mill Place. St Patrick's day at 20 min past 10 AM ...
> March 28th 1831 ... Died at Millbrook, and buried Emily Jane 1st April, aged 1 year and 11 days after 8 days illness.

The Marines depart for Portugal: the speech bubbles sum up much that Cottell sees as being wrong in the corps of the period. Amongst gripes of both being left behind and being sent to Portugal, the odd comment on the wasted cost of new uniform is made, whilst General Cockburn advises, 'Now Major, after every action write me, never mind the Admiralty dispatches; if I send another battalion I will come myself!!!'
(James Cottell, © National Museum of the Royal Navy)

'Cockburn hangs back'. (James Cottell, © National Museum of the Royal Navy)

In November the previous year, Cottell had been able to record happier news about his eldest son: 'Novr 22nd … Joseph joined the *Revenge* as a volunteer of the 1st class, Capt Hillier, appointed by Sir George Cockburn'.

Just eight weeks after Emily's death, Cottell was ordered back to sea, joining *Caledonia* as her captain of marines and soon to sail for Portugal during a civil war. Many of the paintings in his sketchbook were made

A common sailor joins in lampooning Cockburn sending the Marines to Portugal. (James Cottell, © National Museum of the Royal Navy)

173

'From Valenca across the Minho – May 6th '33'.
(James Cottell, © National Museum of the Royal Navy)

during this time when he traced Wellington's route across the Peninsula. Many marine officers resented that an army officer, Sir James Cockburn, had been put in charge of their corps, and Cottell drew several cartoons which lampooned him.

'Douro from Paso ad Regua – April 29th '33'.
(James Cottell, © National Museum of the Royal Navy)

Throughout his career, Cottell had returned to Barnstaple to take part in elections, his diary recording six journeys to vote, the longest a four-day, 230-mile journey from Grantham: 'June 8th 1826, went to Barnstaple, voted for Mr Alexander ... Hodgson 401, Alexander 377, Nolan 126.' Although with a population of nearly five thousand, under a thousand voters in Barnstaple were responsible for the election of two Members of Parliament, and by the end of the nineteenth century the borough had been disenfranchised.

The people of Exeter met on 15 October 1831 to protest against the Reform Bill. Cottell was at sea at this time but his interest in West Country politics will have ensured his knowledge of this event. (James Cottell, © National Museum of the Royal Navy)

Retirement and the last shilling: 1835–1842

By June 1834, the civil unrest in Portugal was coming to an end, and Cottell received orders to return to England. The simple: 'July 10th 1834 ... Disembarked', marks Cottell's final diary entry relating to his military service. Not untypical for the time, Cottell had run up debts whilst away in Portugal, and he wrote to Major-General Sir George Cockburn on 20 March 1835, but received a dusty reply:

Sir, In reply to your letter of the 19th Inst, No1720, with its enclosures from Captain Cottell of the Plymouth Division of Royal Marines, forwarded to you by his commandant requesting to be placed on reserve half-pay in consequence of his inability to resume his professional duties, being and having been several months in confinement for debt with no prospect of making any arrangement with his creditors for his early release. I am commanded by my Lords Commissioners of the Admiralty to acquaint you that under the circumstances of this officers case and agreeably to your recommendation their Lordships are pleased to place him on the reserved half-pay list in compliance with his request.

Unfortunately, the death of his agent, Mr Madden, and an inability to agree terms with his successors led to Cottell being imprisoned. Unable to perform his duties, he was forced to seek permission to be placed on the half-pay list, and only after seven months in Exeter jail was Cottell able to agree terms with his creditors. He was declared bankrupt with debts of £1,700 and was ordered to pay £73 per year, which left him just £54 to provide for his family.

On his release, Cottell wrote to the Admiralty seeking to return to the full-pay list: several other officers in similar circumstances had been

Cottell titled this picture *The Last Shilling*; his final years were overshadowed by his financial failure. (James Cottell, © National Museum of the Royal Navy)

reinstated. Sir George Cockburn, First Sea Lord and brother of Sir James Cockburn – the senior officer lampooned by Cottell – refused to allow Cottell to return to the full-pay list because he had requested and not been required to go on half-pay: 'Having laid before my Lord Commissioners of the Admiralty your petition of the 23rd Ultimo, stating the circumstances which induced you to be placed on half-pay, and requesting to be replaced on full pay in your original standing, or to be placed on the retired full pay I am commanded by their Lordships to acquaint you that your request cannot be complied with.'

Cottell was to try repeatedly over the next seven years to return to the full-pay list. Not only was he on reduced pay, but his wife would not be allowed a pension on his death. His requests were in vain, and he died on 30 April 1842, still on half-pay.[7] However, he lived long enough to record the birth of his first grandchild: 'Feby 10th 1841 … Camilla brought to bed of her first child, a boy, Cottell Edward'.

Elizabeth was to live on for thirty-five years as a widow, until she died aged eighty-seven on 29 June 1877. The following day, the Cottell's eldest daughter Elizabeth Maria acted as the official informant, recording her mother's death at Bedminster register office.

Medals and rewards

Cottell in his cartoons constantly refers to Sir George Cockburn as 'The Cock that Burns', and is unafraid in these private reflections to show his frustration with both Cockburn's appointment and the lack of recognition for service at Trafalgar.
(James Cottell, © National Museum of the Royal Navy)

177

Cottell painted many cartoons and wrote several letters complaining that the Battle of Trafalgar was not celebrated and that no government medal had been awarded for the battle, writing to a Bristol journal: 'Nov 18th 1840 … Mr Editor, How is it that the Battle of Waterloo be celebrated at Bristol by hoisting the colours on all the churches and the ringing of bells, while that of Trafalgar is allowed to pass unnoticed?'

A soldier questions why the sailor and marine wear their medals on their backs.
In the background, *Tonnant* struggles into Gibraltar after Trafalgar.
(James Cottell, © National Museum of the Royal Navy)

After the Battle of Waterloo, the government awarded a medal to every man who had taken part. The naval veterans of Trafalgar had been presented with an unofficial medal paid for by the industrialist Mathew Boulton, whilst the crew of *Victory* had received a similar unofficial medal from Alexander Davidson, Nelson's prize agent. To make matters worse for those who valued their medals, soldiers could wear their Waterloo medals, but sailors and marines were not allowed to wear their unofficial Trafalgar medals.

Grit it brave Ned!, you have shown them clearly,
The ****** disgrace when paid for so dearly,
We boast of Victories, at Trafalgar and Waterloo,

The inequitable distribution of medals for the Napoleonic wars
was a theme Cottell returned to many times in his paintings.
(James Cottell, © National Museum of the Royal Navy)

Where the reds gained honours but not so the blue,
Trafalgar was single handed against Spain and France,
And Waterloo not gained, till the allies did advance.

Cottell wrote on the back of a tiny piece of card: 'After the Battle of
Trafalgar Mr Boulton voluntarily presented medals at his own expense
which were worn by those heroes but our good King did not think sailors
worthy of honorary distinction and they were forbidden from wearing
them'. Not until 1848 did the government relent and announce the award
of the Naval General Service Medal. All the naval veterans of the war were
to receive a medal with the clasp for each action they had taken part in.
However, the veteran had to be living to make his claim, and of the 18,425
sailors and marines at the Battle of Trafalgar, only 1,561 survived to claim
their official medal. Cottell was not amongst them, though he did receive
£44 4s 6d prize money and a further £100 12s 1d parliamentary grant for his
service at Trafalgar.

Two of Cottell's diaries are known to have survived. The first uses the
briefest of notes to record the most important events that occurred
throughout his life. The original was destroyed during the Blitz, but a copy

Three wounded marine veterans present their protests to General Cockburn:
the first has lost an arm, the second a leg and the last an eye.
(James Cottell, © National Museum of the Royal Navy)

made by his grandson has survived.[8] An account book used by James whilst he lived in France during the 1820s is also extant, in which much of the normality of life on half-pay is recorded.[9] In addition, the Cottell family had several letters and documents written or owned by James, whilst much of Cottell's official correspondence with the Admiralty is at Kew. A descendant, Michael Cottell, collected together many of Cottell's paintings and ephemera which had been dispersed around the family, and in 2005 Cottell's paintings were exhibited at Uppark. After Michael's death, his widow Anita generously donated all the material to the Royal Marines Museum, where it is now cared for by the National Museum of the Royal Navy.

The Rise and Fall of the Bourbon Armada, 1744 to 1805: From Toulon to Trafalgar

Larrie D Ferreiro

The Bourbon Family Compacts

The Bourbon Armada, the combined forces of the French Marine Royale and the Spanish Real Armada, had its roots in the Bourbon Family Compacts, a series of three treaties between France and Spain that lasted from 1733 until 1792. These treaties were the result of the War of the Spanish Succession (1701–1715), fought between two coalitions led by (respectively) Britain and France, over whether a Habsburg or a Bourbon would control the Spanish Empire. It ended with a Bourbon king, Felipe V, firmly ensconced on the Spanish throne. At the same time, the Real Armada was formed when Spain's nine previously separate fleets were combined into one centralised navy. Almost immediately upon the end of the war, France and Britain created the Anglo-French Alliance as a hedge against the newly-upstart Spain. This period of relative peace lasted until 1731, when Britain entered into a new alliance with Austria, at the time France's adversary.[1] The young French King Louis XV knew that he needed a powerful partner to face the British-Austrian alliance. Spain had also found itself vulnerable against the same alliance, so it was perhaps inevitable that the two nations, united by a common adversary and by family ties (both were descended from Louis XIV; Felipe V was Louis XV's uncle) would join forces.

On 7 November 1733, the first Bourbon Family Compact between the two nations was signed in the Spanish palace of El Escorial outside Madrid. The treaty agreed that the two nations would act in concert to promote their mutual interests, and support each other in gaining new territories – the Duchy of Lorraine for France, and the kingdoms of Naples and Sicily for Spain. The Treaty of El Escorial (the official title of the first compact) was quite far-reaching, providing, among other things, that France would support Spain's claims on several Italian states and Gibraltar. Spain, emboldened by the Family Compact, immediately sent forces in 1733 and 1734 to capture the Italian islands of Ischia and Procida, and conquered the kingdoms of Naples and Sicily. The only joint operation that France and

Spain carried out under the First Family Compact was not naval but scientific; the Geodesic Mission to the Equator (1735–1744), in which French and Spanish scientists proved that the Earth was not spherical but rather flattened at the poles.[2]

The success of the Bourbon Armada at the
Battle of Toulon/Cap Sicié, 1744

The War of the Austrian Succession (1740–1748) brought France and Spain back into conflict with Britain over the control of the Habsburg throne. Spain had actually been fighting with Britain since 1739 over trade in the Caribbean, but the entry of France, Prussia, Austria and a host of other nations widened the conflict throughout Europe. In the early years of the war, France and Britain were on opposing sides of the conflict, but not yet directly at war with each other. In September 1743, Britain and Austria strengthen their alliance with the Treaty of Worms, which forced France to also strengthen its alliance with Spain. The Second Family Compact between Louis XV and Felipe V was signed at Fontainebleau on 25 October 1743, in which the two nations specified their war aims and reaffirmed their perpetual alliance.[3]

Britain was already blockading the Spanish ports of Cadiz, Ferrol and Cartagena, and in 1742, established a blockade of the French port of Toulon, where a Spanish squadron under Captain-General Juan José Navarro had taken refuge after landing troops in Italy and subsequently being battered by storms. For almost two years, the British fleet under Thomas Mathews kept the Spanish ships bottled up in port, while allowing French ships to come and go. On 9 February 1744, a war council between Navarro and his French counterpart, the elderly Vice-Admiral Court de La Bruyère, determined that French fleet based in Toulon would combine with the Spanish squadron to break the blockade together, even though France was not yet technically at war with Britain. The Bourbon Armada was composed of sixteen French ships, which would form the van and centre, while the twelve Spanish ships, including the massive 114-gun *Real Felipe*, would form the rear. On 19 February at 2pm, the fleet of twenty-eight ships set sail to give battle to the thirty-one British warships waiting for them off the Isles d'Hyères.

For several days, light winds prevented the two fleets from forming into proper lines of battle. Finally, on the evening of 22 February, the British rear began to engage the Spanish rear, and continued through the following day. Navarro outgunned and outmanoeuvred Mathews, though it was not until late afternoon that the two French squadrons were able to wear and

Sir Thomas Mathews, Welshman, Vice-Admiral of the Red and Commander-in-Chief of the English Mediterranean fleet, 1742–44. In the background is Hyères Bay, Toulon; the stern of Mathews's flagship, the 90-gun *Namur* is on the extreme left, and the 90-gun *Neptune* on the right.
(Claude Arnulphy, © National Maritime Museum, Greenwich, London)

join the battle, finally driving the British off and allowing Navarro and Court de La Bruyère to escape to Cartagena. France declared war on Britain soon afterwards. The Battle of Toulon or Cape Sicié was the first military success for the Bourbon Armada, despite the fact that it had been formed not by strategic design, but out of tactical necessity. Mathews was court-martialled for his defeat, while Navarro was given the title Marqués de la Victoria.[4] Ultimately, the War of the Austrian Succession finished largely *status quo ante bellum*, leading to another great war in just six years.

The failure of the Bourbon Armada in the Seven Years War, 1761–1763
The Seven Years War began in 1754 as a series of skirmishes between French and British forces vying for control of the Ohio Valley in North America. Within two years, it included Prussia, Austria, Russia and other European nations, while fighting spread across the globe. Starting in 1759, Britain won a stunning string of victories at sea and on land, decimated the French fleets and occupied their strongholds from Canada to the Caribbean to Asia. Spain was not in the war at this point but, among other factors, it became increasingly fearful that France and Britain would make peace and leave Spain helpless. France's navy, meanwhile, was being mauled by the

British navy, which out-built and out-captured France's navy by a ratio of ten to one.[5]

In early 1761, Louis XV and the new Spanish King Carlos III agreed to revive their alliance against Britain. France's foreign minister Choiseul and the Spanish ambassador Grimaldi signed the Third Bourbon Family Compact in Paris on 15 August 1761. It provided for Spain to declare war on Britain the following year, provided no peace had been concluded, while France promised to support Spain if attacked. Word of the secret Family Compact leaked to Britain, which in January 1762 pre-emptively declared war on Spain. During the remaining months of the Seven Years War, France and Spain made two attempts to form a joint Bourbon armada, neither of which went beyond the planning stage before the preliminary peace treaties were signed in November of that year.[6]

In March 1762, a French squadron under Chef d'Escadre Coubon-Blénac arrived in the Caribbean and, unable to attack Jamaica, proposed to the Spanish officials in Havana to use his squadron to help defend that crucial port from an impending British assault. The Spanish officials in Cuba rejected that offer, and within a few months Havana was in British hands. In April, Carlos III proposed to France a joint Bourbon invasion of Britain. The focus of planning was on their navies, for while Britain's coasts were protected by its wooden walls of warships, the island itself had only a smattering of regular troops and militia. If France and Spain could land troops, Britain could easily be overrun. The plan called for a squadron of twenty Spanish ships from Ferrol and Cadiz to attack and drive off British squadrons which had been blockading Brest and Rochefort. The French squadrons would then join to create the combined Bourbon armada that would escort 30,000 troops from Dunkirk and Calais to invade Britain. The Spanish government planned for the squadron to depart Ferrol on 1 October. However, the British assault on Havana reordered Spain's priorities, while the French troops slated to invade Britain were instead called up to fight in Germany. By July 1762, plans for a Bourbon armada were called off.[7]

The final Treaty of Paris that ended the Seven Years War was signed on 10 February 1763, which resulted in Spain losing Florida, and France losing Canada and giving Louisiana to Spain. Britain was now unchallenged as the dominant power in Europe and the world, and with the French and Spanish navies now decimated, there seemed little that they could do to regain their standing and their territories.

The policy of *revanche* and rebuilding the Bourbon Armada, 1763–1770

Almost before the ink was even dry on the Treaty of Paris, French military officers were spreading out across the south of England, gathering intelligence on the British navy and potential landing sites on the coast. This was part of comprehensive Bourbon strategy of *revanche* (revenge) against Britain, developed by Choiseul and Grimaldi (newly appointed as foreign minister), whose centrepiece would be a combined assault on England. The attempted assault in 1762 had failed because France and Spain could not co-ordinate their fleets in haste. This time, the two ministers believed, their advance planning would ensure success.[8]

Both Choiseul and Grimaldi knew it would take five or more years for both navies to rebuild a credible offensive capability against the British fleet. In addition to intelligence-gathering, they also planned to create an effective, unified Bourbon armada. At the beginning of 1763, France only had forty-seven ships of the line, while Spain had just thirty-seven (eighty-four ships combined), far short of the numbers needed to defeat the 145 ships of the British navy. Though both ministers committed to building more ships, they also recognised that this was insufficient to defeat the British navy. A wholesale reformation and integration of the navies on both sides of the Pyrenees was in order. In France, Choiseul issued a sweeping Naval Ordinance in 1765 that streamlined the bureaucracy, enforced a strict series of rates that standardised the types and dimensions of ships so they would manoeuvre and fight as one unit, and set up the world's first professional corps of shipbuilders, whose task was to use scientific principles in the design and construction of vessels, with the goal of making each ship better than its British counterpart.[9]

Grimaldi's task, on the other hand, was to rebuild the Spanish fleet along the same lines as the French fleet, so they could operate in unison. That meant importing not just French technology but also French know-how. In 1765, Grimaldi asked Choiseul to send French engineers who could bring both Spanish shipbuilding and naval artillery up to French standards. For the first request, Choiseul sent Jean-François Gautier, a mid-level shipbuilder, to be placed in charge of all Spanish ship construction. Gautier quickly discarded the older, sturdier Spanish designs and began constructing lighter, faster warships in the French mode, following the instructions of Choiseul's Naval Ordinance. The French shipbuilder fully understood Grimaldi's objectives: 'My duty is to regard French and Spanish vessels as forming a single Armada.'[10]

For the second request, Choiseul dispatched, also in 1765, the Swiss-French artillery engineer Jean Maritz to Spain, where he established foundries that employed the same technique recently introduced in France of solid-casting the cannon and drilling the bore, which gave cannon greater power and precision. Maritz followed the new French guidelines for gun sizes and calibres, so that the older Spanish hotchpotch of naval guns was soon replaced by a standardised set of cannon that could fire more accurately and at longer ranges.[11] These changes to hulls, masts and artillery meant that the new generation of Spanish warships would manoeuvre and fight identically to French ships of the line. Now, just a few years after the Treaty of Paris, France and Spain were well advanced in planning a war with Britain, and were on their way to having an armada that could accomplish it.

The war plan that was agreed to by both nations in 1767 called for a surprise assault by a combined fleet of 140 ships of the line (eighty French, sixty Spanish) against Britain's fleet, which now numbered 120 ships of the line. The main force would escort a fleet of smaller landing boats to descend on Portsmouth and the Sussex coast, laying waste to critical parts of the naval infrastructure. The invasion would stop short of a full-out assault on London, which could frighten other continental powers. Instead, French diversionary forces would attack Scotland, while Spanish forces would descend on Gibraltar with the aim of recovering the strategic territory it had lost years earlier.[12]

Just as the two nations were well on their way to becoming ready for an assault on Britain, in 1770 a political crisis in the Falkland Islands put a halt to them. In that year, the governor of Buenos Aires sent a large amphibious force to remove the British garrison on the island. Britain geared for war, while Spain called on France to honour the Bourbon Family Compact by coming to its aid. King Louis XV came down firmly against it. The crisis was diffused the following year when Spain disavowed the military action. But the crisis soured Louis XV on the *revanche* strategy against Britain, while making Spain's Carlos III doubt the worth of the Bourbon Family Compact and indeed of any further dependence on France. The invasions plans were put on shelves in Versailles and Madrid.

The Bourbon Alliance floundered for several years, until 1774 when Louis XV died, and the nineteen-year-old Louis XVI succeeded him to the throne. At just the same time, the political situation in America was coming to a boil. The new king appointed Charles Gravier, Comte de Vergennes, as his foreign minister. Vergennes was committed to working with his counterpart Grimaldi to renew the close relationship with Spain. As it happened, a new conflict just brewing in the British colonies of America would provide the two Bourbon powers with an opportunity to re-establish their policy of *revanche* against Great Britain, and lead them directly into the War of American Independence.[13]

The success of the Bourbon Armada in the War of American Independence, 1779–1783

The longest-lived and most successful employment of the Bourbon Armada was actually in the service of another cause, the independence of the American colonies from Great Britain. In April 1775, the shots fired at the battles of Lexington and Concord signalled the beginning of a war that had actually been brewing for several years. Taxes, the lack of any representation in Parliament, and the increasing restrictions on trade all drove the American colonists to take up increasingly violent protests against British policies. But America began the war stunningly incapable of fending for itself; it had no navy, little in the way of artillery, and a ragtag army and militia that were bereft of guns and even of gunpowder. Without the help of France and Spain, the Americans knew they could not survive. In 1775, its colonial leaders reported to a secret French envoy to Philadelphia that 'they are convinced they cannot defend themselves without a seafaring nation to protect them, and the only two powers which are able to help are France and Spain.'[14]

The two Bourbon powers at first provided materiel support to the United States, which had declared independence in 1776, but by the following year it was apparent that the Americans could not win the war without direct military intervention. France agreed to an alliance with the United States in February 1778, after which it sent naval forces under the Comte d'Estaing to assist in the fighting. But during his campaigns in the summer and autumn of 1778, d'Estaing failed to recapture either Newport or Savannah as was intended, which left the Americans despairing for a French-Spanish alliance. As George Washington told the Congress that November:

> The truth of the position will entirely depend on naval events. If France and Spain should unite, and obtain a decided superiority by sea ... France with a numerous army at command, might throw in what number of land forces she thought proper to support her pretensions, and England without men, without money, and inferior on her favourite element could give no effectual aid to oppose them.[15]

Spain had opted to stay out of the alliance in 1778 due to many reasons. One critical factor was that they still had a treasure fleet at sea carrying $50 billion equivalent in silver, and did not want to risk it being attacked by the

British navy.[16] But once it was safely in port at the end of the year, Spain was free to reactivate the mutual assurance clauses of the Bourbon Family Compact. The Treaty of Defence and Offensive Alliance against England between France and Spain was signed at the Palace of Aranjuez on 12 April 1779. It was, in fact, a long list of Spanish demands, punctuated by the occasional concession to French desires, and stipulated that Spain and France would make war against Britain with the intent to acquire Gibraltar and Minorca, co-operate in an invasion of Great Britain, and expel British forces from Florida.[17]

The Comte de Vergennes and his new Spanish counterpart, the Conde de Floridablanca, dusted off the invasion plans for Britain that had been developed a decade earlier, and now drew up a new scheme. French and Spanish ships of the line would rendezvous at the northern coast of Spain, before turning towards Britain. Once sea control had been established in the Channel, smaller vessels would transport a 30,000-strong army from Brittany and Normandy for the amphibious descent, during which they would occupy the Isle of Wight and Gosport, then destroy the British fleet at Portsmouth.[18]

France and Spain sent spies to Portsmouth and Gosport, where they found under-manned garrisons and weak defensive works. They also stepped up dockyard activities to get their ships into service. Spain was actually the more prepared of the two. The Marqués de Castejón, the Minister of the Navy, and his chief shipbuilder Gautier had overhauled and improved the Spanish dockyard system, so that fast warships based on French design principles were steadily coming off the slipways.[19] The French Minister of the Navy, Antoine de Sartine, was rushing to achieve the number of ships needed for the naval campaigns. Most of the dockyards' efforts were directed at refitting older vessels, which averaged just half the cost of a new-construction ship – the 90-gun *Ville de Paris*, for example, was refitted to carry 104 guns, in order to face British three-deckers like the 100-gun HMS *Victory*.[20]

Both the French and Spanish navies were delayed by an even larger problem that afflicted even the vaunted British navy – lack of manpower. Under the flag of Lieutenant-General of the Navy the Comte d'Orvilliers, the French fleet of twenty-eight ships of the line, plus frigates and other vessels, assembled in early June at Brest. The fleet was short of four thousand sailors, which d'Orvilliers had to supplement with inexperienced army men drafted at the last moment, many of whom boarded the ships already ill from an epidemic which was just beginning to grip the French nation. On 3 June 1779, they set sail, arriving a week later at their rendezvous point at the Sisargas Isles off the coast of Galicia in Spain. The thirty-nine Spanish ships of the line at Ferrol and Cadiz, under the overall command of Captain-General Luis de Córdova y Córdova, also faced delays owing to lack of qualified officers and the need to quickly draft inexperienced hands from the local population. The Cadiz fleet sailed in late June, but due to contrary winds did not reach the rendezvous until 23 July. By then, Spain had issued its declaration of war against Britain. With the campaign now in motion, all sides girded for battle.[21]

France and Spain had prepared meticulously for this invasion as far back as 1765, when Choiseul and Grimaldi first envisioned a combined Bourbon fleet, and had exchanged shipbuilders and artillery engineers so that their ships and weapons could operate side by side. It was therefore astonishing,

Luís de Córdova y Córdova commanded the Spanish fleet during the Anglo-Spanish War 1779–83, when he captured two British convoys totalling seventy-nine ships, including fifty-five ships from a rich convoy composed of East Indiamen sixty leagues off Cape St Vincent. In 1782, he fought the Royal Navy to a stalemate at the Battle of Cape Spartel. (Museo Naval de Madrid).

even by the standards of the day, that these preparations had not extended to developing a common system of communications between the fleets. The problem lay not in the language – all of the Spanish officers spoke French – but in the signal flags. D'Orvilliers' chief of staff, Jean-François du Cheyron du Pavillon, had drawn up the French fleet's signal book. A copy had been sent to Madrid back in March, but it did not reach Pavillon's counterpart, Córdova's chief of staff José de Mazarredo, until shortly before the Cadiz fleet weighed anchor. 'I was very surprised to learn that the signal books had not been printed in Spanish, and that M Mazarredo was obliged to copy them by hand since his departure from Cadiz,' complained d'Orvilliers to Sartine. 'I assure you that never before have two squadrons at sea had to improvise their signals, but that is what I have been forced to do.'[22] As soon as the Spanish fleet arrived, Pavillon set to work with Mazarredo, producing ten signal books in one week to distribute to the rest of the ships. Unfortunately, that left the French and Spanish commanders no time to train and exercise together before entering into battle.

With the two fleets joined into a single armada, they were arranged into seven squadrons. D'Orvilliers was in overall command of four combined squadrons while Córdova, aboard his massive 112-gun flagship *Santísima Trinidad*, led an all-Spanish squadron of observation, which would operate in reserve to attack the British during battle. Two more squadrons would patrol the Azores to protect Spanish convoys returning from the Americas. On 29 July, the combined Armada of 150 vessels, larger even than the 128 ships of the original Spanish Armada of 1588, left the Sisargas Isles, bound for the English Channel. Within days, the crews began succumbing to disease; within a few days, eighty were dead and 1,500 ill. The doctors were at a loss to explain it, some pointing to scurvy as the cause. It was, in fact, part of a massive dysentery outbreak, one of the largest on record until that time. On top of the epidemic, it took the Armada a full two weeks, fighting calms and contrary winds, to round the Brittany peninsula, finally entering the English Channel on 16 August.

The British learned of d'Orvilliers' departure from Brest on 12 June. On 16 June, the twenty-eight ships of the line in the Channel Fleet departed Portsmouth under Vice-Admiral Sir Charles Hardy, flying his flag in HMS *Victory*. Although, like the French and Spanish, the British ships were under-manned and their crews sickly, they nevertheless sped west to the Scilly Isles to intercept d'Orvilliers before he could enter the Channel. But the long-anticipated showdown between the Bourbon and British fleets never came. Hardy's fleet patrolled back and forth for a month, though it was too far west to catch sight of d'Orvilliers when he arrived. When the

Admiral Sir Charles Hardy, prominent in the Seven Years War and governor of New York 1755–57. (George Romney, © National Maritime Museum, Greenwich, London)

Armada was finally sighted off Plymouth on 16 August, the coastal towns immediately girded for an invasion, issuing arms and calling up militia, while back in London stocks dropped sharply on the news. But the Bourbon fleet was steadily losing its ability to threaten the British population. Their resupply ships never made their rendezvous, leaving the Armada increasingly short of victuals and water. Meanwhile, dysentery continued to ravage the crews. On the flagship *Ville de Paris*, 307 men fell ill, one-third of its 1,100 crew, necessitating that a frigate be stripped of much of its crew just to keep the flagship operational.

191

On 18 August, a gale from the east blew the Armada out of the Channel. A week later they finally encountered Hardy's flotilla. D'Orvilliers attempted to engage the Channel Fleet. Hardy knew he was overmatched, so he avoided combat while continuing to lead the Armada back east towards the safety of Portsmouth, where on 3 September he moored to re-provision for battle. The same day, d'Orvilliers received orders from Versailles to end the campaign and return to Brest. The Armada entered port a week later with 8,000 sick and dying sailors aboard, but with only one captured British ship to show for their efforts. Sartine and the other members of the French court immediately denounced d'Orvilliers' failure to engage Hardy's flotilla, but Pavillon leapt to his defence, pointing out that 'the French vessels ... were really more hospitals than ships of war.'[23] The French-Spanish invasion of Britain, which had been the centrepiece of the entire Bourbon strategy and the culmination of a fifteen-year naval build-up, had simply fizzled out.

Despite the failure of the invasion scheme, France and Spain were still committed to the joint Bourbon Armada, for neither nation could take on the British navy by itself. Over the course of the next year they ironed out their operational difficulties, as sixteen French ships of the line joined Córdova's fleet, making several sorties into the Atlantic in order to intercept British ships cruising off the Spanish coast. One of those sorties departed Cadiz on 31 July 1780 with twenty-four Spanish and six French ships of the line. Owing to good intelligence passed to him by Floridablanca, Córdova knew that a massive, lightly escorted convoy was en route to the East and West Indies, and went in search of them. In the pre-dawn darkness of 9 August, Spanish frigates glimpsed a cannon flash and heard a boom one minute later, which Córdova's chief of staff Mazarredo argued must be the convoy just ten miles away, and not the Channel Fleet. Córdova duped the convoy into following him by using the stern lamp of *Santísima Trinidad*, which they mistook for their own escort, the 74-gun HMS *Ramillies*. Dawn saw the fifty-five merchantmen under the guns of the combined fleet, while the copper-bottomed *Ramillies* was able to outrun its pursuers, much to the dismay of the French captains whose uncoppered ships were left in its wake. The convoy returned to Cadiz with an enormous haul. It was the single largest loss of ships the British navy would experience in the war, with over three thousand soldiers, 80,000 muskets and £1.6 million in gold and silver (worth $17 billion today) now in Spanish hands.[24]

The next major action of the combined Bourbon navy, the Siege of Pensacola in 1781, shows how well co-ordinated the French and Spanish fleets had become. Their ships were regularly operating from one another's

Por España y por el Rey: Gálvez at the siege of Pensacola. Bernardo Vicente de Gálvez y Madrid, Viscount of Galveston and Count of Gálvez (1746–1786) served as governor of Spanish Louisiana and Cuba, and later as Viceroy of New Spain. (Augusto Ferrer Dalmau)

ports and being refitted in each other's dockyards, both in Europe and the Caribbean. The problems of signals and tactics that had plagued the combined Armada against Britain had long since been ironed out. The two fleets now operated together routinely, with French captains taking orders from Spanish fleet commanders and vice versa. In January 1781, François-Aymar, Chevalier de Monteil, in command of the French fleet based at Martinique, brought his nine ships of the line to the Havana dockyard to be careened and scraped. The Spanish governor of Louisiana, Bernardo de Gálvez, was also in the city at the same time, planning his assault on the capital of British West Florida at Pensacola. Monteil was eager to assist the Spanish action, and anxious to go into action before he was forced to return to Martinique to protect French commerce from British attacks.

The Spanish fleet in Havana was still under repair from a devastating hurricane just months earlier. Nevertheless, Gálvez was eager to press the attack and convinced the military leaders in Havana to mount an under-manned and under-gunned expedition, with the promise that reinforcements would come as soon as they were ready. Gálvez's fleet departed Havana on 28 February 1781 and began the assault of Pensacola on 9 March. As the siege dragged on, Gálvez's troops ran low on ammunition and supplies; by mid-April the soldiers were down to three ounces of beans per day and were foraging for spent cannon shot. On 19 April, he received word that twenty newly-repaired ships had just arrived from Havana under the flag of the Spanish naval Brigadier General José de Solano, including eight French warships under Monteil, who had agreed to postpone an assault on a British blockade in South America in order to join the invasion. The fleet brought cannon, mortars, siege tools and gunpowder. Most welcome were the battle-hardened troops, under the leadership of General Juan Manuel Cajigal y Niño, which included French-speaking troops from Flanders, and five regiments of French soldiers who had just seen action in the United States and in the Caribbean. The combined French-Spanish army began its assault on the fortress on 24 April, backed by naval artillery from the combined fleet. On 8 May, a fortuitous shot from a Spanish howitzer detonated a British ammunition magazine. Gálvez's combined army quickly overran the British stronghold and forced its commander to surrender all of West Florida.[25]

José de Solano y Bote (1726–1806), Spanish naval officer and explorer, governor of Venezuela from 1763 to 1770 and later governor and captain-general of Santo Domingo (1771–79). (Museo Naval de Madrid)

At the same time that Pensacola was besieged, a combined Spanish-French armada was being prepared to re-take Minorca. The French naval Lieutenant-General Luc Urbain du Bouëxic, Comte de Guichen, arrived in Cadiz in early July to link up with Córdova, with whom he had already sailed during the attempted invasion of Britain two years earlier. Meanwhile, the Duc de Crillon was appointed to lead the amphibious force. Crillon was an ideal choice to lead a joint campaign; he had been a French lieutenant-general in the first part of the Seven Years War, before transferring with the same rank into Spanish service in 1762. As Crillon, Córdova and Guichen made their final preparations for the assault, word came of the victory at Pensacola, which was celebrated with a 21-gun salute. On 21 July, the massive fleet began departing the Bay of Cadiz; fifty-eight ships of the line and seventy-five transports carrying 8,000 troops. Britain's navy was at that time spread across Europe, the Americas, the Caribbean and Asia; they had no more ships left to confront such a massive fleet, or to reinforce Lieutenant-General James Murray's garrison on Minorca.

Even if the British navy were spread thin, they were still a force to be reckoned with. Córdova and Guichen took a long, roundabout route to disguise their ultimate objective; London did not know that it would be Minorca until just days before the force landed near the capital of Mahón, on 20 August, and Murray was caught so off-guard that his 2,700 troops barely had time to retreat to the citadel of Fort San Felipe. Crillon established a blockade of the city, while further Spanish and French reinforcements arrived in October. Crillon now had 14,000 men to occupy the entire island and lay siege to San Felipe, whose garrison endured months of almost constant bombardment while succumbing to diseases like scurvy. When Murray finally hoisted a white flag in February 1782, only 600 men were fit enough to walk out unaided. The victors were appalled by the near-skeletons they had to carry out of the citadel and nurse back to health; the vanquished boasted that their captors could take little credit for seizing a hospital.[26]

With the fall of Minorca, the only British stronghold left in the Mediterranean was Gibraltar, and now the Spanish and French turned their attention to concluding the blockade and siege that had begun back in 1779. In June 1782, the Duc de Crillon was appointed to lead a large-scale naval and land assault, supplementing the Spanish siege forces with thousands of French and Spanish troops who had just conquered Minorca. On 12 September, the 35,000 soldiers surrounding Gibraltar were supplemented with thirty-nine ships of the line under Córdova and Guichen. That evening, Crillon held a *junta de generals* to decide on the attack. Several senior officers wanted to delay the assault until all the preparations were complete, but Crillon had received intelligence that a British relief convoy for Gibraltar was being prepared, and any delay in his attack could jeopardise the whole operation.

On 13 September 1782, the combined assault using floating naval batteries and land-based artillery began. While the Bourbon artillery lobbed shells at dug-in British fortifications, the British artillery commanders were using depressing guns to fire into Spanish trenches and firing red-hot shot at the vulnerable floating batteries, which began to smoke, catch fire and then explode. Over forty thousand artillery rounds were expended during the day-long battle, almost one for every second of the fight. Yet when the smoke and wreckage cleared, the British garrison at Gibraltar remained intact, and would do so through to the end of the war.[27]

Just as Crillon had feared, the British navy had been preparing another convoy to supply the Gibraltar garrison, but unknown to him its departure had been delayed by weather and accidents. On 11 September 1782, thirty-four ships of the line and thirty-one transports bound for Gibraltar left Portsmouth. Above HMS *Victory* flew the flag of Admiral Richard Howe, who had until recently commanded the British naval forces in America. The fleet weathered storms en route, but as they approached Algeciras on the night of 10 October, a particularly violent gale blew in from the southwest. When dawn came, it was clear that the French and Spanish ships were unable to stop the British from entering the bay; many had broken their moorings and were scattered about, with some hove up on shore. Howe's fleet had remained intact and came unopposed into harbour to offload the much-needed provisions.

A week later, Howe's thirty-four ships departed Gibraltar. By then, Córdova and Guichen had collected thirty-six ships intact, and gave chase. Although Córdova's flagship, *Santísima Trinidad*, was coppered, most of the Bourbon fleet was uncoppered, and this greatly slowed them down. Even worse, the difference in performance meant that Córdova's formation was ragged, as the faster coppered ships tried to match speeds with the slower uncoppered ones. By contrast, Howe's fully coppered fleet was able to solidly maintain its formation, and at first he was so confident in his ability to control the battle that he intentionally slowed down to engage his adversaries. When the two met off Cape Spartel in Morocco on 20 October 1782, they exchanged a few desultory rounds before Howe decided that engaging Córdova's larger force presented too great a gamble – after all, he had already accomplished his mission of resupplying Gibraltar – so he ordered a general retreat. Howe's coppered ships were able to open the gap between the two fleets as night fell, and by daybreak the combined Bourbon fleet was twelve miles behind and unable to catch up. The last major European battle of the War of American Independence ended with a whimper, not a bang.[28]

What Howe, Córdova and Guichen could not know is that even as the Battle of Cape Spartel was being fought, representatives of their three governments were already at Versailles, hammering out the details of a series of peace treaties that would end the war and secure the independence of the United States. These treaties were finalised just in time to prevent a massive Bourbon fleet, forty ships of the line, from departing Cadiz in early 1783, which was intended to rendezvous with more than fifty French and Spanish ships in the Caribbean to finally capture Jamaica.[29] That invasion would never come to pass. The Bourbon Armada had successfully fought the British navy across the globe, and forced London to sue for peace.

When the fleets at Cape Spartel disengaged, the commanders and their sailors would have been able to see, across the Straits of Gibraltar on the horizon to their north, a Spanish cape named Trafalgar. Twenty-three years in the future, many of these same men and ships that sparred at the Battle of Cape Spartel would meet again at Cape Trafalgar, in a battle that would change the course of history.

The failure of the French-Spanish Armada and the Battle of Trafalgar, 1803–1805

The French Revolution, which began in 1789, was not a direct consequence of the War of American Independence, but rather of France's own internal strife which had been brewing for decades. The Spanish government was fearful that the French Revolution would spread across the Pyrenees and to its own Caribbean colonies, and distanced itself from its erstwhile ally. The French Revolutionary Wars began against Austria in 1792, by which time the Bourbon Family Compact was effectively null and void. In February 1793, France declared war on a coalition of nations, including Britain and Spain.[30] Spain fought against France for two years, then finding itself on the losing end of the conflict, switched sides in 1796 to join France in its fight against Britain, with the Second Treaty of San Ildefonso now taking the place of the Bourbon Family Compact, since France was no longer a Bourbon monarchy but rather a republic.

But by then, both France and Spain had lost much of their naval strength. The Spanish navy lost the Battle of Cape St Vincent in 1797, despite outnumbering the British almost two to one, and the French navy was devastated a year later at the Battle of the Nile. The French navy's officer corps was hit particularly hard by the Reign of Terror: generally members of the hated aristocracy, they were imprisoned, guillotined, shot or exiled in disproportionate numbers compared with their army counterparts. As in the previous wars, the French and Spanish navies would have to combine into a single fleet to have any chance of defeating Britain.[31]

They would have that chance in 1805, soon after the war had resumed, with France and Spain once again united against Britain. Spain had already ceded Louisiana to France, and Buonaparte sold the entire territory to the Americans in order to pay for the new war effort. A major part of that effort would be a planned invasion of Britain, drawn in part from the invasion plans of 1765 and 1779. In order for the assault to proceed, a combined French-Spanish fleet would have to first take control of the English Channel, before a flotilla of invasion barges would cross the narrow stretch to land in Kent. While Buonaparte's plan broadly resembled the previous ones, the scale would be vastly different; where the 1779 invasion had 30,000 troops on shore, Buonaparte had mustered almost ten times that number between Boulogne and Bruges for this invasion.[32]

The naval side of the assault failed before the invasion flotilla could even get underway. The two navies had learned some lessons from their previous experience but forgotten others. By now all ships were coppered, but as with the invasion attempt twenty-six years earlier, the French and Spanish fleets had not trained together to perform complex battle manoeuvres. In early 1805, Buonaparte developed a complicated and ultimately unworkable strategy to have the fleets break out from their ports on the Atlantic and Mediterranean, evade the British blockade, race across the Atlantic to rendezvous in the Caribbean, then race back to the English Channel to support the invasion flotilla. As the spring and summer progressed, only the Toulon fleet was able to accomplish its breakout, and by August the necessary fleet rendezvous with the invasion flotilla had failed. In the autumn, Buonaparte ordered the combined French-Spanish fleet to depart its base at Cadiz to transport troops for the planned invasion of Naples. Under French Vice-Admiral Pierre Charles Silvestre de Villeneuve and Spanish Captain-General Federico Gravina, thirty-three ships of the line sortied from Cadiz on the evening of 20 October and headed for the Straits of Gibraltar. Waiting for them in the offing were twenty-seven ships under the flag of Admiral Horatio Nelson.

As the two fleets closed near Cape Trafalgar the morning of 21 October, officers in both fleets would have recognised the scene. The Battle of Cape Spartel had been fought within sight of Trafalgar twenty-three years earlier. Robert Moorsom and Philip Durham had been junior officers at Spartel, and now commanded their own British ships of the line. In the Spanish fleet, Spartel veterans Federico Gravina, Antonio de Escaño, José Gardoqui and Ignacio María Álava were now flag officers, while Cosme Damián Churruca and Francisco Asedo commanded ships. The sense of déjà vu would have been all the stronger, as the flagships *Victory* and *Santísima Trinidad*, along with *Britannia*, *Rayo* and *San Justo* fought in both battles.[33]

But there the comparisons ended. Where the Battle of Cape Spartel was inconclusive, the Battle of Cape Trafalgar was an overwhelming British victory that indelibly marked the century to come. Nelson decisively cut the French-Spanish battle line in two places and destroyed it in detail. By the end of the day, the British fleet had captured or wrecked two-thirds of the French and Spanish ships, while Nelson was fatally wounded and died a national icon. Buonaparte was thereafter reduced to continental operations, as he could no longer count on his navy to carry out any major overseas campaigns. The impact went far beyond the European sphere – after Trafalgar, Britannia unquestionably ruled the waves across the entire globe; for the next hundred years, until the First World War, no other navy would contest its command of the ocean.[34]

The Bourbon Armada in context

The Bourbon Armada was originally formed as part of the Bourbon Family Compact, and was created due to the inability of either France or Spain to defeat the British navy on its own. The First Family Compact, signed in a period of relative peace, did not result in any joint naval actions. The Second Family Compact was signed during the War of the Austrian Succession, and although the joint action at the Battle of Toulon in 1744 was a success, this was not due to any advance planning, since the French and Spanish squadrons sailed and fought independently of each other, with little strategic co-ordination. The Third Family Compact initially brought no result during the Seven Years War; two attempts at creating joint Bourbon fleets were abandoned even before they were begun. However, the interwar build-up of the Bourbon armada from 1765 to 1778, emphasising common shipbuilding and artillery standards, brought both navies to a high level of materiel readiness.

The War of American Independence showcased the capabilities and possibilities of the Bourbon Armada. Although the first joint operation, the planned 1779 invasion of Britain, was a failure – in part due to haste, lack of operational planning or training, but mostly due to an unforeseen dysentery outbreak – the French and Spanish navies quickly learned how to operate together. Their ships regularly used each other's ports and dockyard facilities, operational orders and signals were unified, and even command structures appear to have been well integrated. Indeed, had the planned 1783 invasion of Jamaica taken place, the combined Bourbon fleet of almost a hundred ships would certainly have captured Britain's most important naval base in the West Indies.

The failure of the French-Spanish fleet in 1805 at Trafalgar was largely due to the same problems that plagued the 1779 invasion – haste and the lack of operational planning and training – but had the fleet not been decimated by Nelson, there is a good chance the combined Armada would have gone on to overcome these difficulties and stood toe-to-toe against the British fleet.

This paper has provided an overview of a little-studied aspect of naval warfare during the age of sail, coalition warfare between allied navies. Far more research can and should be done to clarify the political calculus of the joint Bourbon Armada, the command structures used during the campaigns, signalling, communications and tactics employed, the relationships between French and Spanish officers, and the logistics and support infrastructure for the fleets. Two centuries before NATO was conceived, the Bourbon Armada demonstrated how effective a coalition can be against a common adversary.

Smuggling and Blockade-Running during the Anglo-Danish War of 1807–14

Jann M Witt

Between 1792 and 1815, Great Britain and France fought for the political and economic predominance of Europe, but while both nations were busy disrupting their respective sea trades, neutral shipping prospered. Thus the small kingdom of Denmark for many years was not only able to maintain its neutrality, but to benefit economically from this bitterly fought war.[1]

Since the end of the Northern War with Sweden in 1720, Denmark had remained neutral. From the middle of the eighteenth century onwards, the Danish state – then consisting not only of the present-day kingdom of Denmark, but, among other territories, also of the kingdom of Norway, as well as the duchies of Schleswig and Holstein (now part of Germany but which were then connected to Denmark by a personal union) – had established itself as an important maritime nation. Besides the Danish capital Copenhagen, several ports of the duchies of Schleswig and Holstein had become the home of large merchant fleets, operating in the European and international sea trade.[2]

During the War of American Independence, as well as during the wars of the French Revolution, the Danish merchant fleet took advantage of the protection offered by its neutral flag. But once British policies against neutral trade became more and more repressive, tensions grew. These conflicts culminated in the forming of the second League of Armed Neutrality of several northern European nations in 1800, initiated by the Russian Tsar Paul I after the model of a similar defensive alliance of neutral powers during the War of American Independence.[3]

When the second Armed Neutrality threatened to block British access to the Baltic, the British counter-strike was swift and hard, since a large amount of the vital naval stores, such as wood, hemp and tar, needed for the maintenance of the Royal Navy came from the Baltic. On 2 April 1801, a British squadron under command of Admirals Sir Hyde Parker and Lord Horatio Nelson destroyed the Danish fleet in the bloody Battle of Copenhagen. Nevertheless, Denmark still was able to maintain her neutrality for a few more years.[4]

Only in 1806 did things start to change. After his victory over Prussia and the conclusion of peace with Russia, Buonaparte had but one enemy left: Great Britain. The French emperor was definitely overlord of the Continent, but his power ended at the high-water mark, since after the decisive victory in the Battle of Trafalgar on 21 October 1805 Great Britain literally 'ruled the waves'.[5]

Buonaparte had just one chance to force Great Britain into defeat – by economic, not by military means. By his famous Berlin decree on 21 November 1806, Buonaparte officially established the Continental System, banning all British trade goods and products from the Continent, intending to crush his enemy's export-orientated economy. Not only the parts of Europe under the direct control of France, but also Russia, seeking political reconciliation with France, joined the Continental System. Together, both great powers agreed to persuade the minor powers in the Baltic area to join the embargo against Great Britain – if necessary, by use of force. This would have locked Great Britain out of the Baltic and thus cut one of her most important lifelines, the supply of vital naval stores.[6]

When intelligence about the Franco-Russian plot reached the British government, it struck back as determinedly as six years before. The British sent a fleet commanded by Admiral Lord James Gambier to Copenhagen to exert pressure on the Danish government and to keep access to the Baltic

Taking away the Danish fleet. Contemporary British caricature. (Author collection)

202

A heavily armed and highly manoeuvrable Danish gunboat of the early nineteenth century.
(Author collection)

open for British ships. After their arrival before Copenhagen, the British delivered an ultimatum, demanding that the Danish should consent to an alliance against France and hand over, as a pledge for their future well-behaviour, their fleet to the British within a week. Caught between the Scylla of British sea power and the Charybdis of the far superior French army, a small power such as Denmark could only lose. If they gave in to British demands, Buonaparte would attack, if not, the British forces would besiege the Danish capital.[7]

In the end, the Danish government, with the courage of the desperate, refused the British ultimatum, and on 2 September 1807, the British started a bombardment. For five long days the Danish, with utmost bravery, defended their burning capital, but in the end capitulation was inevitable. This attack and the subsequent seizure of the Danish fleet caused a deep hatred of the British among the Danish population, which lasted for many years and drove Denmark into the arms of Buonaparte. One direct effect of the outbreak of the war between Denmark and Great Britain was the collapse of Danish-British trade, which came near to a total economic disaster for Denmark.[8]

The Danish naval forces, however, recovered amazingly rapidly from their defeat. Within the narrow margins of its remaining military potential, the Danish navy tried to maintain a close embargo on British goods and tried – albeit in vain – to close the passages to and from the Baltic Sea – the

Øresund or Sound, the small passage between the Danish island of Sjælland and Sweden, as well as the Storebelt, or the 'Great Belt', the route between the Danish islands of Fyn and Sjælland. With their few remaining warships and a large fleet of quickly constructed gunboats, they began to wage a form of seaborne guerrilla warfare against British shipping.[9]

Most notably, gunboats proved to be an effective weapon in the Danish fight against blockade-runners and enemy merchant ships. Open, flat-bottomed and of shallow draught, such vessels were ideally suited for a *guerre de course* in coastal waters: armed with a heavy guns fore and aft, these gunboats could be sailed as well as rowed. Swift and highly manoeuvrable, they specialised in quick, surprise sorties from fortified bases. They preyed on enemy merchant ships, which were easy prizes for them, especially when unescorted. In a dead calm, a squadron of these frail vessels could even menace a ship of war. A more traditional navy would have been wiped out in a short time by the mighty British fleet, but in the narrow and shallow waters of the Baltic, these handy vessels proved to be a hard match for the heavily armed, but much more ponderous, warships of the Royal Navy.[10]

Not only gunboats fought against the British, but also privateers. The use of privateers was the classical weapon of minor maritime nations,

A Danish privateer between 1807 and 1814. (Author collection)

mainly aimed at the enemy's sea trade. By an officially issued document, called a letter of marque, privately owned ships were empowered to serve as private ships of war – thus the term 'privateer' – against the enemy nations specified in the document.[11]

Since merchant shipping had slumped, many Danish shipowners and merchants invested in privateers in the hope of rich profits. Between 1807 and 1813, a total of 556 Danish ships were commissioned as privateers to prey on British merchant vessels in the North Sea and the Baltic, and in the beginning, the Danish privateers brought in quite a number of captured British merchantmen.[12] Quite typical for Danish privateers of this period was the jagt *Johanne* of Copenhagen, Chresten Holm commander, a small one-masted vessel, commissioned in 1813, armed with two 3pdr guns and a crew of twenty-five.

During the entire period of war, the British – although officially in a state of war with Denmark, Prussia and Russia, and between 1810 and 1812 also with Sweden – were able to maintain their access, as well as their economic contacts, to the Baltic region. A strong naval squadron commanded by Vice-Admiral Sir James Saumarez kept open the approaches to the Baltic and protected merchant vessels sailing in and out.[13] Not only British-flagged ships were involved in this trade. Many vessels belonged either to American owners or to owners in Scandinavia. Thus ships were owned by subjects of states formally at war with Great Britain, and more or less reluctantly allied with France, and blockade-running and smuggling was often considered as a form of resistance, if not as a patriotic duty. So the Continental System was increasingly undermined, not only economically, but also politically. By an elaborate scheme of licences, these neutral and even enemy ships were granted free access to British ports and protection by the Royal Navy from warships and privateers.[14] The British allowed all foreign ships in possession of such a licence permission to call in at British ports and to export British goods, unhindered by British warships and privateers. To prevent misuse, and an uncontrolled breach of the British blockade of France, the entire licence system was under strict control by British officials. For instance, ships in possession of a licence were obliged to sail only in large convoys, escorted by British ships of war. This escort was not only intended to protect the merchant vessels from enemy attacks, but also to keep a controlling eye on them.[15]

The British convoys met at fixed points of rendezvous and sailed during the annual shipping season from 15 April to 15 October every fortnight, according to a strict schedule. But the British system of licences and convoys only regulated the passages between Great Britain and the Baltic region. In the Baltic, the convoys dispersed, the ships then sailing individually to their destined ports. No longer protected by the Royal Navy, they had to rely on disguise and deception alone. One popular way of disguise was 'neutralisation'. To achieve this, a vessel was sold pro forma to a new owner of neutral nationality, thus changing the vessel's nationality and flag. Furthermore, most ships were equipped with counterfeited documents. As a consequence, the forging of foreign documents and the pretence regarding the neutrality of the ship and its cargo almost became some kind of art.[16]

For its loyalty to Buonaparte and the participation in the Continental System, the Danish state paid an enormous price, since the economic consequences of war, blockade and embargo proved to be disastrous. Besides the export of rural and forest goods to Great Britain, shipping had been the backbone of the Danish economy before the war. The ruin of merchant shipping after 1807 thus had considerable effects on the entire economy: seamen became unemployed, as well as shipyards and ship-builders, and many merchants went bankrupt. In this desolate economic situation, smuggling seemed to be the only recourse.[17]

By seizing the Danish-ruled island of Heligoland in August 1807, the British had secured themselves a first-class base for running the Danish blockade. They transformed the little island, situated about forty-five nautical miles west of the Schleswig-Holstein coast and predominantly inhabited by fishermen and their families, into a fortified warehouse, stuffed

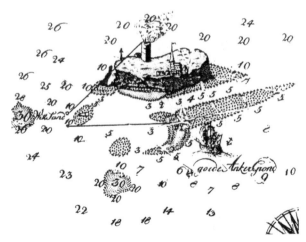

Detail of an eighteenth-century map showing the island of Heligoland. (Author collection)

with all the goods desired on the Continent, mainly colonial commodities like coffee, tea and tobacco. Within a short period of time, Heligoland became a smuggler's nest, accommodating a large number of merchants of various grades of respectability. From Heligoland, these merchants ran the blockade, and landed their contraband – more or less secretly – not only in ports like Husum or Tönning, but also in numerous small landings. Soon the port of Tönning became the most important place of trans-shipment for smuggled goods on the west coast of the Danish state. The small town became a prosperous seaport, until the collapse of the smuggling trade in 1812 due to the breakdown of the Continental System.[18]

Although Denmark was one of the most loyal allies of Buonaparte's France and fully supported the Continental System, the embargo was not entirely maintained, even by the Danish authorities. In theory, any trade with Great Britain was strictly forbidden, but there were some exceptions to the embargo. Both sides allowed limited trade with Norway, since the Norwegians depended heavily on the import of grain and other supplies. Given British naval supremacy, the Danish King, regardless of his political dependency on France, had no choice but reluctantly to allow his subjects to use British licences and to accept the British system of convoys and licensed trade to secure the supply of Norway. Likewise, the British, for humanitarian reasons, allowed the continuity of trade with Iceland, the Faroe Islands, Greenland and Norway, while King Frederick temporarily withdrew all letters of marque and stopped privateering warfare in Norwegian waters. Nevertheless, the question whether the Danish themselves also issued licences for the trade with Great Britain remains unanswered.[19]

Regardless of the complicated question of licensing, the Danish intensified their struggle against smuggling and blockade-running over the years. In 1810, Buonaparte issued an edict that all ships, including vessels sailing under neutral flags, which transported a cargo of British origin should be confiscated and considered as good prizes – notwithstanding any documentary statement of origin. On 8 September 1810, King Frederick issued a similar order.[20] However, although Buonaparte and his allies were able to curtail the illicit trade in 1811 and to increase the economic pressure on Great Britain to a certain extent, they never succeeded in making the Continental System impenetrable. Despite all restrictions, smugglers and blockade-runners again and again found ways to elude the strict embargo controls.[21]

A quite impudent case of blockade-running occurred in 1811 in Tönning. The leader in this affair was one Hendrik van Nievervaart, a Dutch merchant from Dordrecht, apparently somewhat reduced in his circumstances due to the economic crisis caused by the Continental System. Nievervaart devised a scheme to run the blockade by the means of a fake privateer and the capture of an allegedly enemy merchant vessel.[22]

For his intended scheme, Nievervaart had used Georg Christian Hasse, a local merchant from Tönning, as legal frontman. In the name of Hasse, he had fitted out a privateer called *Vigilantia* under command of Captain Jan Jansen, born on the north Friesian island of Föhr, famous for its highly skilled seamen in the eighteenth and early nineteenth centuries. Nievervaart himself was listed as secretary in *Vigilantia*'s muster roll. Under the pretence of a privateering cruise, *Vigilantia* left Tönning, but instead of preying on the enemy merchant shipping, the vessel sailed directly to the English port of Hull, where Nievervaart had prearranged a rendezvous with a Dutch brig named *Fortuna*, Hemme Hendrick de Groot master.

After *Vigilantia*'s crew had assisted in rigging the brig, *Fortuna* with a cargo of coal, accompanied by *Vigilantia*, left Hull. Under way, both ships fell in with a British man-of-war, but after an examination they were allowed to proceed to the island of Heligoland, where *Fortuna* completed her load with a cargo of coffee, and from where both ships made sail back to Tönning. Here, Nievervaart claimed *Fortuna* to be a prize, taken off the coast of Norway. Thus by making a false declaration, he tried to get the brig and her cargo officially condemned as lawful prize. If he succeeded, he would have been allowed to sell the ship and its cargo legally.[23] In other words, using privateering as cover and by declaring his merchant goods as lawful prize, Nievervaart was trying to run the Continental System. The cleverly contrived *Vigilantia* scheme failed because of the vigilance of the ever-distrustful Danish authorities.[24] Both ships, *Vigilantia* and *Fortuna*, were seized by the local authorities and their crews examined. During the investigation, the authorities indeed found sufficient evidence that *Vigilantia* had visited Hull under pretence of cruising against British merchant shipping.[25] This affair was too important to be handled by the local authorities alone, and a special examination board, called a 'combined commission' (*combinirte Commission*) was established on the order of the Danish King.[26]

Under interrogation by the 'combined commission', Nievervaart proved as creative in his excuses as he had been in the design of his elaborated blockade-running scheme. At first, he tried to wriggle himself out by claiming that rather than smuggling, industrial espionage had been the true objective of his enterprise, and that he had tried to figure out the construction of British spinning machines to earn a reward of one million francs offered by Buonaparte for this technical information. But very soon the 'combined commission' found out Nievervaart's complete lack of technological knowledge. The commission established that this defence was only an excuse to escape punishment.[27] Even less credible in the eyes of the commission was Nievervaart's excuse of having been totally ignorant of the rules of the Danish instructions to privateers. Not only was Nievervaart listed as *Vigilantia*'s secretary and thus responsible for any misuse of the ship's letter of marque, but as a merchant he should also have had a certain knowledge of the regulations concerning the Continental System.[28] The commission noted that a Dutch translation of the Danish 'Instructions to privateers' had been found aboard *Vigilantia*, apparently written by Nievervaart himself. Thus, the commission declared, Nievervaart was not only acquainted with the Danish privateering regulations, but that he had violated them wilfully.[29]

After a careful examination of the case of *Vigilantia*, and interrogation of all individuals involved, the commission on 25 November 1811 pronounced its judgement on Nievervaart, Captain Jansen and two merchants from Tönning also involved. Captain Jansen was declared to have forfeited his right to command a ship under the Danish flag. Additionally, he was sentenced to serve four years of hard labour in the fortress of Rendsburg.[30] Nievervaart was sentenced to two years of penal servitude, thus losing his respectability – a hard sentence, because by losing his respectability Nievervaart also lost the confidence of his fellow citizens, essential for every businessman.[31] The two merchants accused, Albrecht Keller and Georg Christian Hasse, received prison sentences of only two and four weeks, respectively. Regarding the two ships *Vigilantia* and *Fortuna*, the commission declared both should be forfeited to the Royal Danish Treasury.[32]

In its judgement, the commission emphasised to the Danish authorities that Nievervaart's and Jansen's crimes were not minor offences, but serious felony.[33] Clearly, the harsh sentences against Nievervaart and Jansen were intended as a deterrent to warn all potential imitators to keep their hands from smuggling.[34] Doubtless the commission's fear was well founded, as many Danish merchants and seamen turned to risky enterprises such as privateering, smuggling or licensed trade.[35] Despite the intensification of the Continental System and the imposition of harsh sentences on smugglers and blockade-runners, France and her allies failed not only in making the embargo impenetrable, but also in destroying the British economy. Quite the contrary happened in 1811: while he strictly forbid his allies any economic contact with Great Britain, Buonaparte himself undermined his own embargo by granting licences to supply the French economy with the import of badly needed raw materials. Thus Buonaparte deprived himself of the chance to defeat Great Britain economically – exactly at the very moment that the British economy was slipping into a deep crisis. Only the breakdown of the Continental System after Buonaparte's assault on Russia in 1812 brought economic relief to Great Britain.[36] While Great Britain recovered commercially, the Danish economy collapsed and, in January 1813, this breakdown culminated in the national bankruptcy of the Danish state, deeply affecting the duchies of Schleswig and Holstein and resulting in a loss of confidence in the Danish government among the duchies' residents. This became one of the causes for the national conflicts between the Danish- and German-speaking populations in Schleswig-Holstein in the nineteenth century.[37]

One year later, military collapse followed economic breakdown. When in January 1814, Danish troops had to surrender to an allied army under command of the Swedish Crown Prince Bernadotte, formerly one of Buonaparte's leading generals, Denmark had to agree to the humiliating peace treaty of Kiel, under which Denmark lost one-third of its landmass when it had to hand over Norway to Sweden.[38]

There is still a lot of research needed to examine the role of Denmark in the maintenance and breaking of the Continental System in detail. All in all, a close look at the Anglo-Danish war reveals a rather confusing picture. From 1807 to 1814, Denmark was one of the most loyal allies to Buonaparte's France. Nevertheless, the attitude of the Danish authorities was quite contradictory. On the one hand, letters of marque were issued and the authorities severely punished merchants and seamen convicted of smuggling and blockade-running. At the same time, official licences were granted by the Danish authorities to support Norway and the Danish Islands in the Atlantic with supplies of grain and other essentials. Likewise, despite all political adversities, Danish merchants and seamen maintained their economic contacts with Great Britain. Thus it can be established that in Denmark a form of resistance against the Continental System existed.

Contributors' Biographies

Allan Adair served in the Royal Navy from 1969–2007 and as Commander British Forces, Gibraltar, he oversaw the commemorations of the bicentenary of the Battle of Trafalgar. His interest in family history was sparked in 1994 when he noticed on the board on his office in HMS *Excellent* that another Adair had held the same appointment in 1897.

Ben Armstrong 'BJ' is an Assistant Professor of War Studies and Naval History at the US Naval Academy, served in the USN as a search and rescue and special warfare support pilot and on the staff of the Secretary of the Navy. A graduate of Annapolis, he earned his PhD at King's College London. He is the series editor of the *21ˢᵗ Century Foundations* books from the Naval Institute Press.

John D Bolt, USMC reserves, is a PhD candidate at the University of Portsmouth, studying the nineteenth-century Royal Marines and how the organisational culture of the corps developed in the port cities of Portsmouth, Plymouth and Chatham.

Anthony Bruce took degrees at Lancaster University and the University of Manchester, and was a director at Universities UK 1992–2010. His published works include *The Purchase System in the British Army* (1980), *An Illustrated Companion to the First World War* (1989), *The Last Crusade* (2002), *A History of the War in the Middle East, 1914–18* and *Encyclopedia of Naval History* (1989).

David Clammer taught history and has a MA in curriculum studies. He is the author of *The Zulu War* (1973), *The Victorian Army in Photographs* (1975), and *The Last Zulu Warrior* (1977). He now lectures on polar history aboard expedition ships and contributed to *Exploring Polar Frontiers: An Historical Encyclopedia* (2003). Born in the shadow of Admiral Hardy's monument, he is an authority on Dorsetshire history during the Napoleonic period. His other current research is on the lives of the women who marched with Wellington's army in the Peninsula.

Sim Comfort joined the US Navy in 1960 and read the Hornblower stories while posted in Guam. Sim Comfort Associates, formed in the 1970s, has published seven maritime titles about objects and relics which have a strong bearing on the age of fighting sail, all of which may be viewed at www.simcomfort.co.uk.

Alex Craig is a graduate of Langside College, Glasgow, and former Royal Marines reservist, who moved to Canada in 1970. He has been the Assistant Curator of the Princess of Wales Own Regimental Museum in Kingston, Ontario, and is presently working for the Hastings and Prince Edward Regimental Museum in Belleville, Ontario. His book, *Rockets, Bombs and Bayonets*, won the RMHS literary award for 2013.

Larrie D Ferreiro is the author of *Brothers at Arms: American Independence and the Men of France and Spain Who Saved It*, a 2017 Pulitzer Prize in History finalist. He teaches history and engineering at George Mason University in Virginia, Georgetown University in Washington DC and the Stevens Institute of Technology in New Jersey. He has served for over thirty-five years in the US Navy, US Coast Guard and Department of Defence.

Tom Fremantle served for ten years in the Royal Navy before spending most of his working life in the engineering industry. The bicentenary of Trafalgar awakened a growing interest in his forebear and namesake, Thomas Fremantle. More recently he discovered another great-great-great-grandfather, Philip Gidley King, and the determination to tell his story more widely has inspired this present article.

Peter Hore is a former naval officer, now author, biographer, and freelance obituarist at the *Daily Telegraph* in London. He has written over a thousand obituaries, specialising in anyone with webbed feet, and also the First Aid Nursing Yeomanry (FANY) and female agents in the Second World War. His latest two biographies (2016) are *Lindell's List* about Mary Lindell, nursing heroine in the First World War and MI9 agent in the Second World War, and *Enigma: The Untold Story*, the life of David Balme who captured Enigma from *U-110* in May 1941. Peter has been editor of the *Trafalgar Chronicle* since 2015.

Major-General Julian Thompson served for thirty-four years in the Royal Marines. Since leaving he has spent his time advising a major London insurance broker, working with a company specialising in operating in remote or hazardous locations, and researching logistics and armed conflict at King's College London, where he is now a visiting professor in war studies. He has published seventeen books of military history and his latest is *The Royal Navy: a Hundred Years of Warfare in the Modern Age* (2016).

Dr Charles Neimeyer is the Director of Marine Corps History and the Gray Research Center at Marine Corps University, Quantico, Virginia. After twenty years in the US Marine Corps, including service at the White House, he retired as a lieutenant-colonel in 1996. He is the author of numerous historical monographs and national security affairs articles, most recently *War in the Chesapeake: The British Campaigns to Control the Bay, 1813–1814* (2015), which won the prestigious Simmons-Shaw award of the Marine Corps Heritage Foundation for the best scholarly history by a federal historian.

John Rawlinson is the Director of Visitor Experience at the National Museum of the Royal Navy. Previously he worked at the National Trust and has written extensively on the Seven Years War, and he leads battlefield studies of the Quebec campaign. He has published several articles on Royal Marines uniforms including *Personal Distinctions, Royal Marines Uniforms and Insignia from 1664 to the Present Day* (2014).

Robert K Sutcliffe is the author of *British Expeditionary Warfare and the Defeat of Napoleon 1793–1815* (2016), holds an MSc in Business Management and a PhD. His special interests are the Admiralty and the strength and disposition of the navy, the Royal Marines and Royal Marine Artillery. He is also a Fellow of the Institute of Chartered Accountants, specialising in business turnaround, chairman of a company operating in the healthcare software development sector and also of a museum trust.

Jann M Witt has studied history, political science and public law at the universities of Kiel and Ealing. He has worked as a journalist and lecturer, and since 2006 has been historian of the Deutscher Marinebund and curator of the Marine-Ehrenmal in Laboe. He lectures in naval history at the Marineschule, Mürwik, and has published numerous books and papers on maritime and naval history.

Britt Zerbe was a Research Fellow at University of Exeter, where he completed his doctorate in maritime history, and he is the author of the much-praised *The Birth of the Royal Marines, 1664–1802*.

Notes

The Marines: The Early Days

1 Britt Zerbe, *The Birth of the Royal Marines, 1664–1802* (The Boydell Press, 2013), p22.

2 Ibid, p25.

3 Seymour's 4th Foot, Saunderson's 30th Foot, Villiers's 31st Foot, and Fox's 32nd Foot. A succession of amalgamations, name changes, and cuts in the years between 1714 and the present day have seen these regiments becoming: 4th Foot – part of The Duke of Lancaster's Regiment; 30th Foot – part of The Duke of Lancaster's Regiment; 31st Foot – part of The Princess of Wales's Royal Regiment; 32nd Foot – part of The Rifles.

4 A Spanish coastguard cut off the ear of one Captain Jenkins, or so the captain claimed. Jenkins was brought before the House of Commons to exhibit his ear in a bottle. Winston Churchill wrote: 'whether it was in fact his own ear or whether he had lost it in a seaport brawl remains uncertain, but the power of this shrivelled object was immense'. Winston Churchill, *History of the English Speaking Peoples*, Purnell, vol 5, chapter 2, p2104.

5 Zerbe, p44.

6 Ibid, p45.

7 Despite the imposition of a tariff on the price of commissions imposed by George I, who disapproved of purchase, there was a wide variation in the price of commissions. See Alan J Guy, *Colonel Samuel Bagshawe and the Army of George II* (Army Records Society, 1990), pp13–14 and 38 for a résumé of the system.

8 See also orders for the Officers of Marines on Board HMS *Mars*, 31 May 1799, in Brian Lavery (ed), *Shipboard Life and Organisation, 1751–1815* (Navy Records Society), pp227–33.

9 See Andrew Lambert, *The Challenge: Britain Against America in the Naval War of 1812* (Faber & Faber, 2012).

10 Admiral Carden in early 1915, at the start of the Dardanelles campaign.

11 Richard Brooks, *The Royal Marines: 1664 to the Present* (London: Constable, 2002), p10.

The Marines in Boston, 1774–75

1 Britt Zerbe, *The Birth of the Royal Marines 1664–1802* (Woodbridge: Boydell Press, 2013), p229. See also Thomas Boas, *"For the glory of the Marines". The organisation, training, uniforms, and combat role of the British Marines during the American revolution* (Devon, Pennsylvania: Dockyard Press, 1993).

2 John Montagu, Earl of Sandwich, *The private papers of John, Earl of Sandwich: First Lord of the Admiralty, 1771–1782*, ed George R Barnes and John Owen (London: Navy Records Society, 1932), vol I, p55.

3 General Thomas Gage to Vice-Admiral Samuel Graves, 17 February 1774, in *Naval documents of the American Revolution (NDAR)*, (Washington, DC: Government Printing Office, 1964), vol I, p31.

4 Major John Pitcairn to Lord Sandwich, 14 February 1775, in John Montagu, Earl of Sandwich, vol I, p58.

5 Major John Pitcairn to Lord Sandwich, 4 March 1775, in John Montagu, Earl of Sandwich, vol I, p60.

6 Ibid, p61.

7 Allen French, 'The British expedition to Concord, Massachusetts, in 1775', *The Journal of the American Military Foundation*, I (1937), pp1–17; Major John Pitcairn's Report to General Gage, 26 April 1775: www.digitalhistory.uh.edu/active_learning/explorations/revolution/account3_lexington.cfm.

8 'A circumstantial Account of an attack that happened, on the 19th April, 1775, on his Majesty's Troops by a number of the people of the Province of the Massachusetts-Bay', in *NDAR*, vol I, p195. See also David H Fischer, *Paul Revere's ride* (New York: Oxford University Press, 1994).

9 Nathaniel Philbrick, *Bunker Hill. A city, a siege, a revolution* (London: Doubleday, 2013), p128.

10 John Barker, *The British in Boston being the diary of Lieutenant John Barker of the King's Own Regiment from November 15, 1774 to May 31, 1776*, ed Elizabeth E Dana (Cambridge, Massachusetts: Harvard University Press, 1924), p35.

11 Cyril Field, *Britain's sea-soldiers. A history of the Royal Marines and their predecessors* (Liverpool: The Lyceum Press, 1924), vol I, p151.

12 Ibid.

13 'Narrative of Vice Admiral Samuel Graves', 19 April 1775, in *NDAR*, vol I, p193.

14 Craig J Brown, Victor T Mastone and Christopher V Maio, 'The revolutionary war battle America forgot: Chelsea Creek, 27–28 May 1775', *The New England Quarterly*, 86:3 (2013), pp398–432.

15 Vice Admiral Samuel Graves to General Thomas Graves, 25 May 1775, in *NDAR*, vol I, pp523–4.

16 General J Burgoyne to Lord Stanley, 25 June 1775, in C Field, vol I, pp154–6.

17 Ibid, p155.

18 Richard M Ketchum, *The battle for Bunker Hill* (London: Cresset Press, 1963), p121. See also Richard Frothingham, *History of the siege of Boston and the battles of Lexington, Concord, and Bunker Hill* (Boston: Charles C Little and James Brown, 1896).

19 Samuel Gillespie, *An historical review of the Royal Marine Corps, from its original institution down to the present era, 1803* (Birmingham: M Swinney, 1803), p196.

20 Quoted in Field, vol I, p158.

21 Account of Adjutant Waller, Royal Marines, 22 June 1775, in Samuel Adams Drake, *Bunker Hill: The story told in letters from the battlefield* (Boston: Nichols and Hall, 1876), p29.

22 John Clarke, *An impartial and authentic narrative of the battle fought on the 17th of June, 1775 ...* (London, 1775), p17.

23 Major John Tupper to Lord Sandwich, 21 June 1775, in *NDAR*, vol I, p731.

24 Account of Adjutant Waller, p29.

25 Ibid, p28.

26 Ketchum, p134.

27 Quoted in Ketchum, p137.

28 Major John Tupper to Lord Sandwich, 21 June 1775, in *NDAR*, vol I, p731.

29 Drake, op cit, p10.

30 Major John Tupper to Lord Sandwich, 21 June 1775, in *NDAR*, vol I, p731.
31 Zerbe, p242.

Leathernecks: The US Marine Corps in the Age of the Barbary Pirates

 1 David Humphreys, US Minister to Lisbon, Portugal to Michael Morphy, US Consul, Malaga Spain, 6 October 1793 in *Naval Documents Related to the United States Wars with the Barbary Powers* [hereinafter referred to as BW], vol 1 (Washington DC: Government Printing Office, 1939), p46.

 2 Edward Church to Secretary of State, Thomas Jefferson, 22 September 1793, in BW, vol 1, pp44–5.

 3 To the Secretary of State from James Simpson, US Consul, Gibraltar, 25 November 1793 in BW, vol 1, p55.

 4 Samuel Calder to the House of Dominick Terry and Company, Cadiz, Spain, 3 November 1793 in BW, vol 1, p54.

 5 Allan R Millett, *Semper Fidelis: The History of the United States Marine Corps* (New York: The Free Press, 1991), p27.

 6 Secretary of the Navy Benjamin Stoddert to Captain Stephen Decatur, 11 July 1798, in *Naval Documents Related to the Quasi-War Between the United States and France & Naval Operations, February 1797 to October 1798* (Washington, DC: Government Printing Office, 1935), pp192–3.

 7 Ian W Toll, *Six Frigates: The Epic History of the Founding of the US Navy* (New York: WW Norton & Company, 2006), pp117–120.

 8 Michael A Palmer, *Stoddert's War: Naval Operations during the Quasi-War with France, 1798–1801* (Columbia, SC: University of South Carolina Press, 1987), pp185–7; Toll, p133.

 9 Richard B Parker, *Uncle Sam in Barbary: A Diplomatic History* (Gainesville, FL: University Press of Florida, 2004), p135.

10 Glenn Tucker, *Dawn like Thunder: The Barbary Wars and the Birth of the US Navy* (Indianapolis, IN: Bobbs-Merrill, Co, 1963), pp227–8.

11 Jonathan R Dull, *American Naval History, 1607 – 1865* (Lincoln, NE: University of Nebraska Press, 2012), p46; Toll, pp164–5, 167.

12 Toll, p197.

13 Joseph Wheelan, *Jefferson's War: America's First War on Terror, 1801–1805* (New York: Carroll & Graf Publishers, 2003), pp199, 203–6; Tucker, pp297–302.

14 Louis B Wright and Julia H MacLeod, *The First Americans in North Africa: William Eaton's Struggle for a Vigorous Policy Against the Barbary Pirates, 1799–1805* (Princeton, NJ: Princeton University Press, 1945), p151; Parker, p146.

15 William Eaton to Dr Francisco Mendrici, 13 December 1804 in BW, vol 5, pp185–6.

16 William Eaton to the Secretary of the Navy, 13 February 1805 in BW, vol 5, p351.

17 William Eaton to the Secretary of the Navy, 13 February 1805 and Samuel Barron to William Eaton, 22 March 1805 in BW, vol 5, pp349–50, 439.

18 Wright and MacLeod, pp158–9. This was the same route essentially used by Field-Marshal Bernard Montgomery against the Axis forces of Irwin Rommel in 1941.

19 Extract of a Letter to an Officer aboard the US Brig *Argus*, from Midshipman Paoli Peck, dated Malta, 4 July 1805, in BW, vol 5, pp361–3.

20 Extract from the Journal of William Eaton, US Navy Agent for the Barbary Regencies, 8 April 1805, in BW, vol 5, pp490–1.

21 William Eaton to Captain Samuel Barron, US Navy, Derne, 29 April 1805, in BW, vol 5, pp553–4; Wright and MacLeod, pp172–3.
22 William Eaton to Captain Samuel Barron, US Navy, Derne, 29 April 1805, in BW, vol 5, pp554–5. George Mann was a midshipman on *Argus* who was given permission by Isaac Hull to accompany Eaton in his attack on Derna.
23 Max Boot, *Savage Wars of Peace: Small Wars and the Rise of American Power* (New York: Basic Books, 2002), pp27–8.
24 Ibid, p28. Stephen Decatur, Jr met an unfortunate end and was killed in a duel in 1820 in Bladensburg, Maryland. Many believed Decatur had the potential to become an American version of Lord Horatio Nelson.

'Against the Common Enemies'

1 Brian Kilmeade and Don Yaeger, *Thomas Jefferson and the Tripoli Pirates: The Forgotten War that Changed American History* (New York: Sentinel, 2015).
2 A B C Whipple, *To the Shores of Tripoli: The Birth of the US Navy and Marines* (New York: William Morrow, 1991), p140. Benjamin Armstrong, 'The Most Daring Act of the Age: Principles for Naval Irregular Warfare', *Naval War College Review*, 63 (2010), pp106–18. The Nelson quote may be apocryphal, the historiography on the subject is mixed: Frederick Leiner, 'Searching for Nelson's Quote', *Naval History*, 26 (2012), pp48–53.
3 Smith to Preble, 22 May 1804, *Naval Documents Related to the United States Wars with the Barbary Powers*, ed by Dudley W Knox, 6 vols (Washington, DC: Government Printing Office, 1939-44), III (1941), p427 (henceforth *Barbary* III). Izard to Izard, 20 Feb 1804, *Barbary* III, pp416–17. Glenn Tucker, *Dawn Like Thunder: The Barbary Wars and the Birth of the US Navy* (New York: Bobbs-Merrill, 1963), p285.
4 Cathcart to Preble, 19 Feb 1804 and Preble to Cathcart, 19 Feb 1804, *Barbary* III, pp435–8.
5 Preble to Smith, 23 Oct 1803, *Barbary* III, pp160–2. Glenn Tucker, pp163–4, 252.
6 Preble Diary, 29 Nov 1803, and 7 Dec 1803, US Library of Congress, *Edward Preble Papers 1680–1912*, Box 28 (henceforth EPP).
7 *Dictionary of National Biography*, vol 1, ed Leslie Stephen (New York: McMillan, 1885), pp67–8. *The Dispatches and Letters of Vice Admiral Lord Viscount Nelson*, vol 5, January 1802–April 1804, ed Nicholas Harris Nicolas (London: Henry Colburn, 1845). Gibbs to Preble, 21 Feb 1804, *Barbary* III, p448. Cathcart to Acton, 5 Mar 1804, *Barbary* III, p476. Broadbent to Preble, 6 Mar 1804, *Barbary* III, p478.
8 Preble to Broadbent, 18 Mar 1804, *Barbary* III, p500. Acton to Cathcart, 27 Mar 1804, *Barbary* III, p538.
9 Preble Diary, 9 May 1804, EPP, Box 28. Cathcart to Acton, 22 Apr 1804, *Barbary* IV (1942), p50. Preble to Acton, 10 May 1804, *Barbary* IV, pp90–1.
10 Acton to Preble, 13 May 1804, *Barbary* IV, pp97–8. Preble Diary, 13 May 1804, EPP, Box 28. Acton to Preble, 14 May 1804, *Barbary* IV, pp99–100.
11 'Naval Operations Against Tripoli', Jefferson to Congress, 20 Feb 1805, *Barbary* IV, pp293–4. Glenn Tucker, pp292–3.
12 Whipple, pp154–7. Preble to Smith, in 'Naval Operations against Tripoli', *Barbary* IV, pp294–5. Preble Diary, 3 Aug 1804, EPP, Box 28.
13 Glenn Tucker, pp302–5. Preble to Smith, in 'Naval Operations against Tripoli', *Barbary* IV, pp296–7.
14 Beaussier to Preble, 6 Aug 1804, *Barbary* IV, pp369–70. Preble to Smith, 7 Aug 1804,

Barbary IV, pp298–9. Spence to Spence, 12 Nov 1804, *Barbary* IV, pp351–2. Spencer Tucker, pp70–1.

15 Journal of John Darby, 7 Aug 1804, *Barbary* IV, pp384–5. Preble Diary, 7 Aug 1804, EPP, Box 28. Whipple, p160.

16 Preble to Smith, 9 Aug 1804, *Barbary* IV, p301. Spencer Tucker claims that Preble rejected the Pasha outright (Spencer Tucker, p73), but his diary clearly describes the counter-offer: Preble Diary, 10 Aug 1804, EPP, Box 28.

17 Preble to Ball, 16 Jan 1804, *Barbary* III, p332. Preble to Villets, 16 Jan 1804, *Barbary* III, p333. Ball to Preble, 17 Jan 1804, *Barbary* III, p335.

18 Preble to Higgins, 11 Aug 1804, *Barbary* IV, p396. Cargo Manifest, US Ketch *Intrepid*, 11 Aug 1804, in *Barbary* IV, p398.

19 Preble to Schomberg, 2 Aug 1804, *Barbary* IV, pp332–3. Cargo Manifest, ship *Conception*, 12 Aug 1804, in *Barbary* IV, p402. Higgins to Preble, 12 Aug 1804, *Barbary* IV, p404.

20 Preble to Commanding Officers, 20 Aug 1804, Orders Book, EPP, Box 49.

21 Preble Diary, 20 & 22 Aug 1804, EPP, Box 28. Haraden Logbook, 23 Aug 1804, *Barbary* IV, p451.

22 Preble Diary, 12–14, 17 Aug 1804, EPP, Box 28. Preble to Smith, 24 & 28 Aug 1804, *Barbary* IV, pp302–3. Whipple, pp164–5.

23 US Ketch *Intrepid* Cargo Manifest, 11 Aug 1804, *Barbary* IV, p398. Preble to Israel, 22 Aug 1804, *Barbary* IV, p446. Haraden Log, 25 Aug 1804, *Barbary* IV, p461. Preble Diary, 9 July 1804, EPP, Box 28. Haraden Log, 29 Aug 1804, *Barbary* IV, p483.

24 'Description by Charles Ridgely', 4 Sep 1804, *Barbary* IV, pp507–9. Glenn Tucker, pp324–7. Preble to Smith, 4 Sep 1804 *Barbary* IV, p306.

25 Preble to Smith, 5 Sep 1804, *Barbary* IV, p307.

26 Hull Journal, 10 & 11 Sep 1804, *Barbary* V (1944), pp14, 16. Barron to Cathcart, 7 Sep 1804, in *Barbary* V, p2. Whipple, pp169–70.

27 Preble to Decatur, 24 Sep 1804, *Barbary* V, p49. Preble to Decatur, 23 Dec 1804, *Barbary* V, p210. Glenn Tucker, pp336–7.

28 Howard Nash, *The Forgotten Wars: The Role of the US Navy in the Quasi War with France the Barbary Wars 1798–1805* (New York: A S Barnes and Company, 1968), pp280–9. Preble to Smith, *Barbary* IV, pp293–308. Treaty of Peace and Amity between the United States and Tripoli, 4 Jun 1805, *Barbary* VI, pp81-82.

29 Alfred Thayer Mahan, *The Interest of America in Sea Power, Present and Future* (Boston: Little Brown, 1897), pp107–8.

Captain Ingram, the Sea Fencibles, the Signal Stations and the Defence of Dorset

1 Marshall, John, *Royal Naval Biography* (London: Longman, Hurst, Rees, Orme, and Brown, 1823), vol 2, pt 2, p7.

2 The National Archives, Kew (henceforth TNA), ADM 1/1989, Letters from Captains.

3 Dorset History Centre (henceforth DHC), D/DOY: A7/1.

4 Clammer, David, 'Pride Of Service: The Dorset Volunteer Rangers 1794–1802', *Journal of the Society for Army Historical Research*, 90 (2012), pp205–4.

5 Steel's *Original and Correct List of the Royal Navy.* Published monthly.

6 TNA ADM 2/135, Orders and Instructions.

7 TNA ADM 2/769, f520, Secretary's letters.

8 TNA ADM 1/1450, Letters from Captains.

9 TNA ADM 1/2066. A revised edition was published with the resumption of the war in 1803.

10 TNA ADM 1/1450.

11 No whole poster exists, but the clerk who had wrapped up bundles of Sea Fencible pay lists cut a poster into strips and used it as tape: it took the author some while to realise this and put the text together.

12 TNA ADM 28/63 & ADM 28/65, Sea Fencibles Pay Lists, Coast of Dorset.

13 TNA ADM 28/67, Sea Fencibles Pay Lists. Coast of Dorset; includes Bridport, Burton, Swyre, Puncknowle & Abbotsbury.

14 TNA ADM 49/110, ff5–6, Signal Stations.

15 TNA ADM 1/1513, B431–9, Letters from Captains.

16 TNA ADM 1/1990, I36, Letters from Captains.

17 TNA ADM 1/1991, Letters from Captains.

18 TNA ADM 49/110, f123, Signal Station Papers 1803–07.

19 TNA ADM 17/96, ff38–39, Signal Stations: Accounts.

20 TNA ADM 17/98, f35, Signal Stations: Accounts.

21 TNA ADM 1/1992, Letters from Captains.

22 Nicholas Harris Nicolas, *The Dispatches and Letters of Vice Admiral Lord Viscount Nelson* (London: H Colburn, 1844), vol 4, pp444–6.

23 TNA ADM 1/1992, f46.

24 TNA ADM 1/581(5) No 9, Report Letters from Admirals unemployed.

25 Hardy, W M, *Old Swanage or Purbeck Past and Present* (Dorchester: Dorset County Chronicle, 1910), p3.

26 TNA ADM 1/1992, I55.

27 TNA ADM 1/1802, f226, Letters from Captains.

28 TNA ADM 49/113, f115, Signal Stations: Abuses.

29 TNA ADM 1/3092, Letters from Lieutenants.

30 TNA ADM 1/1990, I36.

31 TNA ADM 49/110, f23.

32 TNA ADM 49/113, f113.

33 Ibid, f115.

34 A Aspinal (ed), *Correspondence of the Prince of Wales*, vol 3 (London, 1965), pp456–8.

35 TNA ADM 1/1992, I44.

36 C W Thompson, *Records of the Dorset Yeomanry* (Dorchester 1894), p72.

37 A M Broadley and M A Bartelot, *Nelson's Hardy, His Life, Letters and Friends* (London 1909), p118.

38 H G Mundy (ed), *Journal of Mary Frampton from the Year 1779 until the Year 1846* (London, 1885), p123.

39 TNA ADM 1/1992, I53.

40 Ibid, I54.

41 Ibid, I21.

42 DHC Copy in Lieutenancy Papers D52/6/65.

43 TNA ADM 1/1992, I50.

44 DHC Lieutenancy Papers D52/6/64.

That Matchless Victory: Trafalgar, the Royal Marines and Sea Battle in the Age of Nelson

1 One of the best, most recent collected volumes handling various elements of the battle is R Harding (ed), *A Great and Glorious Victory: New Perspectives on the Battle of Trafalgar* (Barnsley, 2008).

2 R Monaque, 'Trafalgar 1805: Strategy, Tactics and Results', *Mariner's Mirror*, 91 (2005),

pp241–50; J Zulueta, 'Trafalgar – The Spanish View', *Mariner's Mirror*, 66 (1980), pp293–318.

3   C White, 'The Nelson Touch: The Evolution of Nelson's Tactics at Trafalgar', *Journal of Maritime Research*, July (2005), pp1–16.

4   J Corbett, *The Campaign of Trafalgar* (London, 1910); A Schom, *Trafalgar: Countdown to Battle, 1803–1805* (London, 1990); R Gardiner (ed), *The Campaign of Trafalgar, 1803–1805* (London, 1997).

5   C Field, *Britain's Sea-Soldiers* (Liverpool, 1924) I & II; B Edwards, *Formative years 1803 to 1806* (Southsea, 2005); R Brooks, *The Royal Marines, 1664 to the Present* (London, 2002).

6   National Maritime Museum (hereafter NMM), NMM BGR/8 Lt William Clarke, Reflections of service Afloat and Ashore by a Marine Officer, 1803–1816, p24.

7   B Zerbe, *Birth of the Royal Marines, 1664–1802* (Woodbridge, 2013).

8   P Hore, 'Introduction: A very British Way in War', in P Hore (ed), *Seapower Ashore: 200 Years of Royal Navy Operations on Land* (London, 2001), pp9–25; J W Fortescue, *A History of the British Army* (East Sussex, 2004), IV-Part II, p797.

9   B Lavery, *Nelson's Navy: The Ships, Men and Organisation, 1793–1815* (London, 1989), p145.

10 The 1691 Instructions by Admiral Russell were in general used throughout the eighteenth century, in J S Corbett (ed), *Fighting Instructions, 1530–1816* (Naval Records Society, 1905), vol 29, p175.

11 Regulations and Instructions relating to Marines serving on board His Majesty's Ships in The National Archives of England and Wales (hereafter TNA) ADM 96/3, 1759, pp5–6; Regulations and Instructions relating to Marines serving on board His Majesty's Ships in TNA ADM 106/308, 1804, p5.

12 Advices in H Richmond (ed), *Papers Relating to the Loss of Minorca in 1756* (Naval Records Society, 1913), vol 42, p23.

13 Orders for the Officers of Marines on Board HMS *Mars* in B Lavery (ed), *Shipboard Life and Organisation, 1731–1815* (Naval Records Society, 1998), vol 138, p232.

14 Sir James Douglas to Elphinstone, 28 November 1775, in W G Perrin (ed), *The Keith Papers*, I (Naval Records Society, 1927), vol 62, p25.

15 John MacIntire's work was continued to be used up to the early twentieth century in the officers' library of the Royal Marine Barracks, Eastney.

16 J MacIntire, *A Military Treatise on the Discipline of the Marine Forces, When at Sea* (London, 1763), v–vi.

17 MacIntire, p109.

18 MacIntire, p118.

19 Richard Spry to ships at Plymouth, 31 May 1771 in D Bonner-Smith (ed), *The Barrington Papers*, I (Naval Records Society, 1937), vol 77, p431.

20 Quarter Bill, HMS *Goliath*, 1805 in Lavery, *Shipboard Life and Organization, 1731–1815*, pp278-85; Watch, Quarter and Station Bills, HMS *Indefatigable*, 1812, in Lavery, *Shipboard Life and Organization, 1731–1815*, pp303–8.

21 R Knight, *The Pursuit of Victory* (London, 2005), p517.

22 Court Martial of William Cuming, NRS, J D Byrn (ed), *Naval Courts Martial, 1793–1815* (Naval Records Society, 2009), vol 155, p594.

23 Charles Middleton, 13 October 1779 in J Laughton (ed), *Letters of Lord Barham*, I (Naval Records Society, 1907), vol 32, p300.

24 R Mackay and M Duffy, *Hawke, Nelson and British Naval Leadership, 1747–1805* (Woodbridge, 2009), p46; Court Martial of Captain Thomas Fox in R Mackay (ed), *The Hawke Papers, 1743–1771* (Naval Records Society, 1990), vol 129, p73.

25 T O'Loghlen, *The Marine Volunteer* (London, 1766), p114.

26 O'Loghlen, pp113–14.

27 O'Loghlen, p115.

28 MacIntire, p113; O'Loghlen, p113.

29 MacIntire, p111.

30 St Vincent's Standing Orders for the Mediterranean Fleet of 22 June 1798, in Lavery (ed), *Shipboard Life and Organization, 1731–1815*, p219.

31 Captain John Scaife to Admiralty in TNA ADM 1/2473, 24 September 1759.

32 Royal Marine Museum (hereafter RMM), RMM 11/13/93, John Howe Biography, vol 1, p23.

33 Proceedings on board His Majesty's Ship *Blanche* in TNA ADM 1/317, 05 January 1795.

34 Captain Caldwell to Admiral Jervis in TNA ADM 1/317, 11 January 1795.

35 W Robinson, *Jack Nastyface* (Annapolis, 1973), p48.

36 Letter to Lt Nicholas brother in NMM AGC/N/11, Letter of 2 Lt Paul Harris Nicholas, p2.

37 N A M Rodger, 'Honour and Duty at Sea, 1660–1815', *Historical Research*, 75 (2002), 445.

38 Major Rotely, Lewis (1785–1861), Royal Marines. The spellings 'Roteley' (eg on his gravestone) and 'Roatley' also occur.

39 Not dated but presumably after the battle, located in RMM, 11/12/42, Lt Rotely Letters, Journal 9-10.

40 Watch, Quarter and Station Bills in HMS *Indefatigable*, 1812 in Lavery (ed), *Shipboard Life and Organization, 1731–1815*, pp300–15.

41 Proceedings on board His Majesty's Ship *Blanche* in TNA ADM 1/317, 05 January 1795; O'Loghlen, *The Marine Volunteer*, p115.

42 T Mante, *The history of the late war in North-America, and the islands of the West-Indies, including the campaigns of MDCCLXIII and MDCCLXIV against His Majesty's Indian enemies* (London, 1772), p215.

43 A C T White, 'An Early Experiment in Bayonet Fighting', *Journal of the Society of Army Historical Research*, vol X (1930), p216.

44 P & D Ayshford, *Ayshford Complete Trafalgar Roll*, SEFF, 2004 [CD-ROM].

45 TNA ADM 1/3338, Memorial of Lt Luke Higgins Portsmouth Division.

46 Plymouth West Devon Record Office (hereafter PWDRO), PWDRO, 86/1 Letter to Family from Jacob Richards on HMS *Euryalus*, 29 November 1805.

47 Field, *Britain's Sea-Soldiers*, pp254–5.

48 James, *The Naval History of Great Britain*, IV, p39.

49 Tables 1–3 are sourced from P & D Ayshford, Ayshford Complete Trafalgar Roll, SEFF, 2004 [CD-ROM] and B Zerbe, 'A Social and Military History of the Royal Marines in the Age of Nelson', MA thesis, University of Exeter (2007); information has been verified in the ship's muster books at TNA.

50 Ayshford, *Ayshford Complete Trafalgar Roll*, CD-ROM.

51 R Mackenzie, *The Trafalgar Roll: The Ships and the Officers* (London, 1913), pp165–72.

52 T Jackson (ed), *Logs of the Great Sea Fights, 1794–1805* (Navy Records Society, 1900), II, p266.

53 W Clowes, *The Royal Navy* (London, 1900; reprint Chatham, 1997), V, p154.
54 'Admiral Nelson after action report, 03 August 1798', *The Naval Chronicle*, vol 1 (January to June 1799), pp174, 63–6; *Whitehall Evening Post (1770)* (London), Tuesday, October 2, 1798.
55 RMM 11/13/93 in John Howe Biography, vol 1, p23.

Loyal Au Mort: The Adairs at the Battle of Trafalgar
1 P H McKerlie, *History of the Lands and their Owners in Galloway* (1870), p85.
2 A Knight Banneret could only be conferred by the sovereign on the field of battle.
3 Christopher Hibbert, *Nelson, a Personal History*, London (1994), p31, and Tom Pocock, *Horatio Nelson*, London (1987), p51.
4 *The Trafalgar Roll*, Col R H Mackenzie (1913), p22 states incorrectly that Charles William Adair was the second son.
5 *The Globe and Laurel*, No 120, 7 Oct 1905, vol XII, p112.
6 *Navy Lists*, *Royal Marine Lists*, *Army Lists* and the RMM database.
7 Turner Bequest, Tate Gallery.
8 Even the National Maritime Museum's website offers for sale a reproduction of the picture with Adair wearing a blue jacket.
9 *Nelson's Trafalgar, the Battle that Changed the World*, Roy Adkins, New York (2004), p124, and *Trafalgar – the Men, the Battle, the Storm*, Tim Clayton and Phil Craig, Hodder & Stoughton (2004), p172.
10 Various spellings of his surname are seen, but Rotely is correct (it is how he addressed his father; RMM 1981/435/14).
11 RMM 1981/435/55. Lt Rotely's letter to the editor of *The Times*, undated.
12 RMM 1981/435/46. Lt Rotely's draft address to a meeting of Swansea citizens, *c*1845.
13 RMM 1981/435/56. Lt Rotely's letter to the editor of *The Cambrian*, undated. Does not appear to have been published.
14 Col Cyril Field RMLI, *Britain's Sea Soldiers*, Liverpool (1924), pp255–6.
15 Tim Clayton and Phil Craig, *Trafalgar – the Men, the Battle, the Storm*, Hodder & Stoughton (2004), p 203.
16 Although, of course, Nicholas was not close to the scene.
17 *Cassell's World of Adventure* (1889). It is also quoted in *Naval Anecdotes* (1806).
18 Iain Ballantyne and Jonathan Eastland, *HMS Victory*, Barnsley (2005), p145, citing the Rotely Papers RMM 11/12/42.
19 *Naval Chronicle*, XV, p109.
20 Lt Col Brian Edwards RM, *Formative Years 1803–1806*, RM Historical Society, Portsmouth (2005), p77.
21 Turner Bequest, Tate Gallery.
22 Roy Adkins, *Trafalgar, the Biography of a Battle*, UK (2004), p145.
23 Mary McGrigor, *Defiant and Dismasted at Trafalgar*, Leo Cooper (2004), based on the original biography of Sir William Harwood, James Allan (1841), p118.
24 RMM 1981/435/14. Letter from Lt Rotely to his father, Victory, St Helier, 4 Dec 1805.
25 *The Gentleman's Magazine*, Dec 1805, p1172.
26 *The Globe and Laurel*, No 6 of June 1946, vol LIV, p170.
27 FHL Film Number 916924 (www.ageofnelson.org/TrafalgarRoll incorrectly states the marriage date as 11 Nov 1800).
28 *Hampshire Chronicle*, 8 July 1797.
29 *The Hereford Journal*, 5 July 1797.

30 TNA ADM 106/3028/763 and The Trafalgar Archives, National Archives.

31 FHL Film Number 1469266 IT 1.

32 England & Wales, Prerogative Court of Canterbury Wills, 1384–1858 (accessed through www.ancestry.co.uk).

33 She may have been pregnant, but there is no evidence that Ann gave birth to a second child after Charles William's death.

34 TNA ADM 106/3028/763.

35 TNA ADM 51/1595.

36 TNA ADM 107/45 and ADM 107/8/196.

37 *DNB*, vol xvi, p427; *The Gentleman's Magazine* (1826), i, p46; Marshall, vol ii, p779; Ralfe, vol IV, p112. See also Peter Hore, *Nelson's Band of Brothers: Lives And Memorials* (Barnsley: Seaforth and the 1805 Club, 2015), pp163–4.

38 *The Gentleman's Magazine*, May 1826, pp464–5.

39 Col R H Mackenzie, *The Trafalgar Roll* (1913).

40 Adkin, *Trafalgar*, p525.

41 Unpublished letter from *Sirius*'s Master William Wilkinson (051030wwwd) and The Dublin Journal No. 10,745, 17 December 1805. The debate surrounding the fate of Nelson's slayer and who, if anyone, avenged him is a complex one with a number of claimants to which the marines of *Temeraire* can be added. For a synopsis of the debate see J Spence, *Nelson's Avenger and the Smugglers of Plymouth Sound* (2009), appendix 1, pp185–96.

42 TNA ADM 106/3030/894.

43 James, *Naval History*, vol IV, pp233–4.

44 *The Gentleman's Magazine*, May 1826, pp464–5.

45 *The Annual Register or General Repository of History, Politics, and Literature for the Year 1806*, London (1807), p71.

46 They had five sons and four daughters, but none produced any heirs, and the Loughanmore Estate was eventually passed to Amelia's great-nephew General Sir William Thompson Adair.

47 Private conversation between CGRM Lieutenant-General Sir Robin Ross KCB OBE and the author, 29 July 1994.

Marine Stephen Humphries 1786–1865

1 TNA ADM 158.

2 See also TNA ADM 27/11/5: he remitted part of his wages (9s 4d per month) on 1 December 1805 to his mother, Nancy Tolley (paid in Bridgnorth).

3 According to the ship's muster book, he joined *Achilles* on 23 April 1805.

4 *Achilles,* or *Achille* as she was known properly, was in Collingwood's lee division at the Battle of Trafalgar. Her first opponent was the Spanish *Montañés* (74) and she was then closely engaged for hour with the Spanish *Argonauta* (80) before the enemy ceased firing. Next the French *Achille* (74) engaged her in passing, leaving *Achilles* in single combat with the French *Berwick* (74). *Berwick* was completely subdued and *Achilles* took possession of her. *Achilles* lost thirteen killed and fifty-nine wounded.

5 He was awarded £1 17s 6d of prize money but does not appear to have claimed his Naval General Service medal and clasp.

6 On 25 September 1806, a squadron of French frigates escaped from Rochefort carrying troops for the West Indies, but were hunted down by a squadron under Commodore Sir Samuel Hood, who gave the signal for general chase. The French *Armide* struck to the

British *Centaur*, *Minerve* to *Monarch*, and *Infatigable* and *Gloire* to *Mars*. All four frigates were added to the Royal Navy.

7 Humphries was discharged from *Achille* on 29 February 1812.

8 He means 1816: see footnote 9.

9 In the attack on Algiers *Impregnable* lost a midshipman, thirty-seven seamen, ten marines and two boys killed and two midshipmen, 111 seamen, twenty-one marines, nine sappers and miners and seventeen boys wounded. The total for the fleet, excluding the Dutch squadron, was 128 killed and 690 wounded.

10 This is an error by Humphries: Buonaparte surrendered onboard *Bellerophon* on 15 July 1815 and was removed to *Northumberland* in Torbay on 6 August prior to his exile on St Helena on 6 August 1815, ie a year before the Bombardment of Algiers.

11 A son, William (1820–97) was born in the West Indies and returned home with Stephen. The following year Stephen married a Plymouth lass, Susannah (1801–86), and they eventually set up home in Acton Round, near Bridgnorth, Shropshire.

12 He died in June 1865 in Acton Round, where his grave at the church of St Mary the Virgin was restored by his family in 2005 and a plaque placed inside the church. The editor is grateful to his descendants for permission to print Stephen Humphries' memoir in the *Trafalgar Chronicle*: it was first published by Beverly Humphries in Coolangatta, Queensland, in 2005.

The Royal Marines Battalions in the War of 1812

1 Horatio Nelson and Nicolas Harris Nicolas, *The Dispatches and Letters of Vice Admiral Lord Viscount Nelson* (London: Henry Colburn, 1846), vol VI, pp iv, 22–34, 113–15.

2 Edward Frazer and L G Carr-Laughton, *The Royal Marine Artillery 1804–1923* (London: The Royal United Service Institution, 1930), vol 1, pp23–35. The Instructor of Mathematics and the Theory of Projectiles, a Mr Joseph Edwards, was provided with lodgings at Chatham and a salary of £3 a week.

3 Later Colonel-Commandant Sir Richard Williams (1764–1839), who served during the American War of Independence, the Great War 1792–1815, and as the senior RM officer in British North America and West Indies Station during the War of 1812. As well as being the first commanding officer of the Royal Marine Artillery, he commanded the Portsmouth Division of Royal Marines 1827–35.

4 Frazer and Carr-Laughton, vol 1, pp37–8. The 'Iron Coast' was the French name for the heavily defended coast between Cape Grisnez and Cape d'Alprech, north and south of Boulogne.

5 Ibid, p36.

6 ADM 196/58/49. Brevet-Major George Elliot Balchild (1790–1846) served in bomb vessels on the coast of France 1805/6, seriously wounded at the Dardanelles 1807, worked with Colonel Congreve on his rocket system in 1813, joined the Marine Battalions with Lt J H Stevens, present at Craney Island and Battle of Plattsburgh. Continued working as an experimental officer in Royal Navy, testing ship design, and died suddenly in HMS *Ocean* in 1846, and was buried in the English Cemetery, Cadiz.

7 ADM 196/66/10 and ADM 196/58/67. Major-General John Harvey Stevens RMA (?–1866). Served in the Caribbean 1806/7, Walcheren in 1809, flotilla service in the mortar brig *Gallant* 1809, Cadiz, Tarifa, Algeciras, Chippawa 1810–12, rocket service in the Chesapeake and Canada 1813–15, and Algiers 1816 in *Queen Charlotte*. See also Fraser & Carr-Laughton, vol 2, p955, and Paul Harvey Nicolas, *Historical Records of The Royal Marine Forces* (Cambridge: Cambridge University Press, 2012). First published 1845.

8 *Hampshire Telegraph*, 18 March 1813.

9 William Kingsford, *The History of Canada 1808–1815* (Toronto: Rowsell & Hutchison, 1895), p421.

10 William James and Captain Frederick Chamier, *The Naval History of Great Britain* (London: Richard Bentley, 1837), vol VI, p227.

11 ADM 9/3/824 Officers' services & ADM 1/2262/7 Captain's letters. Captain Daniel Pring (*c*1788–1846), who commanded the 16-gun brig *Linnet* during the Battle of Plattsburgh. He anchored *Linnet* across the head of the American line and did great damage, and fought until she was almost sinking. Promoted to captain in 1815, he briefly commanded the navy on Lake Erie before retiring to his home at Ivedon Penn, near Honiton.

12 Nicolas, p258.

13 Jon Latimer, *1812: War with America* (Cambridge, Mass.: Belknap Press of Harvard University Press, 2009), p278. Captain William Holtaway RM had a premonition of death. He told Lieutenant J C Morgan RM to 'look after his accounts'. See also J C Morgan, *The Emigrant's Note Book and Guide* (London: Longman, Hurst, Rees, Orme, and Brown, 1824), p333. Further details of Holtaway are not known. See also Frazer and Carr-Laughton, p249. Commodore Sir James Lucas Yeo after battle report to the Admiralty.

14 Brian J Orr, *Bones of Empire* (Kingston, Ontario: LULU Publishers, 2013), p324, and Kingston Gazette, 25 May 1814. Lieutenant James Lawrie RM, 2nd Battalion, Royal Marines in North America, was Yeo's secretary, and first into Fort Ontario on 6 May 1814.

15 Nicolas, pp 256–61, and Colonel Cyril Field, *Britain's Sea Soldiers* (Liverpool: The Lyceum Press, 1924), p296.

16 *Naval Chronicle*, vol 16, p175, vol 21 p176, vol 33 pp39, 88. Captain Alexander Anderson RM (?–1814). Killed in action at the Battle of Cumberland Bay on 11 September 1814 and is buried along with Captain George Downie RN and other officers from both sides in Riverside Cemetery, Plattsburgh, NY.

17 Scott S Sheads and Graham Turner, *The Chesapeake Campaigns 1813–15* (London: Osprey Publishing, 2014), p29.

18 Major-General Robert Ross (1766–1814) fought in Egypt, Syria, Italy, Holland, and the Peninsular War, commander of the British army at Bladensburg and the capture of Washington, killed during the Battle of North Point and buried at Halifax, NS.

19 Lieutenant-General George Lewis (1774–1854) fought at the Battle of Cape Ortegal 1805, the Peninsular War, Holland, commanded the 3rd Battalion RM and fought at Bladensburg, Washington and Baltimore.

20 Field, p302. Second-Lieutenant William Hammond: no record of service as a private soldier or NCO, but named as the First Sergeant of Royal Marines in HMS *Albion* in 1813. Promoted to ensign and adjutant in charge of colonial marines by Admiral Cockburn in July of 1814.

The First Royal Marine Battalion's Peninsular War 1810–1812

1 TNA, ADM, 2/1193.

2 The Marines became Royal Marines in 1802. The Royal Marine Artillery was established by an Order in Council 18 August 1804 to take over the manning of bomb and mortar vessels from the Royal Artillery, following a court ruling that army officers were not subject to naval orders following a naval court martial of a Royal Artillery officer.

3 Robert K Sutcliffe, *British Expeditionary Warfare and the Defeat of Napoleon, 1793–1815* (Woodbridge, 2016), pp195–203. The evacuation of Corunna is described in detail.

4 Arthur Wellesley, 1st Duke of Wellington, will be referred to as Wellington throughout this paper, although the title was not bestowed on him until 11 May 1814. He was elevated to viscount following the Battle of Talavera in 1809.

5 David Gates, *The Spanish Ulcer* (Cambridge, Mass, 1986), p150.

6 Christopher D Hall, *Wellington's Navy, Sea Power and the Peninsular War* (London, 2004), p145.

7 Ian Fletcher, *The Lines of Torres Vedras 1809–11* (Oxford, 2003).

8 The Admiralty were very concerned that the French Toulon fleet would seize the moment to cause mischief at Lisbon or Cadiz.

9 NMM, YOR/2, Berkeley to Charles Yorke, First Lord of the Admiralty, undated memorandum.

10 NMM, AGC, B/3, letters to Vice-Admiral Berkeley from Major-General John Randall McKenzie, Abrantes, 15 May 1809 and Berkeley's response.

11 Sutcliffe, *British Expeditionary Warfare*, p220. Comprehensive details of the evacuation plans.

12 Hall, *Wellington's Navy*, pp94–5, 100; John Gurwood, *Dispatches of Field-Marshal the Duke of Wellington*, vol 7 (reprinted, Cambridge, 2010), pp39 and 64, Wellington to Berkeley, 9 and 24 Dec 1810. Berkeley requested Wellington to secure extra payment for naval officers and seamen serving ashore. It was finally agreed that lieutenants would receive 10s per day, midshipmen 6s and seamen 1s 6d.

13 Gurwood, *Wellington's Dispatches*, vol 4, p235, Wellington to Berkeley, 15 Jun 1810.

14 Sutcliffe, *British Expeditionary Warfare*, pp134–5.

15 Marshal Andre Massena, Duke of Rivoli, Prince of Essling (1758–1817). His army arrived before the lines of Torres Vedras on 11 October 1810; they remained there for just a month.

16 NMM YOR/2, Berkeley to Charles Yorke, First Lord of the Admiralty, 9 Dec 1810.

17 TNA ADM 1/342, Berkeley to the Admiralty, 22 Nov 1810.

18 Gurwood, *Wellington's Dispatches*, vol 6, 272, Wellington to Berkeley 3 Nov 1810.

19 TNA ADM 1/342, Wellington to Berkeley, 10 Nov 1810.

20 NMM YOR/2, Yorke to Berkeley, 25 Nov 1810. It is not known what that particular service was.

21 Edward Fraser and L G Carr-Laughton, *The Royal Marine Artillery 1804–1923* (London, 1930), p158. Lieutenant Lawrence succeeded as commanding officer in July 1811 when Captain Burton returned to England for health reasons.

22 NMM YOR/2 Berkeley to Yorke, 9 Dec 1810.

23 Colonel C Field, *Britain's Sea Soldiers* (Liverpool, 1924), p290.

24 Gurwood, *Wellington Dispatches*, vol 7, p70, Wellington to Berkeley, 25 Dec 1810.

25 Sutcliffe, *British Expeditionary Warfare*, p217. Wellington's army represented a significant proportion of the whole British Army; the Secretary of State for War, Lord Liverpool recognised that if it was trapped in Portugal then it would be a major political and military disaster. He authorised the retention of a large number of transports at Lisbon for this purpose and instructed Wellington and Berkeley to ensure that any evacuation could be executed at short notice.

26 Fraser and Carr-Laughton, *The Royal Marine Artillery*, pp160–1.

27 Lieutenant-Colonel Brian Edwards, *Formative Years 1803–1806, A perspective of the Royal Marines in the Navy of John Jervis, Earl St Vincent and Horatio Lord Nelson* (Southsea, 2005), p144. Lieutenant Robert Fernyhough, *Lavinia* (48) on the Tagus to the Lieutenant-Colonel of the 1st Battalion of the Rifle Brigade, 1810.

28 NMM YOR/2, Berkeley to the Admiralty, 2 Apr 1811.

29 NMM KEI 37/1, Popham, off Castro, to Lord Keith, 13 Jul 1812.

30 TNA ADM 1/343, Berkeley to the Admiralty, 8 Mar 1811.

31 TNA ADM 1/343, Berkeley to the Admiralty, 11 Apr 1811.

32 TNA ADM 1/343, Lieutenant Geddes to Berkeley, 4 Aug 1811.

33 Marmont, Marshal August Frederic Louis Viesse de, Duke of Ragusa (1774–1852). He replaced Massena as commander of the Army of Portugal in May 1811; he was defeated at Salamanca in July 1812. Soult, Marshal Nicolas Jean de Dieu, Duke of Dalmatia (1769–1851). Caffarelli Du Falga, General Marie Francois Auguste, Count (1766–1849), commander of the Army of the North in Spain, May 1812 to January 1813.

34 Christopher D Hall, *Wellington's Navy Seapower and the Peninsular War* (London, 2004), p200. Popham had a contentious naval career: he is described as greedy and ambitious, yet energetic, imaginative and determined. See also Hugh Popham, *A Damned Cunning Fellow, The Eventful Life of Rear-Admiral Sir Home Popham 1762–1820* (Tywardreath, Cornwall, 1991).

35 NMM KEI 37/1. Captain Sir Home Popham, *Venerable*, near the Bar of Bilbao, to Lord Keith, 25 Jun 1812.

36 This is not intended to be a judgement on the guerrilla activity: for further insight see Charles J Esdaile, *Fighting Napoleon, Guerrillas, Bandits and Adventurers in Spain 1808–1814* (Bury St Edmunds, 2004) and John Lawrence Tone, *The Fatal Knot, The Guerrilla War in Navarre and the Defeat of Napoleon in Spain* (North Carolina, 1994).

37 NMM KEI 37/ 1, Diary of the proceedings of the squadron on the North Coast of Spain from 29 June to 14 July 1812.

38 This was achieved by knocking off the trunnions, the pivots which supported the gun on the carriage, much more effective than spiking the guns, which was choking up the firing vent with a large nail or spike, exacerbated by filling the bottom with a cylinder of hardwood with a shot ball muffled in felt above it.

39 NMM KEI 37/1, Diary of proceedings 29 June to 14 July 1812.

40 NMM KEI 37/1, A diary of proceedings of the squadron appointed to the north coast of Spain between 15 and 27 July 1812.

41 Hall, *Wellington's Navy*, p203.

42 Porlier, Juan Diaz, Marques de also known as El Marquesito.

43 Gurwood, *Wellington Dispatches*, vol 6, 101, Wellington to Home Popham, 2 Oct 1812.

44 Paul Harris Nicolas, *Historical Record of The Royal Marine Forces*, vol 2 (reprinted New York, 2012), p240.

The 'Blue Colonels' of Marines: Sinecure and Shaping the Royal Marine Identity

1 Alexander Gillespie, *An historical review of the Royal Marine Corps: from its original institution down to the present era, 1803* (Birmingham: Mr Swinney, Printer, 1803), p144.

2 'Proposal of an Establishment of Marines', 29 March 1755, TNA ADM 2/1152, pp1–5.

3 Julian Thompson, *The Royal Marines: From Sea Soldiers to a Special Force* (London: Pan Books, 2001), p16.

4 Britt Zerbe, *The Birth of The Royal Marines, 1664–1755* (Woodbridge: Boydell Press, 2013), p56.

5 Thompson, p16.

6 TNA ADM 2/1156, pp251–3.

7 Cyril Field, *Britain's Sea-Soldiers*, vol I (Liverpool: The Lyceum Press, 1924), pp132–3.

8 *The Times* (London, England), Monday, Jun 08, 1795, Issue 950608, p2.

9 Zerbe, p63.

10 Field, pp132–3.

11 Gillespie, p1.

12 The Rotely Papers, RM 1981/435/8.

13 Rotely, RM 1981/435/10, RM 1981/19, RM 1981/435/28.

14 'Obituary of Eminent Persons', *Illustrated London News* (London), 18 May 1861, p477.

15 Major Alistair Donald, 'The "Blue Colonels" of Marines', *The Sheet Anchor*, Royal Marines Historical Society, vol XXIX, no. 2 (Winter 2004), p52.

16 *Gazetteer and London Daily Advertiser* (London), Tuesday, 14 June 1763.

17 House of Commons debate (HC), 12 February 12, 1812, vol 21, cc753–61, c761–2.

18 HC, 12 February 1812, c757.

19 HC, 12 February 1812, c757.

20 HC, 12 February 1812, c761.

21 *Hampshire Telegraph and Sussex Chronicle* (Portsmouth), 1 November 1830, Issue 1621, p6.

22 *Hampshire Telegraph and Sussex Chronicle*, 1 November 1 1830, Issue 1621, p6.

23 HC, 14 February 1833, vol 15, cc660–713, p660.

24 HC, 14 February 1833, c687.

25 HC, 14 February 1833, c712.

26 HC, 14 February 1833, c712.

27 HC, 14 February 1833, c713–16.

28 Donald, p53.

29 Sir George Grey Aston KCB, *Memories of a Marine: An Amphibiography* (London: John Murray, 1919), p224.

30 Aston, p232.

31 Aston, p290.

32 Thompson, pp2–3.

Captain Philip Gidley King, Royal Navy, Third Governor of New South Wales

1 The Journal of Philip Gidley King, Lieutenant RN, 1787–1790, University of Sydney Library, Digital version 2003 Kinjour; Appendix I Letter Gideon Johnston to Mrs King 7 May 1775, vol 8, p1.

2 Ibid, Appendix II.

3 Eg Steel's Navy List of December 1782 and Rif Winfield, *British Warships in The Age of Sail, 1714–1792* (Barnsley, Yorkshire: Seaforth Publishing, 2007).

4 Jonathan King and John King, *Philip Gidley King; a biography of the third governor of New South Wales* (Australia: Methuen, 1981), p10.

5 Ibid, p10.

6 King's journal, 1787–1790, p4.

7 The Journal of Lt William Bradley of HMS *Sirius* 1786–92, copyright Trustees of the Public Library of New South Wales; facsimile edition, Ure Smith 1969, National Library of Australia Registry number Aus 68-1986.

8 Bradley, p11. William Dawes (1762–1836) astronomer, engineer, botanist, surveyor, explorer, abolitionist and colonial administrator. He joined the Marines in 1779 and was wounded at the Battle of the Chesapeake in 1781. In 1788, Dawes built an observatory on what is now Dawes Point, Sydney, constructed batteries at the entrance to Sydney Cove, laid out the government farm and first streets and allotments in Sydney and Parramatta.

9 Ibid, p6.
10 Ibid, p8.
11 Ibid, p12.
12 Ibid, p13.
13 Ibid, p15.
14 Ibid, p17.
15 King's journal, p19.
16 Ibid, p21.
17 King, in his journal, uses the term 'Native' or 'native', and occasionally 'Indian', to refer to the Aborigines. The attitude of both King and Phillip to them is one of compassion, and a desire to understand them, which might today be construed as condescension. King and his fellows were confronted by people who looked and behaved very differently from what they regarded as normal; it is not surprising that they were initially nervous.
18 Ibid, p27.
19 Ibid, p29.
20 Ibid, p29.
21 King's account states of La Pérouse, 'he has found all ye Astronomical & Nautical works of Capt. Cook to be very exact & true & concluded by saying ... "Enfin, Monsieur Cook a tout fait qu'il n'a me rien laisse a faire, que d'admirer ses oeuvres"', King's journal, p33.
22 Ibid, p38.
23 King biography, p48.
24 King's second spell on Norfolk Island is described in his second Journal 1791–1796 held in manuscript form by the National Library of Australia, call number MS 70 NLA Object 26005434.
25 *Historical Record of New South Wales*, vol 4, p xxv. Ed F M Bladen, Sydney, government printer 1892–1901. This and the subsequent volume 5 cover King's governorship, reproducing all available correspondence. He wrote to Sir Joseph Banks, for example, 'There are two things which set me much at variance with those about me – first my determination that the public shall not be cheated; and next, that the King's authority shall not be insulted.'
26 In less than two years, Bligh's authoritarian regime had led to a total breakdown of government and to the arrest of Bligh by a group of officers supported by John Macarthur, now a civilian. It was the arrival of General Macquarie as governor which began to restore the order and productivity of King's governorship.
27 King biography, p157.

Captain James Cottell: The Pictorial Life of a Trafalgar Veteran
1 The quotations attributed to James Cottell throughout this article are from his diary and account book in the NMRN archives, references RMM 2012/115/91 and RMM 2012/115/92. Other Cottell artefacts are RMM 2012/115/94, a bosun's call taken from a French man-of-war at the Battle of Trafalgar, and RMM 2012/115/95, flax taken from HMS *Sirius* before she was set alight by her crew and eventually blew up off the coast of the Isle de France in August 1810.
2 RMM 2012/115/89. Letter, dated 31 October 1798 and addressed to Mr James Cottell (uncle of Captain James Cottell RM), Taunton, Somersetshire. It was written by Captain R Williams RM aboard HMS *Robust*, Lough Swilly, Ireland. The letter relates to the death in service with the Royal Marines of James Cottell's older brother William. William Cottell

died from wounds received aboard the third rate ship of the line HMS *Robust*, while in action off the Irish Coast. *Robust* was involved in the capture of the French third rate ship of the line *Hoche* off the Irish Coast.

3 Johnson, Paul, *The Birth Of The Modern: World Society, 1815–30* (London: Weidenfeld & Nicolson, 1991).

4 Nicolas, Paul, Lieutenant RM, 'The Battle of Trafalgar', in *The Casket* (Philadelphia: Atkinson, 1828), p116.

5 Fraser, Edward, *The Enemy at Trafalgar* (London: Chatham Pub, 2004).

6 A full account of *Tonnant* at Trafalgar is inappropriate for this is article: this summary is drawn from Laird Clowes's *The Royal Navy* and Nicolas's *Dispatches and Letters of Lord Nelson*.

7 RMM 2012/115/88. Written after Captain James Cottell's death based on his own letters written to the Admiralty during the 1830s seeking re-employment, c1840s. The letter is entitled: Services of the late Captn James Cottell, Reserves Half pay list Royal Marines.

8 RMM 2012/115/92. Transcription of a diary kept by Captain James Cottell RM throughout his adult life from the 1790s until his death in 1842. The original diary is believed lost, possibly during the Blitz on the city of Bristol during the Second Word War. This transcription was undertaken by his grandson Reverend Charles Rowland Cottell (1865–1943).

9 RMM 2012/115/91. Diary, belonged to Captain James Cottell RM dated 1820, St Servan, Brittany, France. The small book is used as a diary and as a ledger.

The Rise and Fall of the Bourbon Armada, 1744–1805: From Toulon to Trafalgar

1 Jeremy Black, *The Collapse of the Anglo-French Alliance, 1727–1731* (New York: St Martin's Press, 1997).

2 José María Blanco Núñez, *La Armada Española en la Primera Mitad del Siglo XVIII* (Madrid: IZAR Construcciones Navales, 2001), pp108–14; Larrie D Ferreiro, *Measure of the Earth: The Enlightenment Expedition that Reshaped Our World* (New York: Basic Books, 2011).

3 Allan J Kuethe and Kenneth J Andrien, *The Spanish Atlantic World in the Eighteenth Century: War and the Bourbon Reforms, 1713–1796* (Cambridge: Cambridge University Press, 2014), pp157–8.

4 Blanco Núñez, *La Armada Española en la Primera Mitad del Siglo XVIII*, pp190–203.

5 Jan Glete, *Navies and Nations: warships, navies and state building in Europe and America 1500–1860*, 2 vols (Stockholm: Academitryck AB Edsbruk, 1993), vol 1, p272.

6 Jonathan Dull, *The French Navy and the Seven Years' War* (Lincoln, NE: University of Lincoln Press, 2005), pp200–4.

7 Dull, *The French Navy and the Seven Years' War*, pp224–6; Cesáreo Fernández Duro, *Armada española desde la unión de los Reinos de Castilla y Aragón,* 9 vols (Madrid: Imprenta Real, 1894–1903), vol 7, pp53–8.

8 Ramon E Abarca, 'Bourbon "Revanche" Against England: The Balance of Power, 1763–1770', PhD thesis (Notre Dame: University of Notre Dame, 1965).

9 Larrie D Ferreiro, *Ships and Science: The Birth of Naval Architecture in the Scientific Revolution, 1600–1800* (Cambridge: MIT Press, 2007), pp286–7.

10 Larrie D Ferreiro, 'Spies versus Prize: Technology Transfer Between Navies in the Age of Trafalgar', *Mariner's Mirror*, 93:1 (2007), pp16-27; José María Sánchez Carrión, *De Constructores a Ingenieros de Marina: Salto tecnológico y professional impulsado por Francisco Gautier* (Madrid: Fondo Editorial de Ingeniería Naval, 2013), p236.

11 Ivan Valdez-Bubnov, *Poder naval y modernización del Estado: política de construcción naval española, siglos XVI–XVIII* (Madrid: Iberoamericana, 2011), pp312–19.

12 Sudipta Das, *De Broglie's Armada: a plan for the invasion of England, 1765–1777* (Lanham, MD: University Press of America, 2009) pp18–20; Ramon E Abarca, 'Classical Diplomacy and Bourbon "Revanche" Strategy, 1763–1770', *The Review of Politics*, 32:3 (June 1970), pp313–37; Hamish M Scott, 'The Importance of Bourbon Naval Reconstruction to the Strategy of Choiseul after the Seven Years War', *The International History Review*, 1:1 (Jan 1979), pp17–35.

13 Larrie D Ferreiro, *Brothers at Arms: American Independence and the Men of France and Spain Who Saved It* (New York: Knopf, 2016), p31.

14 Henri Doniol, *Histoire de la participation de la France à l'établissement des États-Unis d'Amérique*, 6 vols (Paris: Imprimerie National, 1886-1899), vol 1, p288.

15 Theodore J Crackel et al (eds), *The Papers of George Washington Digital Edition*, Revolutionary War Series, 22+ vols (Charlottesville: University of Virginia Press, Rotunda, 2007; http://founders.archives.gov), vol 18, pp149–52.

16 José María Blanco Núñez, *La Armada Española en la Segunda Mitad del Siglo XVIII* (Madrid: IZAR Construcciones Navales, 2004), pp117–20.

17 Juan Hernández Franco, *Aspectos de la política exterior de España en la época de Floridablanca* (Murcia: Real Academia Alfonso X El Sabio, 1992), pp178–9.

18 Paul del Perugia, *La tentative d'invasion de l'Angleterre de 1779* (Paris: Alcan, Presses universitaires de France, 1939), pp71–3; Alfred Temple Patterson, *The Other Armada: The Franco-Spanish Attempt to Invade Britain in 1779* (Manchester: Manchester University Press, 1960), pp46–53; Jonathan R Dull, *The French Navy and American independence: a study of arms and diplomacy, 1774–1787* (Princeton: Princeton University Press, 1975), pp142–50.

19 Sánchez Carrión, *De Constructores a Ingenieros de Marina*, p118.

20 Patrick Villiers, 'Sartine et la préparation de la flotte de guerre française 1775–1778: refontes ou constructions neuves?', in Olivier Chaline, Philippe Bonnichon and Charles-Philippe de Vergennes (eds), *Les Marines de la Guerre d'Indépendance Américaine, 1763–1783: I. L'instrument naval* (Paris: PUPS, Presses de l'Université Paris-Sorbonne, 2013), pp65–75.

21 I have drawn from the following sources to describe the failed Armada attempt: Patterson, *The Other Armada*, pp160–229; Dull, *The French Navy and American independence*, pp143–58; Perugia, *La tentative d'invasion de l'Angleterre de 1779*, pp75–176; Blanco Núñez, *La Armada Española en la Segunda Mitad del Siglo XVIII*, pp125–7; Patrick Villiers, 'La tentative franco-espagnole de débarquement en Angleterre de 1779', in *Revue du Nord, Le Transmanche et les Liaisons Maritimes XVIIIe–XXe Siècle* (Hors-série no. 9, 1995), pp13–29; Georges Lacour-Gayet, 'La Campagne Navale de La Manche en 1779', *Revue Maritime*, 150 (July 1901), pp1629–73; Cesáreo Fernández Duro, *Armada española desde la unión de los Reinos de Castilla y Aragón*, 9 vols (Madrid: Imprenta Real, 1894–1903), vol 7, pp233–47; Juan Alsina Torrente, *Una guerra romántica 1778–1783. España, Francia e Inglaterra en la mar: Trasfondo naval de la independencia de Estados Unidos* (Madrid: Ministerio de Defensa, Instituto de Historia y Cultura Naval, 2006), pp142–9.

22 Louis Édouard Chevalier, *Histoire de la marine française pendant la guerre de l'indépendance américaine* (Paris: Hachette, 1877), p161.

23 Villiers, 'La tentative franco-espagnole de débarquement en Angleterre de 1779', p28.

24 Blanco Núñez, *La Armada Española en la Segunda Mitad del Siglo XVIII*, pp134–6; David Syrett, *The Royal Navy in European Waters During the American Revolutionary War*

(Colombia, SC: University of South Carolina, 1998), pp136–7.

25 The Siege of Pensacola is described in Carmen de Reparaz, *Yo Solo: Bernardo de Gálvez y la toma de Panzacola en 1781* (Madrid and Barcelona: Serbal/ICI, 1986) and Wesley S Odom, *The longest siege of the American Revolution: Pensacola* (Pensacola: W S Odom, 2009).

26 Eric Beerman, *España y la Independencia de Estados Unidos* (Madrid: Editorial MAPFRE, 1992), pp249–60; Piers Mackesy, *The War for America, 1775–1783* (Cambridge: Harvard University Press, 1964), pp436–8.

27 Tom Henderson McGuffie, *The Siege of Gibraltar, 1779–1783* (London: B T Batsford, 1965), pp83–167; Rene Chartrand and Patrice Courcelle, *Gibraltar 1779–83: The Great Siege* (London: Osprey, 2008), pp57–87; Blanco Núñez, *La Armada Española en la Segunda Mitad del Siglo XVIII*, pp154–60.

28 McGuffie, *The Siege of Gibraltar, 1779–1783*, pp168–75; Blanco Núñez, *La Armada Española en la Segunda Mitad del Siglo XVIII*, pp160–3.

29 Karl Gustaf Tornquist, *The Naval Campaigns of Count de Grasse during the American Revolution, 1781–1783* (Philadelphia: Swedish Colonial Society, 1942), p123.

30 Francis P Renaut, *Le Pacte de Famille et l'amérique: La politique coloniale franco-espagnole de 1760 à 1792* (Paris: Leroux, 1922), pp436–44.

31 Michel Vergé-Franceschi, 'Marine et Révolution, les officiers de 1789 et leur devenir', *Histoire, économie et société*, 9/2 (1990) pp259–86.

32 Das, *De Broglie's Armada*, xi.

33 Agustín Ramón Rodríguez González, *Trafalgar y el conflicto naval Anglo-Español del siglo XVIII* (Madrid: Actas Editorial, 2005); Peter Hore, *Nelson's Band of Brothers: Lives and Memorials* (Barnsley: Seaforth Publishing, 2015). My thanks to the authors Agustín Rodríguez and Peter Hore, as well as Pierre Lévêque, for the help in locating the ships and men who fought both at Cape Spartel and Cape Trafalgar.

34 For the Battle of Trafalgar, see Rodríguez González, *Trafalgar y el conflicto naval Anglo-Español del siglo XVIII*; John D Harbron, *Trafalgar and the Spanish Navy: The Spanish Experience of Sea Power* (London: Conway, 1988); Peter G Goodwin, *The Ships of Trafalgar: The British, French and Spanish Fleets, October 1805* (Naval Institute Press, 2005); Michèle Battesti, *Trafalgar: Les aléas de la stratégie navale de Napoléon* (Saint-Cloud: Éditions Napoléon Ier, 2004).

Smuggling and Blockade-Running during the Anglo-Danish War of 1807–14

1 Paul Kennedy, *Aufstieg und Fall der großen Mächte – ökonomischer Wandel und militärischer Konflikt von 1500–2000* (Frankfurt/M 1991), pp208–12; Jann M Witt, 'Vor Kapern hatte ich viel mehr Furcht wie vor Seegefahren – Eine kurze Einführung in die Geschichte der Kaperei', in Hartmut Roder (ed), *Piraten – die Herren der sieben Meere* (Bremen, 2000), pp90–9; Jann M Witt, 'Frieden, Wohlstand und Reformen – Die Herzogtümer im dänischen Gesamtstaat', in Jann M Witt and Heiko Vosgerau (eds), *Geschichte Schleswig-Holstein* (Heide, 2010), pp183–219.

2 Jann M Witt, 'Unter dem Danebrog in alle Welt – die schleswig-holsteinische Schifffahrt im 18 Jahrhundert', in Jann M Witt and Heiko Vosgerau (eds), *Geschichte Schleswig-Holstein* (Heide, 2010), pp220–8; Ole Feldbæk, *Storhandelens tid, Dansk Søfarts Historie*, vol 3, 1720–1814 (Kopenhagen, 1997), pp215–19.

3 Witt, *Frieden*, pp200–2, 211–19. See also Feldbæk, pp193–5.

4 Jann M Witt, *Horatio Nelson – Triumph und Tragik eines Seehelden* (Hamburg, 2005), pp282–306; Hans Christian Bjerg and Ole L Franzen, *Danmark i Krig* (Kopenhagen,

2005), pp228–41. See also Witt, *Frieden*, pp212–13.

5 Witt, *Horatio Nelson*, pp399–400. See also John B Hattendorf, 'The struggle with France', in J R Hill (ed), T*he Oxford Illustrated History of the Royal Navy* (Oxford, 1995), pp80–119, see pp114–19.

6 Jann M Witt, 'Vom "Schleichhandel und strafbaren Verbindungen mit dem Feinde". Schmuggel und Handelskrieg vor Schleswig-Holsteins Küsten 1807–1814', in Robert Bohn und Sebastian Lehmann (eds), *Strandungen, Havarien, Kaperungen, Nordfriesische Quellen und Studien*, vol 4 (Amsterdam, 2004), pp61–84; Feldbæk, p196; Christian Degn, 'Die Herzogtümer im Gesamtstaat 1773–1830', in Olaf Klose and Christian Degn, *Die Herzogtümer im Gesamtstaat 1721–1830, Geschichte Schleswig-Holsteins*, vol 6 (Neumünster, 1960), pp303–7.

7 Witt, *Frieden*, pp215–17; Witt, *Schleichhandel*, pp61–3; Feldbæk, p196 and Degn, p303–7.

8 Witt, *Frieden*, p215–9; Feldbæk, pp193–5; Bjerg/Franzen, pp242–51; Rolf Gehrmann, 'Handelskonjunkturen in Schleswig-Holstein zur Zeit der Kontinentalsperre, 1807–1813', in Jürgen Brockstedt (ed), *Wirtschaftliche Wechsellagen in Schleswig-Holstein vom Mittelalter bis zur Gegenwart* (Neumünster, 1991), pp145–73.

9 Feldbæk, pp201–6; Bjerg/Franzen, pp252–61; Witt, *Schleichhandel*, pp63–79.

10 Feldbæk, pp201–6; Bjerg/Franzen, pp252–61; Witt, *Schleichhandel*, pp63–79.

11 Reglement für die Kaperfahrten und das gerichtliche Verfahren in Betreff der Prisen für die Herzogthümer Schleswig und Holstein vom 14. September 1807. See also Feldbæk, pp201–6; Witt, *Schleichhandel*, pp63–6; Kay Larsen, *Dansk Kapervæsen 1807–1814* (Kopenhagen, 1972), pp167–205. For privateers in general see David J Starkey, 'Privateering', in T*he Oxford Encyclopaedia of Maritime History, vol 3: Navies, Great Powers: Portugal – Shipyards* (Oxford 2007), pp381–4.

12 Larsen, pp167–205; Feldbæk, pp201–6; Witt, Schleichhandel, pp63–6.

13 Feldbæk, pp201–6; Bjerg/Franzen, pp252–61; Witt, *Schleichhandel*, pp63–79.

14 Gehrmann, pp149–53; Witt, *Schleichhandel*, pp72–4. See also Anthony Nicolas Ryan, 'Trade between Enemies, Maritime Resistance to the Continental System in the Northern Seas (1808–1812)', in Arne Bang-Andersen, Basil Greenhill and Egil Harald Grude (eds), *The North Sea, A Highway of Economic and Cultural Exchange* (Stavanger, 1985), pp181–94.

15 Witt, *Schleichhandel*, pp67–9; Ryan, pp181–2; Feldbæk, pp201–6; Gehrmann, pp153–5.

16 Witt, *Schleichhandel*, pp67–9; Ryan, pp181–2; Feldbæk, pp201–6; Gehrmann, pp153–5.

17 Witt, *Schleichhandel*, p72, Degn, pp320–7; Gehrmann, pp159–61. See also Heinrich Hitzigrath, *Hamburg und die Kontinentalsperre* (Hamburg, 1900); Wernher Mohrhenn, 'Helgoland zur Zeit der Kontinentalsperre', Phil Diss (Köln, 1926).

18 Witt, *Frieden*, pp216–19; Witt, *Schleichhandel*, pp72–3; Degn, *Herzogtümer*, pp320–7; Gehrmann, pp159–61.

19 Witt, *Schleichhandel*, pp72–4; Gehrmann, pp149–50, Feldbæk, pp206–11; Donald A Petrie, *The Prize Game – Lawful Looting on the High Seas in the Days of Fighting Sail* (New York, 1999), pp92–5.

20 Kanzleypatent, betr die Abweisung der mit Colonalwaaren beladenen Schiffe von den Häfen und Ladeplätzen in den Herzogthümern Schleswig und Holstein vom 8 September 1810. See also Witt, *Schleichhandel*, pp74–6; Ryan, pp191–2; Gehrmann, pp149–53.

21 Ryan, pp188–9; Witt, *Schleichhandel*, pp77–8; Kennedy, pp209–11.

22 LASH 65.2 No. 832 I: Bericht der Allerhöchst angeordneten combinirten Untersuchungs-Commission, wegen des Kapers VIGILANTIA von Tönningen und der von demselben

eingebrachten Brigg FORTUNA vom 22 April 1812. See also Witt, *Schleichhandel*, pp78–81.

23 Reglement für die Kaperfahrt und Prisenbehandlung, für die Herzogthümer Schleswig und Holstein vom 28 März 1810. See also Witt, *Schleichhandel*, pp78–81.

24 Reglement für die Kaperfahrt und Prisenbehandlung, für die Herzogthümer Schleswig und Holstein vom 28 März 1810.

25 LASH 65.2 No. 832 I: Pflichtmäßiger Bericht der Oberdirection und des Magistrats der Stadt Tönning an das Schleswigsche Obercriminalgericht auf Gottorf vom 21 September 1811.

26 LASH 65.2 No. 832 I: Befehl über die Arrestanten Kaperführer Jan Jansen, Kapersecretair Hendrik van Nievervaart et. Cons. angeordnete combinirte Commission, 27 September 1811.

27 LASH 65.2 No. 832 I: Bericht der Allerhöchst angeordneten combinirten Untersuchungs-Commission.

28 LASH 65.2 No. 832 I: Bericht der Allerhöchst angeordneten combinirten Untersuchungs-Commission.

29 LASH 65.2 No. 832 I: Bericht der Allerhöchst angeordneten combinirten Untersuchungs-Commission.

30 LASH 65.2 Nr. 832 II: Urtheil der über die Arrestanten Kaperführer Jan Jansen, Kapersecretair Hendrik van Nievervaart et. Cons. angeordneten combinirten Commission vom 25 November 1811.

31 LASH 65.2 Nr. 832 II: Urtheil der über die Arrestanten Kaperführer Jan Jansen, Kapersecretair Hendrik van Nievervaart et. Cons. angeordneten combinirten Commission vom 25 November 1811. For the judicial aspects see also Witt, *Frieden*, pp185–8; Thomas Krause, 'Zuchthaus', in *Handbuch zur deutschen Rechtsgeschichte*, vol V, Adalbert Erler und Ekkehard Kaufmann (eds) (Berlin, 1998), column 1777– 80; Uwe Wesel, *Geschichte des Rechts*, (München, 1997), pp388–90.

32 LASH 65.2 Nr. 832 II: Urtheil der über die Arrestanten Kaperführer Jan Jansen, Kapersecretair Hendrik van Nievervaart et. Cons. angeordneten combinirten Commission vom 25 November 1811.

33 LASH 65.2 Nr. 832 II: Urtheil der über die Arrestanten Kaperführer Jan Jansen, Kapersecretair Hendrik van Nievervaart et. Cons. angeordneten combinirten Commission vom 25 November 1811. See also Witt, *Frieden*, pp185–8; Krause, column 1777–80; Wesel, pp388–90.

34 LASH 65.2 No. 832 I: Bericht der Allerhöchst angeordneten combinirten Untersuchungs-Commission.

35 Witt, *Schleichhandel*, pp80–2.

36 Witt, *Schleichhandel*, pp82–3; Kennedy, pp209–11; Ryan, pp188–90.

37 Witt, *Schleichhandel*, pp83–4; Witt, *Frieden*, pp216–19; Gehrmann, pp152–3 and Degn, pp320–7. For the effects on the political situation in Schleswig and Holstein see Heiko Vosgerau and Frank Lubowitz, 'Zwischen Dänemark und Preußen – zwischen Nationalismus und Modernisierung: Schleswig-Holstein 1815–1920', in *Geschichte Schleswig-Holsteins*, Jann M Witt and Heiko Vosgerau (eds) (Heide 2010), pp229–71, see pp229–49.

38 Witt, *Schleichhandel*, pp83–4; Witt, *Frieden*, pp216–19; Gehrmann, pp152–3; Degn, pp320–7.

The 1805 Club

President: Admiral Sir Jonathon Band GCB DL
Chairman: Peter Warwick

The 1805 Club is a registered charity no. 1071871.

The 1805 Club was established twenty-five years ago to conserve the graves, monuments and artefacts of people associated with the Royal Navy and the merchant service during the era of the Georgian sailing navy. They are a vital yet often neglected part of our naval heritage. No other organisation is dedicated to their preservation.

Since 1990 the Club has conserved sixty-five graves and memorials in Britain and overseas, created three new memorials, arranged high-profile commemorative events, and furthered research through international conferences and its publications with Seaforth Publishing, including *Nelson's Band of Brothers: Lives and Memorials* and the annual *Trafalgar Chronicle.*

To join the 1805 Club go to www.1805club.org and download the membership application form.